Breaking Down the
Monolingual Wall

To all our teachers, and the teachers who have embraced and will embrace what is written here.

Breaking Down the Monolingual Wall

Essential Shifts for Multilingual Learners' Success

Ivannia Soto

Sydney Snyder

Margarita Espino Calderón

Margo Gottlieb

Andrea Honigsfeld

Joan Lachance

Marga Marshall

David Nungaray

Rubí Flores

Lyn Scott

Foreword by Jan Gustafson-Corea

FOR INFORMATION:

Corwin

A SAGE Company

2455 Teller Road

Thousand Oaks, California 91320

(800) 233-9936

www.corwin.com

SAGE Publications Ltd.

1 Oliver's Yard

55 City Road

London EC1Y 1SP

United Kingdom

SAGE Publications India Pvt. Ltd.

Unit No 323-333, Third Floor, F-Block

International Trade Tower Nehru Place

New Delhi 110 019

India

SAGE Publications Asia-Pacific Pte. Ltd.

18 Cross Street #10-10/11/12

China Square Central

Singapore 048423

Vice President and
 Editorial Director: Monica Eckman

Program Director and Publisher: Dan Alpert

Content Development Editor: Mia Rodriguez

Editorial Intern: Lex Nunez

Production Editor: Amy Schroller

Copy Editor: Deanna Noga

Typesetter: C&M Digitals (P) Ltd.

Proofreader: Caryne Brown

Indexer: Molly Hall

Cover Designer: Rose Storey

Marketing Manager: Melissa Duclos

Printed in Canada

Library of Congress Control Number: 2023945231

This book is printed on acid-free paper.

23 24 25 26 27 10 9 8 7 6 5 4 3 2 1

CONTENTS

ACKNOWLEDGMENTS

From David:

Gracias a Dios por darme esta oportunidad to share parts of my story with the world. I would also like to thank my mom Carmen, my dad Hermengildo, my husband Jonathan, and our entire family for their unwavering support and love and for building me up to be the person I am today, including my *Abuelita* Graciela, *Tia* Licha, and *Tia* Gladys who are watching after me from heaven. I am grateful to the thousands of students, teachers, staff members, families, and community members who have shaped me tremendously, including so many teachers from my K–12 education and professors at Chapman and Trinity Universities. I give special thanks to Dr. José Medina for thinking of me to co-author a chapter in this book, and Dr. Olivia Hernández who is the guide and mentor in my dual language leadership work. To my Bonham *familia: los quiero con todo mi corazón.* And last, but not least, to Bendel and Bruno, our two dogs who provided me lots of cuddles and moral support while co-authoring my first chapter ever.

From Ivannia:

I would like to dedicate this book and chapter 1 to the two important men in my life who assisted me with completing the project—my husband Ron Skamfer, and my longtime editor Dan Alpert—as well as each of the authors who agreed to contribute to this project!

First, to Dan Alpert, who believed in this project and that there was another story to tell with *Breaking Down the Monolingual Wall.* Thank you once again for also believing in a project with multiple authors. As usual, I appreciate your wordsmithing, thoughtful feedback, and brotherly kindness.

- Similarly, not one of the men in my life, but I appreciate Mia Rodriguez's partnership in completing the details of this project. Thank you for all that you did to get us to the finish line!

- Thank you also to each author who contributed to this book—Sydney, David, Joan, Andrea, Marga, Margarita, Margo, Rubi, and Lyn. Each of your voices and expertise made this project a success, and I know will impact so many educators and students in the field!

Finally, thank you to my loving husband, Ron, who has supported me throughout this project and countless others! There were some especially difficult times during this project, and his validation and advocacy pushed me to complete all that I had on my plate during my sabbatical year.

Thank you, *gracias, y grazie*!

From Marga:

I would like to dedicate chapter 6 to all bilingual students in Dual Language Programs across the world. You are *nuestro futuro*, and your way of looking at things through different cultural lenses will make our world a better place with you in it.

Second, to my amazing husband Kyle and my wonderful children Maggie and Roberto: Writing this chapter as a newbie and in a language that is not my native one has been a challenge, and you have supported me along the way and cheered me up every time a paragraph was finished.

To Dr. José Medina, who told me to not give up and who found a way to connect me with my amazing chapter co-author, David Nungaray. Everything happens for a reason.

Last, to Ivannia Soto for giving me the opportunity of being part of an amazing *aventura* that I never would have thought I could accomplish.

From Margarita:

I would like to acknowledge Dan Alpert for all his kindness, brilliance, guidance, and support with this and my other publications. I would also like to thank Mia and Luke, Corwin marvels, for their assistance. Additionally, a special thanks to Andrés Henriquez from the Carnegie Corporation of New York for his vision and support of my research.

From Sydney:

First, I would like to express my gratitude to Dan Alpert and Ivannia Soto for their vision and leadership in this project. I greatly appreciate your guidance and the opportunity to contribute to this book. Thank you also to Mia Rodriguez for all you did to support this work and keep us on track. Finally, I would like to thank my longtime colleague, co-author, and friend Diane Staehr Fenner. It is because of you and the work that we have done together that I had an opportunity to write this chapter. I am thankful for all that I have learned from you and the endless amount of encouragement that you have provided over the years.

From Rubí:

To my husband Abraham and my two young *mujeres con propósito* Aly and Abby. Thank you for being my partners in this journey. We share all the success because I wouldn't be who I am personally and professionally without your support and encouragement. Love you always.

Also, to my parents Juliana Torres González and José Luis Flores. *Su valentía y sacrificio me inspiran a crecer como madre, educadora y persona.* Thank you *papi, por ti le echo ganas.* I try every day. Thank you *mami por tu ejemplo de dedicación y perseverancia, ¡por ti es que no me rindo!* To my siblings José Luis, Juliana, and Flor for their resilience and perseverance.

Thank you to Ivannia Soto, Dan Alpert, Mia Rodriguez, and the Corwin team for opening the door for new voices to contribute to our field. Finally, thank you to my CABE *familia*, to all the children I've had the privilege to teach and learn from, and to all the dual language teachers, coaches, and administrators who never stop learning so our multilingual children can thrive (You know who you are!).

From Margo:

A mis estudiantes bi- y multilingües que me han enseñado tanto de sus lenguas y culturas when I began my career, y a todos mis colegas que han compartido sus lenguas y culturas conmigo throughout my career . . . agradezco que me hayan incluído en sus vidas.

Thank you to my Corwin family, Dan, Mia, and Lucas, with whom I have always found solace in their commitment to equity and through which I have gained confidence as a writer over the years. *Gracias, también a* Ivannia, it's been a pleasure working with you, to admire your organizational skills, and to share your pledge to tear down monolingual walls.

From Lyn:

This book and chapter 8 hold greater meaning because of my multilingual students in California, Florida, Kansas, and Massachusetts. They grew up in families and communities that valued their languages and supported their biliteracy development even before national and state policies moved toward dual language policies. I also acknowledge the support of Dr. Ivannia Soto as a colleague, mentor, and editor whose leadership in dual language education and research continues to inspire. *¡Gracias!*

From Andrea and Joan:

We dedicate our chapter to Dan Alpert, Mia Rodriguez, and Ivannia Soto for your shared vision and commitment to collaboration in this book. Our chapter is also dedicated to all the talented dual language educators who collaborate for multilingual learners, their families, and the language-rich communities they serve. We thank you!

PUBLISHER'S ACKNOWLEDGMENTS

Corwin gratefully acknowledges the contributions of the following reviewers:

Analis Carattini-Ruiz
Executive Director of Equity, Inclusion, and Student Support
Alpine School District
American Fork, UT

Christine Kennedy
District Program Facilitator, Multilingual Department
Minneapolis Public Schools
Minneapolis, MN

Elizabeth Scaduto
Director of ENL/ESL K–12 and Adjunct Instructor
Riverhead Central School District (NY) and SUNY Stony Brook University
Riverhead, NY
Stony Brook, NY

Karen Lapuk
Coordinator of Programs for Multilingual Learners
Goodwin University Magnet School System and University of Connecticut
East Hartford, CT

Maribel Guerrero
Dual Language Coordinator and Adjunct Professor
Naperville Community Unit School District 203 and Judson University
Naperville, IL

Marion Friebus-Flaman
Director of Language Acquisition Services
Naperville Community Unit School District 203
Naperville, IL

Soula Katsogianopoulos
Multilingual Language Learner Lead
Seconded from the Peel District School Board
Ontario, Canada

ABOUT THE AUTHORS

Ivannia Soto is a professor of education and the director of graduate programs at Whittier College, where she specializes in language acquisition, systemic reform for English language learners (ELLs), and urban education. Dr. Soto began her career in the Los Angeles Unified School District (LAUSD), where she taught English and English language development to a population of 99.9 percent Latinx, who either were or had been multilingual learners. Before becoming a professor, Soto also served LAUSD as a literacy coach as well as district office and county office administrator. She has presented on literacy and language topics at various conferences, including the National Association for Bilingual Education (NABE), the California Association for Bilingual Association (CABE), the American Educational Research Association (AERA), and the National Council of Urban Education Associations. As a consultant, Soto has worked  with Stanford University's School Redesign Network (SRN), WestEd, and CABE, as well as a variety of districts and county offices in California, providing technical assistance for systemic reform for ELLs and Title III. Recently, Soto also directed a CABE bilingual teacher and administrator program across California.

Soto has authored and coauthored thirteen books, including *The Literacy Gaps: Bridge-Building Strategies for English Language Learners and Standard English Learners; ELL Shadowing as a Catalyst for Change*, a bestseller that was recognized by Education Trust–West as a promising practice for ELLs in 2018; *Moving From Spoken to Written Language With ELLs*; the *Academic English Mastery* four-book series; the Common Core Companion four-book series for English language development; *Breaking Down the Wall*; and *Responsive Schooling for Culturally and Linguistically Diverse Students*. Together, the books tell a story of how to equitably engage and include multilingual learners by ensuring that they gain voice and an academic identity in the classroom setting. Soto is executive director of the Institute for Culturally and Linguistically Responsive Teaching (ICLRT) at Whittier College, whose mission it is to promote relevant research and develop academic resources for ELLs and Standard English learners (SELs) via linguistically and culturally responsive teaching practices.

Sydney Snyder is a Principal Associate at SupportEd. In this role, Dr. Snyder coaches multilingual learner (ML) educators and develops and facilitates interactive professional development for teachers of MLs. She also works with the SupportEd team to offer technical assistance to school districts and educational organizations. She started her teaching career as a Peace Corps Volunteer in Guinea, West Africa. This experience ignited her passion for language teaching, culturally responsive instruction, and ML advocacy. Sydney is co-author of *Unlocking English Learners' Potential: Strategies for Making Content Accessible* and *Culturally Responsive Teaching for Multilingual Learners: Tools for Equity.* She served as an English Teaching Fellow at Gadja Mada University in Yogyakarta, Indonesia. She earned her PhD in Multilingual/Multicultural Education at George Mason University and her MAT in TESOL at the School for International Training. You can connect with her on email at Sydney@ SupportEd.com or on X, formerly known as Twitter, at @SydneySupportEd.

Margarita Espino Calderón is Professor Emerita/Senior Research Scientist at Johns Hopkins University. Dr. Calderón has worked on numerous research and development projects focusing on reading for English learners funded by the USDOE Institute of Education Sciences, the U.S. Department of Labor, and has collaborated with Harvard and the Center for Applied Linguistics on a longitudinal study funded by the NICHD.

The Carnegie Corporation of New York funded her five-year empirical study to develop *Expediting Comprehension for English Language Learners (ExC-ELL)*, a comprehensive professional development model for math, science, social studies, language arts, ESL, and SPED teachers that integrates language, literacy, and content. She also developed two other effective evidence-based programs: *Reading Instructional Goals for Older Readers (RIGOR)* for Newcomers with Interrupted Formal Education. Additionally, the *Bilingual Cooperative Integrated Reading and Composition (BCIRC)* program was developed for dual language instruction and is listed in the *What Works Clearinghouse.*

Dr. Calderón collaborated with George Washington University on a Title III five-year grant to implement and further study *A Whole-School Approach to Professional Development with ExC-ELL* in Virginia school districts.

She is a consultant for the U.S. Department of Justice and Office of Civil Rights. She serves and has served on national language and literacy research panels. Dr. Calderón is also President/CEO of Margarita Calderón and Associates, Inc. Dr. Calderón and her team of ten associates conduct *ExC-ELL* comprehensive multiyear professional development and on-site coaching in schools, districts, and statewide and international institutes. She has over 100 publications on language and literacy for ELs.

Margo Gottlieb is a staunch advocate for multilingual learners and their teachers. As co-founder and lead developer of WIDA at the University of Wisconsin-Madison, over the past 20 years, Dr. Gottlieb has contributed to the design of language development standards frameworks and Can Do Descriptors. As a teacher, teacher educator, consultant, and mentor, she has worked with universities, organizations, governments, states, school districts, and schools in co-constructing linguistic and culturally sustainable curricula and reconceptualizing classroom assessment policy and practice. Dr. Gottlieb has been appointed to national and state advisory boards, has been a Fulbright Scholar, and has presented across the United States and in twenty-five countries. In 2016 she was honored by TESOL International Association "as an individual who has made a significant contribution to the TESOL profession within the past 50 years." Having authored, co-authored, or co-edited over 100 publications, including twenty books and guides, Dr. Gottlieb's third edition of her best-selling book, *Assessing Multilingual Learners: Bridges to Empowerment*, is soon to join her Corwin compendium.

Andrea Honigsfeld is TESOL Professor in the School of Education and Human Services at Molloy College, Rockville Centre, New York. Dr. Honigsfeld teaches graduate courses on linguistics, TESOL methods, and cultural and linguistic diversity. Before entering the field of teacher education, she was an English-as-a-foreign-language teacher in Hungary (Grades 5–8 and adult) and an English-as-a-second-language teacher in New York City (Grades K–3 and adult). She also taught Hungarian at New York University.

She was the recipient of a doctoral fellowship at St. John's University, New York, where she conducted research on individualized instruction. She received a Fulbright Award to lecture in Iceland in the fall of 2002. In the past 20 years, she has been presenting at conferences across the United States, Canada, China, Denmark, Great Britain, Italy, the Philippines, Sweden, Thailand, and the United Arab Emirates.

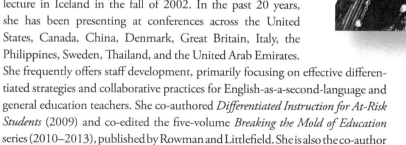

She frequently offers staff development, primarily focusing on effective differentiated strategies and collaborative practices for English-as-a-second-language and general education teachers. She co-authored *Differentiated Instruction for At-Risk Students* (2009) and co-edited the five-volume *Breaking the Mold of Education* series (2010–2013), published by Rowman and Littlefield. She is also the co-author of *Core Instructional Routines: Go-To Structures for Effective Literacy Teaching, K–5 and 6–12* (2014) and author of *Growing Language and Literacy* (2019) published by Heinemann. With Maria Dove, she co-edited *Coteaching and Other Collaborative Practices in the EFL/ESL Classroom: Rationale, Research, Reflections, and Recommendations* (2012) and *Co-Teaching for English Learners: Evidence-Based Practices and Research-Informed Outcomes* (2020). Maria and Andrea also co-authored *Collaboration and Co-Teaching: Strategies for English Learners* (2010), *Common Core for the Not-So-Common Learner, Grades K–5: English Language Arts Strategies* (2013), *Common Core for the Not-So-Common Learner, Grades 6–12: English Language Arts Strategies* (2013), *Beyond Core Expectations: A Schoolwide Framework for Serving the Not-So-Common Learner* (2014), *Collaboration and Co-Teaching: A Leader's Guide* (2015), *Coteaching for English Learners: A Guide to Collaborative Planning, Instruction, Assessment, and Reflection* (2018), *Collaborating for English Learners: A Foundational Guide to Integrated Practices* (2019), and *Co-Planning: 5 Essential Practices to Integrate Curriculum and Instruction for English Learners* (2022). She is a contributing author of *Breaking Down the Wall: Essential Shifts for English Learner Success* (2020), *From Equity Insights to Action* (2021), and *Digital-Age Teaching for English Learners* (2022). Nine of her Corwin books are bestsellers.

Joan Lachance is an Associate Professor of Teaching English as a Second Language (TESL) at the University of North Carolina at Charlotte (UNCC). Dr. Lachance directs the TESL graduate programs and undergraduate TESL Minor. She is the co-author of the *National Dual Language Education Teacher Preparation Standards* and the Director of the CAEP Specialized Program Association in Dual Language Education called "EMMA: Education for a Multilingual Multicultural America." She received her undergraduate degree in Secondary Education, Modern Languages and Linguistics from Florida International University. With Spanish as the language of program delivery, she completed graduate coursework to earn her master's degree in School Counseling from Pontifical Catholic University in Poncé, Puerto Rico. Dr. Lachance completed her doctoral work in Curriculum and Instruction, with an emphasis on Urban Education, Literacy, and TESL at UNCC.

Dr. Lachance's research agenda encompasses dual language teacher preparation, academic literacy development, and authentic assessment with multilingual learners, which has resulted in over twenty-five publications, including articles, book chapters, technical reports, and state-level curriculum guides since she has joined UNCC. She serves on several journal editorial boards and is a board member of the Multistate Association for Bilingual Education, Northeast (MABE). With the publication of her latest Corwin book, she is specializing one aspect of her work further into collaboration and co-teaching for multilingual learners in the dual language context. She continues to work to support dual language education for the preservation of Native American languages, currently and most honorably collaborating with a K–8 school serving the Eastern Band of the Cherokee Indians (EBCI).

In addition to her faculty position, Dr. Lachance's service agenda has resulted in over 100 conference presentations, invited panels, keynotes, and roundtables to support the North Carolina Department of Public Instruction and the nation at large. Her service specializes in professional learning for teachers, school counselors, and school administrators. She co-created materials and professional learning institutes for myriad North Carolina state-led initiatives, including *Using the WIDA Standards, The North Carolina Guide to the SIOP Model, The North Carolina Guide to ExC-ELL,* and *Dual Language/Immersion Program Support.* The presentations, webinars, and asynchronous learning opportunities share innovative practices for multilingual learner academic language development, equitable active multilingual learner engagement, dual language program development, sociocultural nuances in school counseling, and international comparative education.

For fun, Dr. Lachance enjoys camping (it's really glamping!) with her husband Carl, their son, and their two rescue dogs. She is passionate about science, astronomy, the outdoors, hiking in the Blue Ridge Mountains, and the preservation of the Appalachian Trail. While she lives and works in North Carolina, she shares her heart deeply with New Mexico and has a passion for the Native American Pueblo Languages, their ways of living, and *everything Hatch green chilis.* Finally, she is a former dual language parent, who reached the point of watching multilingualism come to life in her own home.

Marga Marshall is an Educational Consultant with experience in bilingual education in Spain and California. She opened the first TK–8 Two Way Dual Immersion English/Spanish School in Concord, California, as part of the district's Magnet schools. Prior to becoming a principal, Marga Marshall was a bilingual teacher, an instructional coach, an English Learners coach, and a Dual Language coach. As an educator for over 24 years, her passion is bilingualism, biliteracy, and offering students the opportunity to learn a second language. Marga Marshall has always developed relationships with the community, staff, and teachers. Her leadership also involves watching students grow, providing the opportunity to learn in a multicultural and collaborative environment through the emphasis on collaboration, critical and creative thinking, and supporting teachers and staff so that they can

reach their greatest potential while strengthening a connection between school and home and fostering a positive school culture. Marga Marshall has presented at state and national conferences on best practices for the bilingual classroom; Creating Culturally Competent Schools; Number Talks in bilingual classrooms; Foundations for a Strong, Successful, and Sustainable Dual Language Program; Guiding Principles for Dual Language Education strategies; and Foundations in Designated and Integrated ELD. Her work and collaboration with parents, community, and paraeducators has also led Marga Marshall to do online and in-person presentations for parents and paraeducators with strategies on how to support students during Distance Learning and at home and Biliteracy and Literacy Development from Home to School.

She was awarded the MDEA Community Involvement Award during the 2015–2016 school year and is the recipient of the MDEA Outstanding Administrator Award for the 2017–2018 and 2020–2021 school years. She was also nominated as the ACSA Region 6 Elementary Principal of the Year for the 2018–2019 school year.

During her leadership at Holbrook Language Academy, her school was voted best Bilingual School by Parents Press for three consecutive years, and she wrote the entry for the CSBA Golden Bell Awards—an award that promotes excellence in education by recognizing outstanding programs— leading Holbrook Language Academy to be the recipient of the 2021 Golden Bell Award in the Category of English Learners/Biliteracy. As an Educational Bilingual Consultant, Marga Marshall partners with districts providing expert, customized consulting and professional learning in the areas of biliteracy and English Learner education.

David Nungaray is a forever dual language teacher and school leader at heart no matter what his current work title is. The children and families he worked with as an educator are one of his guiding forces in the work he continues to do in education. As a son of Mexican immigrants, native Spanish speaker, gay educator, and a first-generation college graduate, David Nungaray is passionate about educational excellence and ensuring that school systems best meet the needs of all learners. He began his journey in education in 2010 as a founding corps member of Teach for America-San Antonio, where he served as a fourth dual language teacher. In his first year of teaching, David Nungaray was the district's Elementary Rising Star Teacher of the Year. Currently, David Nungaray works as a bilingual consulting partner at a national nonprofit where he oversees partner-ships in Texas and supports national strategy for integrating multilingual learners into all the work at the organization. He has led teams focused on partnering with districts through strategic planning, (bi)literacy visioning and implementation, dual language supports, stakeholder and family engagement, high-impact tutoring, learning acceleration, and state-wide high-quality instructional materials adoption. With almost thirteen years of experience in education, David Nungaray served as the principal of one of the flagship dual language schools in San Antonio ISD (SAISD) prior to his time at TNTP. During his tenure as principal, the school community revised and renewed their in-district school charter and established a partnership with the University of Texas-San Antonio to create the first dual language teacher residency lab network of schools in Texas. David Nungaray also served as co-chair of the Bexar County COVID-19 PreK–12 Consultation group in San Antonio, focused on guiding the reopening of schools in the county. Prior to his role as principal, he co-founded one of the first schools in the Innovation Zone of SAISD, which spanned PreK–12th grade, as associate principal. The school focuses on project-based learning and also has a teaching and school administrator residency model. David Nungaray serves on multiple nonprofit boards focused on education, and he holds his master's degree in school leadership from Trinity University, where he has served as an adjunct professor in multilingual education, school leadership, and special education.

Rubí Flores is a native from San Luis Potosí, Mexico. Rubí is the Director of Professional Learning at the California Association for Bilingual Education. She has extensive expertise working with schools on implementing and refining Dual Language and Multilingual Learner Programs. Prior to this role, Rubí Flores served as a bilingual teacher, ESL specialist, dual language teacher, dual language instructional coach, dual language program coordinator, and biliteracy curriculum developer. She has worked in schools across California, El Salvador, Oklahoma, and Texas. Rubí Flores earned a bachelor's degree in bilingual education from Texas State University and a master's degree in bilingual and bicultural curriculum and instruction from the University of Texas at Austin. She is a member of the Proyecto Maestría leadership development program through the University of Texas. Rubí Flores holds a multiple subject teaching credential with a bilingual teacher authorization in California and in Texas. She has presented her work with dual language programs and biliteracy instruction at CABE, NABE, TABE, Adelante! Dual Language Conference, La Cosecha, CARLA, and at multiple county- and district-level conferences and events in California, Texas, and México. Her current work focuses on developing teacher capacity to support multilingual learners through coaching, presenting authentic methods for biliteracy instruction, and teaching strategies that support Spanish and English academic language development in Dual Language and Multilingual Learner settings. As an immigrant and first-generation college graduate, Rubí Flores is committed to honoring her parents' courage to seek a better future by creating and acting as advocate for culturally sustaining and high-quality professional learning programs that will promote linguistic justice for multilingual learners. Connect with Rubí at thebiliteracycoach@gmail.com.

Lyn Scott, a native of the rural Midwest, is a credentialed dual language teacher in Massachusetts and California teaching in two-way immersion and transitional bilingual education classrooms for over two decades. As an elementary teacher, Dr. Scott joined colleagues and parents in restructuring their neighborhood public school into a multiage, dual language immersion public school. Inspired by the work of Paulo Freire, he immersed himself in Brazilian culture early in his teaching journey, reflecting on adult literacy pedagogies relevant to the dual language development of young learners in American schools. Lengthy experiences in China, Sweden, and Taiwan stimulated his curiosity in national language policies impacting language diversity, schooling, and migration. His advocacy for linguistic human rights includes all students having access to education in their home language in addition to English and other languages. His doctoral dissertation at the University of California, Berkeley, investigated language policy in Mexican American homes in Arizona and California. Since 2012, Dr. Scott has served as a faculty member of the California State University system, currently an Associate Professor in the Department of Teacher Education at Cal State East Bay. He is past president of the California Association for Bilingual Teacher Education and co-author of *Community-Owned Knowledge: The Promise of Collaborative Action Research* published in 2022. Dr. Scott is biliterate in Spanish, Portuguese, Swedish, and English and conversational in Mandarin Chinese.

FOREWORD

"To learn a new language is to open another window from which to see the world."

—Chinese proverb

We are living in a wonderfully innovative and expansive time where our languages, cultures, and vast life experiences open windows and build bridges to an ever-evolving and connected global society that impacts all aspects of our lives. As educators, we possess the privilege and the responsibility to ensure that our educational systems, our pedagogies, and our practices expand and focus on a multitude of options for all students (and their parents and families). Uplifting the gift of multilingualism and multiculturalism is at the heart of that. We are called to be fully engaged in creating classroom communities that reflect and value the languages and cultures of our students and to elevate the values of equity, justice, kindness, empathy, and love across our classrooms—locally, nationally, and across global borders.

Transformative educators do this by providing innovative educational opportunities that promote and build multilingualism and biliteracy for students in grades PK/TK–12 (and beyond) instructional settings. Having access to a multilingual-, multicultural-, and biliteracy-focused education is both a privilege and a right of all students in the United States. Our charge is to focus on building bridges to multilingual and multicultural educational programs and breaking down the walls focused on monolingual, monoethnic, and monocultural teaching and learning. Through a broad resource bank of research and rich instructional practices, there is no question that we have the knowledge, wisdom, experience, and know-how to make this type of learning experience an enriching and successful reality for all students!

Dynamic student data throughout the United States shows that multilingual and multicultural education is a must. Nationally, 21 percent of all students speak a language other than English at home, and close to 10 percent of those students are identified as English Learner students (students who are acquiring English as a second language). While *English Learner* and *English Language Learner* continue to be recognized as the official terms used in state and federal systems, a nationwide alternate movement has begun to use assets-based terms such as *multilingual learners, emergent bilingual learners, biliteracy learners*, and so on to identify students who have a primary language other than English and are additionally learning English, uplifting the concept that students are speaking and learning in more than one language and are becoming multilingual. With almost 50 million students in the United States, over 10 million already come from multilingual backgrounds and have the potential to excel in their multilingual skills if they have access to a multilingual/biliteracy–based instructional program. According to a report distributed by the U.S. Department of Education and the Office of English Language Acquisition (2019–2020), fifty languages or language categories appear in one or more of states' top five lists of languages spoken in their communities. Spanish is on the top five list of forty-five states and is spoken by more than 75 percent of all students across the United States. Other languages such as Arabic, Chinese, Vietnamese, Portuguese, Haitian Creole, Hmong, Cushitic, Tagalog, and Russian, representing smaller percentages, complete the list of the top 10 languages spoken in U.S. schools. This rich linguistic foundation across our nation provides the perfect momentum for the growth of multilingual/dual language programs in our schools.

Now, more than ever, we have the momentum to recognize the natural potential to grow and increase multilingual/dual language instructional options for all students. Indeed, the drive continues across the nation to build on the assets of students' languages and cultural backgrounds and to increase the development of additive educational models that expand students' access to multilingualism (such as dual language, one-way immersion/developmental language education, and heritage language programs) rather than providing a subtractive monolingual, English-only education model that reduces the value and potential of students' languages and cultures. *Breaking Down the Monolingual Wall: Essential Shifts for Multilingual Learners' Success* comes just at the right time to highlight the *why* and the *how* of multilingual and dual language education as an imperative for true student success. It provides a lighted pathway that takes into account the complex history of multilingual education in the United States, and it opens new and familiar doors to the systemic and pedagogical approaches that are essential to creating multilingual and dual language success. In this context, preserving and learning languages becomes an issue of equity and civil and human rights.

For decades, the historical context of multilingual education in the United States has followed a curved pathway of policy, pedagogy, practice, and hard-fought advocacy that drives, uplifts, and motivates us still today. These legal and policy decisions are numerous: *Mendez v. Westminster* (1947); *Brown v. Board of Education* (1954); *Lau v. Nichols* (1974); *Castañeda v. Pickard* (1978/1981); California's Prop 227 (1998) followed 18 years later by Proposition 58 (2016); Colorado's Amendment 3 (2002); Massachusetts Question 2 (2002); the California State Seal of Biliteracy (2011) and its growth to approval in forty-nine states; California's English Learner Roadmap Policy (2017); and many, many others. This timeline of legal and legislative battles reflects both additive and deficit approaches to multilingual and dual language education that have compelled us to pivot from theories of English-only or English-dominant instructional programs and embrace the powerful potential and possibilities of multilingual and dual language education.

The comeback surge from our legislative and policy wins has set the stage across the nation for new approaches, updated language, rigorous research, and the implementation of highly impactful programs. We have key tools such as the *Guiding Principles for Dual Language Education* (3rd Edition, Center for Applied Linguistics, Dual Language Education of New Mexico, and Santillana USA), learning standards and frameworks across different states in languages other than English, and state and national organizations, coalitions, government agencies, university programs, and partnerships whose sole mission is to support multilingual and dual language programs. Across the nation we may see that education systems and programs use slightly different terms at times to describe elements and features of their multilingual programs due to their local programmatic and linguistic context; however, overwhelmingly, successful multilingual programs are shifting from the use of *deficit-oriented terminology* (such as language minority, English-only, transitional bilingual, limited English proficient, etc.) *to uplifting assets-based language* (such as biliteracy, multilingualism, multiliteracy, dual language, two-way immersion, dual language immersion, one-way immersion, dual language learners, development bilingual, emergent bilingual, cross-linguistic transfer, translanguaging, multiculturalism, integrated and designated language development, heritage language, world and global languages, and linguistically and culturally responsive and sustaining strategies). Our current U.S. Secretary of Education, Dr. Miguel Cardona, has even widely declared that *bilingualism is **a** superpower!* The time is ***now*** to advance and propel our multilingual and dual language programs to new heights.

With the increased momentum and visibility of the power and impact of multilingual and dual language education, we are wise to proactively be aware of and respond to the challenges and opposition that exist, and to uplift the essential components that are still needed to increase success and transform multilingual and dual language programs to become the norm for all students. Several of these areas are addressed in *Breaking Down the Monolingual Wall: Essential Shifts for Multilingual Learners' Success* and include fidelity to successful program components; the need for more bilingually authorized teachers; high-quality instructional resources; accurate assessment and accountability in the target languages of instruction; updated research studies; being supportive of language and learning needs that arose from the pandemic; ongoing support for leaders of biliteracy programs, attention toward narrowed and weakened support systems; the swinging pendulum toward English-only or English-centric program models; instruction of literacy that ignores the assets of multilingualism; and the last gasp approaches by some to continue to support monolingual and monocultural education.

Inspired by Dr. Ivannia Soto and contributed to by eight additional key authors and researchers, *Breaking Down the Monolingual Wall: Essential Shifts for Multilingual Learners' Success* will propel and guide us to continue moving forward toward building strong, successful, and sustainable multilingual and dual language learning programs. We are extremely fortunate to have the insights, strategies, and pathways that *Breaking Down the Monolingual Wall: Essential Shifts for Multilingual Learners' Success* provides through concrete, practical, and innovative approaches, as we most certainly will continue to face uphill challenges in breaking down monolingual systems in our educational programs. Coming together through research, policy, practice, and advocacy is essential in making multilingualism a reality for all our students and their future impact on our world. When multilingual and dual language programs are accessible for all students, we will indeed provide them with the *superpower of being multilingual!*

In the words of Guatemalan Nobel Peace Prize laureate Rigoberta Menhcu: "When you are convinced your cause is just [and right], it is worth fighting for."

Jan Gustafson-Corea, CEO
California Association for Bilingual Education

From Subtractive Schooling Models to Dual Language Models That Lead to Linguistic and Cultural Equity

THE PREMISE

Many Dual Language Education (DLE) programs are launching with good intentions, but if not careful will create the same inequities that they were intended to counter. Dual language program models were developed to reverse and undo some of the very subtractive schooling inequities that historically have been fostered over time. Other models, such as Transitional Bilingual Education (TBE), or early exit bilingual education, are considered subtractive models because the goal is not bilingualism or biliteracy. Instead, the native language is only viewed as a vehicle to transition students to English. Additionally, while we recognize that all students in DLE programs are learning language and content in two languages, we are specifically focused on equitable dual language programs where students who come from homes where a language other than or in addition to English is spoken in the home and students who come from cultures outside the dominant culture. That is why we use the equitable term multilingual learners (MLLs), which is simply not an assets-based replacement for English learners (ELs). Instead, it refers to a broad group that includes those receiving services (i.e., ELs), those who have exited out, "never ELs" who come from linguistically and culturally diverse backgrounds, and Heritage language learners. When we include this plethora of subgroups, the number of students swells to more than twice that of ELs. The context for this chapter comes from the reality that many DLE programs, even those that start out with the best of intentions, end up privileging native English speakers over language minority students. For example, a recent article in *Education Week*, "The Equity Question of Dual Language Programs," supports the notion that "[d]espite their promise, dual language programs remain rare" (Najarro, 2023). Additionally, that students who need two-way programs (ELs and heritage language learners) must be given priority to such programs. Schools can do this by reserving at least 30 percent of dual language seats for ELs. Similarly, states should avoid building dual language programs in English-only communities when largely EL communities have no such programs.

The following vignette is an example of a school that launched its Dual Language Immersion (DLI) program during the height of the pandemic and struggled to adhere to the definition of an equitable DLE program, by struggling to implement several of the key principles of DLE outlined in the *Guiding Principles for Dual Language Education* (Howard et al., 2018), specifically sociocultural competence and linguistic equity. The school launched with such inequities already in place, because it did not have enough actual ELs in the program. As suggested in the *Education Week* article, the school could have benefited by reserving at least 30 percent of dual language seats for ELs within the district. We want to acknowledge that it is difficult to launch a DLE program, much less during the constraints of a pandemic. Still, there are several things to learn from Mountain Heights Elementary School, both good and areas of growth.

VIGNETTE

During the pandemic (school year 2019–2020), a kindergarten student named Maricela was enrolled in a new DLI program at Mountain Heights Elementary School by her parents, Juana and Ignacio. The parents heard about this new program, before the pandemic, from the school principal when they enrolled Maricela, who is an MLL, in the school over the summer of 2019. After meeting with the principal of the school, Ms. Ortiz, Juana and Ignacio were excited to hear that their local community school was offering a DLI program, which would help Maricela with retaining her primary language and her culture. Both Juana and Ignacio had become concerned that Maricela was already losing her primary language because she was unable to communicate with her grandparents who lived close by.

Mountain Heights Elementary School has an enrollment of about 408 students, who are made up of 14 percent ELs, 90 percent Latinx students, and 62 percent socioeconomic disadvantaged students. Although most of the students in the DLI program at Mountain Heights are Latinx, the school did not have enough Latinx students who were truly ELs to participate in the program. This then created an overrepresentation of students who initially only speak English. In and of itself, this became a driver of inequity for ELs in the program, as well as something that the administration needed to contend with in subsequent years.

The school launched its DLI program with two kindergarten classrooms, two kindergarten DLI teachers, and with the 90/10 model. Students in an additive Dual Language program are often taught in the 90/10 (or 50/50) model. With the 90/10 model, students in kindergarten through first grade receive 90 percent of their instruction in Spanish and 10 percent in English. Each year thereafter English is gradually increased into the program. By fifth grade, instructional time is 50 percent in English and 50 percent in Spanish. The distribution of the 90/10 model is included in figure 1.1.

Please note that the other language being taught is often called the partner *or* target language. *Additionally, that instructional time may include classes such as art, music, and physical education (PE). Some practitioners also include recess and lunch in the calculation of time in the partner language and English. Figure 1.1 represents the percentage of instruction in the partner language and the percentage of instruction in English for the 90/10 Model at Mountain Heights Elementary School.*

FIGURE 1.1 **90/10 Model**

90/10 Model	Percentage of Instruction in Partner Language	Percentage of Instruction in English
K	90	10
1	90	10
2	80	20
3	70	30
4	60	40
5	50	50

When Juana and Ignacio spoke with the principal to enroll Maricela into the DLI program, Ms. Ortiz mentioned a parent center on campus where they offered classes such as English as a Second Language (ESL) and Zumba for parents and that they would be offering additional programs and meetings for DLI parents specifically. She also explained that Maricela's classes would not only be addressing bilingualism and biliteracy but also be focusing on high academic achievement and cultural competence. Juana, especially, was interested in taking classes and the programming offered at the parent center.

She was also interested in understanding more about the DLI program model that her child would be experiencing, especially cultural competence and linguistic equity because Juana had taken a class in multiculturalism at her local community college when obtaining her AA.

As the months went on, Juana and Ignacio were surprised that the only parental engagement provided to DLI parents was back-to-school night. Additionally, during back-to-school night, Juana and Ignacio noticed that there was no evidence of sociocultural competence in Maricela's folder, on the walls, or in the classroom library of books (empowering students with stories that reflect their identity—and their peers' identities—are essential to sociocultural competence. This enables students to understand societal inequities.), which was something that Ms. Ortiz had explained to Juana and Ignacio as central to the dual language program when they enrolled Maricela into the school. Since the cultural and linguistic composition of Maricela's class did not include 30 percent ELs, it was more monolithic than expected, and less diverse than they had hoped when planning for the program. Sociocultural competence, as well as the use of the primary language, were part of the reason that Juana and Ignacio enrolled Maricela into the school because Maricela had begun to lose touch and communication with her grandparents' language and culture. Juana wanted to make sure that her daughter did not lose her language or culture as a result of living in an English-dominant community. The parents asked the teacher about this, and the teacher suggested that students were going to start a project that took them "around the world" to different parts of Latin America during the next six-week unit. Through this project, students would learn more about their own and their classmates' cultures.

> It's interesting to think about what Juana and Ignacio might have been looking for related to building cultural competence. I imagine that they were looking for examples of ways that Maricela might see herself and the experiences of her family and community represented in the curriculum and instructional materials.
>
> **Sydney**

Juana and Ignacio, as well as other parents, were also disappointed that they weren't being offered additional parental programs as promised to them earlier in the year. The group of parents decided to talk to the principal about this. When they discussed this with Ms. Ortiz, she stated that during the start of the pandemic it had been difficult to offer additional parent programs, but she hoped to begin to discuss the Center for Applied Linguistics' *Guiding Principles for Dual Language Education* (Howard et al., 2018) in Spanish with them the following semester, especially how to use the rubrics for self-reflection, which is addressed in the next section.

THE FOUR PILLARS OF DUAL LANGUAGE EDUCATION

While we recognize that all students in DLI programs are learning language and content in two languages, we are specifically focused on those students—like Maricela in the vignette—who come from homes where a language other than, or in addition to English, is spoken in the home and students who come from cultures outside the dominant culture. As the opening vignette demonstrates, inequities in Dual Language programs begin to occur when a school or district struggles to implement all four pillars of DLE.

In the vignette, for example, Mountain Heights Elementary School struggles to implement the third pillar, sociocultural competence (including linguistic equity since there aren't enough true ELs in the program), and the fourth pillar, critical consciousness—the latter is newly proposed by researchers Palmer et al. (2019). All DLI stakeholders—teachers, administrators, and parents—would benefit from professional learning on the four pillars (more in Chapter 2 about this), which are defined in figure 1.2, and thus can assist DLI programs with ensuring that they are being implemented in an equitable manner.

FIGURE 1.2 ## Four Pillars of Dual Language Education

Source: Sketchnote by Claribel Gonzalez, used with permission. (Lachance & Honigsfeld, 2023).

- **Pillar 1: Bilingualism and Biliteracy**—DLE programs are intended to produce fully bilingual and biliterate students. That is, students who can listen, speak, read, and write in two languages. A bilingual student will be able to listen and speak in two languages, while a biliterate student will become a skilled reader and writer of two languages. An advantage of learning to read one's own native language and subsequently learning to read a second language is the potential to become biliterate—a skilled reader and writer of two languages. Additionally, work by Diaz and Klinger (1991), Bialystok (1991), Hakuta (1986), as well as others, has established that bilingualism and biliteracy enhance cognitive and metalinguistic abilities (one type of metacognition is defined as an individual's ability to focus attention on language as an object in and of itself, to reflect on language, and evaluate it). Thus, we expect biliterate students to be able to use all the linguistic repertoires (social and academic) in both languages.

- **Pillar 2: High Academic Achievement**—High academic achievement means performing extremely well in both languages of instruction and in each academic content area, including science, language arts, social science, and mathematics. Additionally, it is only when we offer classes such as music, special education, art, and physical education that we follow best practices. Special education, for example, ensures that we are including all students, and is required by law and/or compliance, while content areas such as music, art, and physical education might be content areas that keep students in school due to interest levels. It is by keeping expectations high, and providing scaffolding support, that students will rise to high academic achievement levels.

- **Pillar 3: Sociocultural Competence**—Tabaku (2020) suggests the change from cross-cultural understanding to sociocultural competence (more about this later and in Chapter 2) is crucial if students are to understand their own identity, as well as the identities of others. In the classroom, this manifests itself as educators embed lessons with stories that reflect their own identity—and their peers' identities—which are essential to sociocultural competence. Teachers can also embed lessons where students can understand societal inequities, including those at their school and in their classroom, and encourage students to work for more equitable environments for themselves and their classmates. Students can also complete ancestry projects, which can allow them to understand their own identities, as well as learn from those of their classmates.

- **Proposed Pillar 4: Critical Consciousness**—Critical consciousness, then, is the latest pillar proposed for strengthening sociocultural competence and increasing equity and social justice in Two-Way Dual Language (TWDL) education. Specifically, Palmer et al. (2019) argue

    that centering critical consciousness—or fostering [it] amongst teachers, parents, and children creates an awareness of the structural oppression that surrounds us and a readiness to take action to correct it—which can then support increased equity and social justice in TWDL education. (abstract)

For example, students may be asked to provide feedback on the curriculum that is being used and to what extent it addresses social justice. Students may also want to discuss what linguistic equity is, to what extent it is experienced in their own classroom with the language that is required of them inside and outside the classroom, and why that is. Students may also want to join food workers at their school site who may be picketing due to low wages.

After meeting with concerned parents of students in the DLI program, Ms. Ortiz, the principal of Mountain Heights Elementary School, chose to unpack Principle 1: Program Structure with teachers (and then share the results with parents) in Spring 2020 by having teachers complete and use the self-reflective rubrics included in the appendices of the *Guiding Principles for Dual Language Education* (Howard et al., 2018). It was also decided that teachers would read more about equitable environments for ELs within the program the following semester by reading about linguistic equity in DLI programs, using the self-reflection rubric results that follow.

FIGURE 1.3   Appendix A: Self-reflection Rubric for Program Structure from *Guiding Principles for Dual Language Education* (Howard et al., 2018)

Principle 1

All aspects of the program work together to achieve the three core goals of DLE: grade-level academic achievement, bilingualism and biliteracy, and sociocultural competence.

Key Points	Comments	Minimal	Partial	Full	Exemplary
Key Point A The program design is aligned with the program mission and goals.					
Key Point B The development of bilingualism and biliteracy is part of the program design.					
Key Point C The development of sociocultural competence is part of the program design.					
Key Point D Appropriate grade-level academic expectations are clearly identified in the program design.					
Key Point E The program is articulated across grades.					
Key Point F There is deliberate planning and coordination of curriculum, instruction, and assessment across the two languages of instruction.					

When discussing the self-reflection rubric results, Ms. Ortiz, in part, decided to start with Principle 1: Program Structure (which includes sociocultural competence and linguistic equity), because these were the lowest areas when teachers completed the self-reflection rubrics. You can see below in Figure 1.4 that linguistic equity was only partially and minimally aligned, as connected to Program Structure. Teacher findings from the *Guiding Principles for Dual Language Education* (2018) self-reflection rubrics were as follows:

- **75 percent of teachers** felt that there **was <u>partial alignment</u> of the development of sociocultural competence** as part of the program design.

- **25 percent of teachers** felt there **was <u>minimal alignment</u> of sociocultural competence** as part of the program design.

FIGURE 1.4 *Guiding Principles for Dual Language Education*

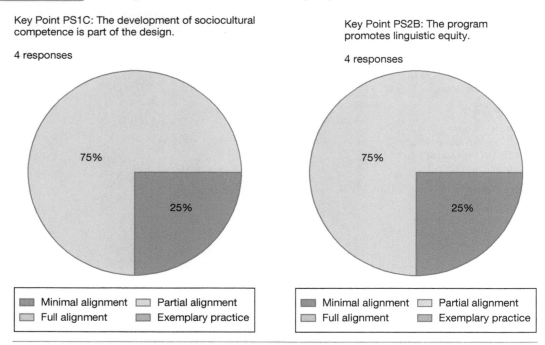

Key Point PS1C: The development of sociocultural competence is part of the design.

4 responses

Key Point PS2B: The program promotes linguistic equity.

4 responses

Source: Howard et al. (2018)

In the discussion that ensued about program outcomes, DLI teachers and the principal wanted a higher percentage of teachers feeling that there was further or more alignment of the development of sociocultural competence as part of program design. Teachers decided to read more about sociocultural competence for this reason. Specifically, teachers started with an article from the Center for Applied Linguistics titled *The Guiding Principles and the Critical Third Pillar: Sociocultural Competence* (Tabaku, 2021).

There were similar results for linguistic equity, with only **75 percent of teachers feeling that there was only <u>partial alignment</u> to the promotion of linguistic equity**. According to the *Guiding Principles of Dual Language Education* rubric, exemplary practice in linguistic equity looks like

- both languages are equally valued throughout the program and the district,

- the home varieties of the two program languages are valued and used as a resource for instruction and for family and community engagement,

- **issues of language status are discussed and revisited as needed, and**

- **particular consideration is given to elevating the status of the partner language.**

The last two bullet points are in bold because the self-reflection rubrics completed by teachers suggested that these two were the greatest areas of need. In particular, the program outcome was that only **25 percent of teachers felt that there was <u>minimal alignment</u> of the program promoting linguistic equity, while 75 percent of teachers felt that there was only <u>partial alignment</u> to the promotion of linguistic equity**. The conversation that ensued was that DLI teachers and the principal wanted a higher percentage of teachers feeling that the DLE program promoted linguistic equity, as well as exemplary practice on the linguistic equity rubric as defined and bulleted previously—issues of language status discussed and revisited as needed, which teachers were doing via the self-reflection rubric exercise, but also a particular consideration given to elevating the status of the partner language. They suggested that periodically self-reflecting and planning around the rubrics, as well as discussing program goals and the research base around the data, would help them get there.

Since Mountain Heights Elementary School did not have enough ELs to participate in the program to begin with, it was already set up for inequities around linguistic equity. So this was something that teachers wanted to immediately rectify for the following school year when recruiting students for the next cohort. As described in the vignette, although DLE models were developed to create equitable environments for multilingual learners, they can inadvertently re-create the same inequities that they were designed to destroy. This happens when multilingual learners are not equally represented, or given a place, within DLE programs.

> The goal of linguistic equity is a critical component of equitable DLE programs. Consider how linguistic equity is discussed in your school or program. What steps can be taken toward increasing linguistic equity in your context?
>
> **Sydney**

THE URGENCY

By carefully integrating linguistic and cultural equity models and characteristics into dual language programs—such as the three pillars of DLE and critical consciousness, a consistent definition and use of Multilingual Learner, an understanding of subtractive and additive program options, as well as the case study in how bilingual teacher certification shortages in one state became a model in creating additional bilingual teaching positions—educators can undo many of the inequities that have developed over time. Additionally, by understanding how dual language programs historically became inequitable, educators can ensure that such inequities are not repeated.

RESEARCH BASE: DLE AS A WAY TO ASSIST SUBTRACTIVE SCHOOL MODELS TOWARD LINGUISTIC AND CULTURAL EQUITY MODELS

In this section of the chapter, we explain how we define and use DLE throughout this book, unpack how DLE programs can assist subtractive school models toward becoming linguistic and cultural equity models, describe the benefits of multilingualism, as well as make clear how the historical impact of subtractive school models came to be so that such inequities are undone.

OUR DEFINITION OF DUAL LANGUAGE EDUCATION

Throughout this book when we discuss DLE, we are referring to:

Dual language as a form of bilingual education in which students are taught literacy and content in two languages. The goals of DLE are **bilingualism** and **biliteracy**. That being so, there should also be sustained instruction in the partner language for at least 6 years (grades K–5). Additionally, at least 50 percent of instruction during the day should be in the partner language throughout the program. Last, language arts and literacy instruction should occur in both program languages.

Two-way or dual language programs are programs where the goal is for students to develop language proficiency in two languages by receiving instruction in English and another language. Similarly, according to the Center for Applied Linguistics (CAL), "[m]any people use the term *dual language* to refer to programs that have a balance of native English speakers and native speakers of the partner language. This model is also called *two-way immersion* or *two-way bilingual immersion*" (Center for Applied Linguistics, 2004).

ASSET-BASED LABELS AND PROGRAMS CONSIDERED SOUND IN THEORY

Another thing that you may notice in this chapter, and throughout this book, is the shift in language around the way that we label students who speak languages other than English as their primary language. Policymakers, state education departments, and school districts still tend to use the label English learner (EL), defined as "[t]he federal statutory classification for the subset of multilingual learners who have been identified as eligible for English language support, which public state and local education agencies are required to provide" (Rutherford-Quach et al., 2021). Instead, the authors of this book have chosen the term multilingual learners (MLLs) because it is an asset-based label, which recognizes and honors the use and development of multiple languages. In this book, we are specifically focused on those students who come from homes where a language other than or in addition to English is spoken in the home and students who come from cultures outside the dominant culture. Multilingual learners is *not* simply an assets-based replacement label for English learners. It refers to a broad group that includes those receiving services (English learners), those who have exited out, "never English learners" who come from linguistically and culturally diverse backgrounds, and Heritage language learners.

Multilingual students also come from a variety of backgrounds regarding language, culture, immigration/visa status, and time spent in the United States. The majority of international students are bi- or multilingual, with some having taken English classes throughout their schooling. Others may be refugee students, who may have limited or interrupted literacy development in both their home languages and English. Another group common in California are long-term permanent residents and the children of immigrants (Generation 1.5) who arrived as young children, learning English in the U.S. school system (Menken, 2013).

Additionally, we have chosen the label MLLs because the language one uses about students matters. We want to honor the language and cultural resources that MLLs have brought with them from home and can further develop and share when they are in DLE programs. According to seminal research by Thomas and Collier (2012), ALL students benefit from dual language education, but it has a clear positive impact on MLLs. When MLLs are only instructed in English, they typically only close half of the achievement gap with English-only speakers, and they tend to fall further behind in school. Thomas and Collier argue that dual language education is the <u>only model</u> that allows MLLs to fully close the achievement gap and even outperform their native English-speaking classmates on standardized tests. As such, DLE programs lead to linguistic and cultural equity, which is why we highlight these program models in this book. The following section discusses the benefits of multilingualism.

THE BENEFITS OF MULTILINGUALISM

What does the research say about the cognitive benefits of bilingualism?

The research on the metalinguistic advantages of bilinguals is strong and suggests bilinguals are aware of their languages at an early age, separating form from meaning, and having reading readiness earlier than monolinguals, which increases reading comprehension (Altman et al., 2018). Similarly, bilingualism increases focus, promotes creativity, and enhances communication skills. Research on language-specific cognitive consequences of bilingualism shows that bilinguals may have a unique perspective of the world, which is unique to that of monolinguals of either language. Since language and culture are intertwined, this is the function that cultivates greater cultural awareness.

Bilingualism enables worldly views because it opens the mind to different and multiple perspectives. As was suggested in the opening vignette, bilingualism links families of different generations together by ensuring that grandparents and grandchildren, as well as other family members, can communicate with each other.

> There are so many amazing benefits of being bilingual. It's important that students have an opportunity to learn about these benefits and have opportunities to celebrate their bilingualism.
>
> **Sydney**

Recent studies also suggest that bilingualism may help fend off the decline of cognitive function in late adulthood and may delay the onset of aging and diseases such as dementia and Alzheimer's disease (Baker & Wright, 2017). This mental health benefit seems to be connected to the fact that multilingual brains are quicker and nimbler. In this way, bilingualism promotes brain health, as well as both activating and stimulating the brain.

Debunking the Myths of Bilingualism

Historically, bilinguals were regarded as having a relatively lower IQ than monolinguals. The ownership of two languages, however, does not appear to interfere with efficient thinking. On the contrary, bilinguals who have two well-developed languages tend to share cognitive advantages (Baker & Wright, 2017). Bilinguals also have advantages in certain thinking dimensions, particularly in divergent thinking (multiple perspectives or ideas to a problem that you are trying to solve), creativity, early metalinguistic awareness (the ability to distance oneself from the content of speech to reflect on and manipulate the structure of language), and communicative sensitivity (Altman et al., 2018).

One particularly compelling research study (Storm et al., 2017) underscored multilinguals' capacity for divergent thinking:

> A sample of bilinguals was randomly assigned to perform alternate uses tasks (AUTs), which explicitly required them to either switch languages or to use only one language while performing the tasks. [The researchers] found that those who were instructed to switch languages during the AUTs were able to generate ideas that were on average more original, than those who were instructed to use only one language during the AUTs, but only at higher levels of habitual language switching. (p. 1)

SUBTRACTIVE AND ADDITIVE BILINGUAL PROGRAM OPTIONS

There are both additive and subtractive bilingual program options. In additive bilingualism, a student's first language continues to be developed while they are learning their second language. These students often have opportunities to use both languages inside and outside of school. If a child is from another culture, the first culture is also honored and respected. With subtractive bilingual program options, students learn the second language at the expense of the first language. Students in subtractive programs may not have opportunities to practice their first language and may feel that their first language and culture are not welcome.

The following chart, adapted from the U.S. Department of Education, Office for Civil Rights, & U.S. Department of Justice (2015), provides a brief overview of some common EL program options, program goals, and the language(s) used for instruction, as well as whether the program is additive or subtractive. Each program also requires specialized training. For example, for a Dual Language Education or Two-Way Immersion program, the goal is for students to develop language proficiency in two languages by receiving instruction in English and another language in a classroom that is typically composed of half primary-English speakers and half primary speakers of the other language. This means that the languages used for instruction would be English and a partner or primary language that the students speak. Please note that each of the program options is unpacked, along with the additive program options highlighted.

Figure 1.5 is helpful for a variety of reasons, including assisting parents and educators with determining programs that are additive and avoiding programs that are subtractive. It is also helpful in making sure that everyone within a system understands the program options, goals, and languages used for instruction when they are selecting the appropriate program for students. The chart also assists educators with using the same language for the programs and options that they are offering their students.

FIGURE 1.5 **Program Options, Goals, Languages Used for Instruction, and Additive and Subtractive**

Program Option	Program Goal	Language(s) Used for Instruction	Additive or Subtractive
English as a Second Language (ESL) or English Language Development (ELD)	Program of techniques, methodology, and special curriculum designed to teach ELs explicitly about the English language, including the academic vocabulary needed to access content instruction, and to develop their English language proficiency in all four language domains (i.e., listening, speaking, reading, and writing).	Usually provided in English with little use of the ELs' primary language(s).	Subtractive
Structured English Immersion (SEI)	Program designed to impart English language skills so that the ELs can transition and succeed in an English-only mainstream classroom once proficient.	Usually provided in English with little use of the ELs' primary language(s).	Subtractive

(Continued)

(Continued)

Program Option	Program Goal	Language(s) Used for Instruction	Additive or Subtractive
Transitional Bilingual Education (TBE), or early exit bilingual education	Program that maintains and develops skills in the primary language while introducing, maintaining, and developing skills in English. The primary purpose of a TBE program is to facilitate the ELs' transition to an all-English instructional program, while the students receive academic subject instruction in the primary language to the extent necessary.	Students' primary language and English.	Additive
Dual Language or Two-Way Immersion	Bilingual program where the goal is for students to develop language proficiency in two languages by receiving instruction in English and another language in a classroom that is usually composed of half English speakers and half primary speakers of the other language.	English and another language.	Additive

For example, Structured English Immersion (SEI) and English Language Development (ELD) are often used interchangeably. Instead, districts should define designated ELD as the protected time of day (e.g., in California, the expectation for Designated ELD is 30–45 minutes at the elementary level and one hour at the secondary level) with a focus on the four domains of language—listening, speaking, reading, and writing—as well as the academic vocabulary needed to access content area instruction. In this way, designated ELD is a time to frontload or provide an overview or review of a concept or skill. SEI, then, is a program designed to eventually impart English language skills necessary to succeed in an English-only classroom and is not meant to sustain the primary language.

As we take a look at analyzing subtractive models, it is important to note that both ESL and Transitional Bilingual Education (TBE), or early exit bilingual education are considered subtractive models. They are considered subtractive models because the goal is not bilingualism or biliteracy. Instead, the native language is only viewed as a vehicle to transition students to English. In TBE Early Exit programs, students are offered native language instruction, but only until second or third grade. All students may have the same common home language (for example, Mandarin), but this is still a subtractive model because English proficiency is the sole goal. Similarly, with TBE Late Exit programs, students are offered native language instruction, but only until fourth or fifth grade. The goal is to use the native language to transition to English, which is an example of a subtractive model. Again, understanding both additive and subtractive models allows educators to both understand and explain such programs to parents, as they are selecting appropriate programs for their children, as well as for teachers and administrators to understand the distinctions in the types of programs that they are offering families.

In the next sections, we discuss the variety of bilingual teacher certification across the country, as well as a case study on the bilingual teacher shortages in one state, California, and what they did to resolve the shortage.

BILINGUAL TEACHER CERTIFICATION ACROSS THE COUNTRY

As suggested previously, the specific certification requirements for bilingual educator positions vary across the country. To demonstrate this, the following figure describes the role, description, and state policies typically required for bilingual teachers and paraprofessionals across the country. Included in the third column, and below the figure, there is also more detail regarding which fifteen states require teachers to hold a bilingual endorsement to teach in a bilingual classroom, as well as the eight states that allow teachers with an ESL credential to teach in bilingual programs. There is no doubt that with a bilingual teacher certification shortage there is also a shortage of bilingual teachers.

FIGURE 1.6 Adapted State Policies Related to Description and Role

Role	Description	State Policies
Certified Bilingual Teachers	• Provide instruction in primary language and/or English to ELs. • Always have both a base credential and an additional endorsement (also called a certification, authorization, credential, or extension).	• At least fifteen states (1) require teachers to hold a bilingual endorsement in order to teach in a bilingual classroom. • In the remaining states, it is unclear from publicly available state policy documents what credentials are required of bilingual teachers.
ESL (or ELD) Teachers in Bilingual Placements	• Provide instruction in English or, in some cases, in the ELs' primary language. • Nearly always have both a base teaching credential and an additional ESL certification. • Typically have to demonstrate additional competencies and/or complete coursework or professional development related to teaching ESL.	• At least eight states (2) allow teachers with an ESL credential to teach in bilingual programs. In these states, districts or schools are responsible for assessing a teacher's language proficiency because there is no state-required language proficiency exam.
Bilingual Paraprofessionals	• Are required to have a high school diploma and, in some cases, an associate degree, two years of post-secondary training, and/or passing scores on a paraprofessional exam.	• A few states, including California, Rhode Island, and Wisconsin, have developed a formalized bilingual paraprofessional role and have provided clear requirements for that role.

(Continued)

(Continued)

Role	Description	State Policies
	• May serve as translators, both for individual ELs immersed in English classes and for events such as individualized education plan or parent meetings, as required by federal law. • May provide small-group or individual instruction to ELs under teacher supervision. • May perform noninstructional duties (e.g. supervising recess, lunch, and school transitions or interacting with parents). • In some cases, they are required to demonstrate content area proficiency, including English, a language other than English, or cultural competency.	• In most other states, there are no clear roles (beyond translation) or official requirements in publicly available state policy documents for paraprofessionals working in a bilingual setting. • Some states specify additional requirements for paraprofessionals working in special education settings, Title 1 schools, or for advanced paraprofessional roles.

(1) *At least fifteen states require teachers to hold a bilingual endorsement to teach in a bilingual classroom. These states are California, Connecticut, Delaware, Idaho, Illinois, Massachusetts, Minnesota, Nevada, New Jersey, New Mexico, New York, Rhode Island, Texas, Utah, and Wisconsin.*

(2) *At least eight states allow teachers with an ESL credential to teach in bilingual programs. These states are Alaska, Colorado, Georgia, Iowa, Maine, Michigan, Oregon, and Washington.*

IMPLICATIONS FOR PRACTICE AND IMPLEMENTATION: CALIFORNIA, A CASE STUDY IN REVERSING BILINGUAL TEACHER SHORTAGES

While there exists a wide variety of specific certification requirements for bilingual educator positions across the United States, there also exists a bilingual teacher shortage in most states. The next section highlights the bilingual teacher shortages in California, which mirrors the bilingual teacher shortages in other states. By highlighting the bilingual teacher shortage in California, as well as systemic efforts to rectify such shortages, we present California as a policy case study in reforming such bilingual teacher shortages.

One of the initiatives that California has had alongside Proposition 58, which reversed Proposition 227 and restrictive English-only policies in the state, has been Global 2030. *Global California 2030*, a document written by then California State Superintendent of Public Instruction, Tom Torlakson, and continued by current State Superintendent of Public Instruction, Tony

Thurmond, operationalized Proposition 58 by setting goals for the number of new dual language immersion programs across the state, as well as setting a goal for the number of new bilingual teacher authorizations per year (California Department of Education, 2018).

Figure 1.7 represents the number of new bilingual teacher authorizations per year between 1994 and 2030. You'll notice that between 1994 and 2016, there is a decline (from 1800 to 700) in the number of new bilingual teacher authorizations due to the restrictive English-only policy in California. Proposition 227, which passed in California in 1998, required that teachers overwhelmingly use English in the classroom setting, further causing the number of bilingual programs to decrease across the state. However, with the passage of Proposition 58 in 2016, which did away with these restrictive English-only programs, we begin to see an incremental increase in the number of new bilingual teacher authorizations per year, which was projected by Torlakson starting in 2019.

FIGURE 1.7 **Number of New Bilingual Teacher Authorizations Per Year**

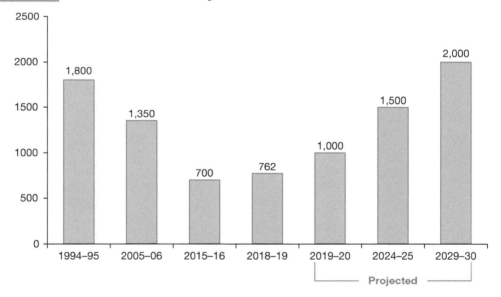

Source: California Commission on Teacher Credentialing (2018)

In Figure 1.8, notice that there were only thirty bilingual teacher preparation programs at state-approved educator preparation programs in 2016, whereas fifty were projected for 2020. When I spoke with the Multilingual Director at the California Commission on Teacher Credentialing in Spring 2021, she stated on the record that nine new bilingual authorization programs were approved in 2020–2021. She also estimated that three to six new bilingual authorization programs would be approved in 2021–2022. Notice that although there is progress, the number of bilingual teacher preparation programs at state-approved educator preparation programs is significantly lower than the projected numbers. This suggests that the projected numbers should be revised, or that new initiatives or incentives for new programs should be provided to make the goals moving forward. At the very least, teacher preparation programs can be surveyed to determine how many might be thinking of adding a bilingual program, as well as why teacher education programs might not want to add a bilingual program at this time.

FIGURE 1.8   Number of Bilingual Teacher Preparation Programs at State-Approved Educator Preparation Programs

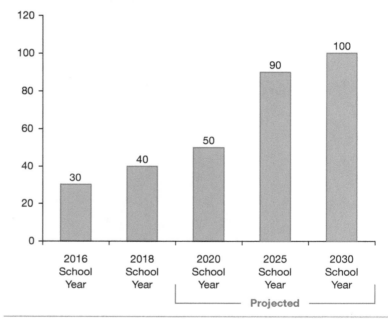

Source: California Commission on Teacher Credentialing (2018)

According to the policy document *Global 2030* (2018), California has been able to turn 20 years of subtractive bilingual policies that extinguished language and multilingual identities at the teacher education level into specific additive policies and goals that now promote bilingualism systematically across the state. The next section discusses how the historical impact of subtractive school models came to be.

HOW THE HISTORICAL IMPACT OF SUBTRACTIVE SCHOOL MODELS CAME TO BE

In this section, the historical perspective of subtractive school models is unpacked. It is our hope that by understanding how dual language programs historically became inequitable, educators can ensure that such inequities are not repeated. Please note that this section is not intended to be an exhaustive list, because we are highlighting subtractive school models in particular. For a more extensive list of key bilingual policies, please see Chapter 8.

Era of Building Programs, Practices, and Approaches

From 1974 to 1981, we find the era of building programs, practices, and approaches on behalf of multilingual learners. Specifically, in this section, we describe three important legislative developments in response to violations that occurred within 7 years. Understanding these violations and the subsequent legislation that furhered the rights of multilingual students and their families allows us to understand such potential violations that may continue to occur in our own contexts. Here, we specifically address three such violations:

- **1974—*Lau v. Nichols*—**This was a violation for not providing ELs language support. Specifically, a lawsuit was filed by Chinese parents in San Francisco in 1974, which led to a landmark Supreme Court ruling that identical education does not constitute equal education under the Civil Rights Act. Instead, school districts must take "affir-mative steps" to overcome educational barriers faced by non-English speakers (Lyons, 1995).

- **1976—California Bilingual-Bicultural Act—**With this act, bilin-gual education became a right for ELs. The California Bilingual and Bicultural Act was also referred to as the Chacon-Moscone Bilingual-Bicultural Education Act of 1976. The purpose of the act was to require California school districts to offer bilingual learning opportu-nities to each pupil of limited English proficiency enrolled in public schools and to provide adequate supplemental financial support to achieve such purpose. Participation in bilingual programs is voluntary on the part of the parent or guardian.

- **1981—*Castañeda v. Pickard*—**The case of *Castañeda v. Pickard* was tried in the United States District Court for the Southern District of Texas in 1978. This case was filed against the Raymondville Independent School District in Texas by Roy Castañeda, the father of two Mexican-American children. Castañeda also claimed the Raymondville Independent School District failed to establish sufficient bilingual education programs, which would have aided his children in overcoming the language barriers that prevented them from participating equally in the classroom.

Era of English-Only Research, Policy, and Accountability

The late 1990s and early 2000s represented the era of English-only research, policy, and accountability. The No Child Left Behind era coincided with English-only and subtractive legislation.

- **2001—No Child Left Behind—**The No Child Left Behind Act (NCLB) passed Congress with overwhelming bipartisan support in 2001 and was signed into law by President George W. Bush on January 8, 2002. This was the name for the most recent update to the Elementary and Secondary Education Act of 1965. The NCLB law—which grew out of concern that the American education system was no longer internationally competitive—significantly increased the federal role in holding schools responsible for the academic progress of all students. The best thing that NCLB did for ELs was to make sure that they, and other sub-groups—such as students with special needs—were also making strides in achievement. States that did not comply risked losing federal Title I money.

- **2006—The National Literacy Panel on Language Minority Children and Youth—**In the mid-2000s, the Stanford Research Institute International and the Center for Applied Linguistics were awarded a contract from the Institute of Education Sciences to convene a National Literacy Panel (NLP) composed of expert researchers from the fields of reading, language, bilingualism, research methods, and education. The charge to the panel was to conduct a comprehensive, evidence-based review of the research literature on the development of literacy among language-minority children and youth. The panel was to produce a report evaluating and synthesizing this research literature to guide educational practice and inform educational policy. In 2006, the NLP published its report, *Developing Literacy in Second-Language Learners*, edited by Diane August and Timothy Shanahan. Several dual language advocates criticized the NLP for not doing enough advocacy for MLLs and for normalizing monolingualism.

Multilingualism Renaissance Era

Both 2015 and 2016 were seminal years for the re-emergence of multilingualism both in California and across the country. With the Every Student Succeeds Act, we begin to see new requirements for the education of ELs. With Proposition 58 in California, we see how one state established a policy—California Education for a Global Economy Initiative—without bilingualism or multilingualism in its name. This proposition was used to redirect the public around the power of multilingualism via goals set out by the California Superintendent of Public Instruction and systemic principles laid out by MLL advocates. More about this and other additive policies next.

- **2015—Every Student Succeeds Act—**Every Student Succeeds Act (ESSA) is the 2015 reauthorization of the 1965 Elementary and Secondary Education Act. ESSA includes a number of new requirements for the education of ELs, including standardized criteria for identifying EL students and inclusion of English proficiency as a measurement of school quality. Unlike its predecessor, the No Child

Left Behind Act, ESSA pushes back on the state's critical decisions such as how quickly schools must improve and how states can intervene with struggling districts, shifting such decision making to state governments—along with provisions within ESSA requiring stakeholder engagement. Unfortunately, ESSA takes no position on promoting multilingualism and is based on a monoglossic view (that bilinguals have two separate linguistic systems).

- **2016—Proposition 58 (California Education for a Global Economy Initiative)**—In 2016, *Global 2030* was written by then California State Superintendent of Education, Tom Torlakson, to guide the systemic implementation of Proposition 58. Some of the goals of *Global 2030* included 1,600 new dual language schools in California, 100 new bilingual authorization programs in teacher education programs, and 2,000 new bilingual teachers. *Global 2030* also guided the implementation of the California EL Roadmap and its four principles:

  o Principle One: Assets-Oriented and Needs-Responsive Schools

  o Principle Two: Intellectual Quality of Instruction and Meaningful Access

  o Principle Three: System Conditions that Support Effectiveness

  o Principle Four: Alignment and Articulation Within and Across System

Era of Advancing Biculturalism

Since language and culture are intertwined, it is clear why the Black Lives Matter movement began to influence education once again in 2020. Although the culturally responsive research base began in 1995, many educators began to see the importance of teaching culture, especially raciolinguistics (the intersection of race and language) and the culturally sustaining research base.

Unfortunately, the backlash movement that has followed, including prohibitions on books and in education, has once again silenced conversations about race, gender identity, and sexual orientation. Multilingual advocates also fear that it is only a matter of time before multilingualism also experiences a similar backlash. This is why it is essential that the third and fourth pillars of dual language education—sociocultural competence and critical consciousness—be taught explicitly and effectively within dual language programs, including the literature below on Culturally Responsive-Sustaining Pedagogies and the Black Lives Matter movement.

The backlash itself can be taught as connected to critical consciousness. Here are additive programs that can be utilized when teaching and addressing pillars 3 and 4.

- **2020—Black Lives Matter**—Although the Black Lives Matter movement officially started in 2013, and the culturally responsive research

> The role of state, district, and school leaders in learning and teaching about sociocultural competence and critical consciousness needs to also live in how we engage staff in professional learning. It's also important to note the education it takes with families and to be transparent about the process to sustain our dual language programs. With changes in cultural trends and leadership, dual language programs need broad coalitions to ensure we stay focused on what we know works for our multilingual students.
>
> **David**

base emerged in 1995, the era of advancing biculturalism and biliteracy officially took hold during the pandemic. The movement returned to national headlines during the global George Floyd protest in 2020, following his murder by Minneapolis police officer Derek Chauvin. An estimated 15 million to 26 million people participated in the 2020 Black Lives Matter protests in the United States. A 2020 Pew Research Center poll found that 67 percent of adult Americans expressed some support for the Black Lives Matter movement. Similarly, in education, we see ethnic studies, humanizing curricula, culturally sustaining pedagogies, raciolinguistics, and translanguaging re-emerge.

- **2021 and Beyond**—Most states have now developed criteria for a Seal of Biliteracy. This addition to a high school diploma has had a huge impact on bilingual program popularity across the country.

CULTURALLY RESPONSIVE-SUSTAINING PEDAGOGIES

The culturally responsive research base has evolved since its first inception in 1995 by founding mother Gloria Ladson-Billings. At that time, Ladson-Billings (1995) laid the foundation with four central tenets of Culturally Responsive Teaching. These tenets focused on student learning by addressing student achievement and helping students accept and affirm their cultural identity, as well as how to develop critical perspectives to challenge inequities. Ladson-Billings's work was then built on by Gay (2002), also a founding mother of Culturally Responsive Teaching, who initially suggested that there are eight attributes of Culturally Responsive Teaching.

Figure 1.9 summarizes the evolving Culturally Responsive Teaching research literature, which continues to grow, and is not an exhaustive list. In fact, we are excited to watch the recent growth in the Culturally Responsive Teaching literature with contributions from antiracist and decolonizing literature, as well as the intersection of race and language with raciolinguistics and translanguaging (Soto et al., 2023).

FIGURE 1.9 Summary of Culturally Responsive Teaching Research Literature (Soto, 2022)

Ladson-Billings's Culturally Responsive Teaching Central Tenets (1995)	• High Expectations • Critical Consciousness • Cultural Competence • Focus on Student Learning (addresses student achievement)

Funds of Knowledge (González et al., 2005)	• Strengths, resources, competencies, and knowledge possessed by households and individuals based on life experiences
	• Necessitates contextualization by educators, or making meaning and connecting school to students' lives
Cultural Proficiency (Nuri-Robins et al., 2006)	• Seeing and responding to cultural differences effectively in a variety of environments
	• Requires movement toward proficiency along a continuum from cultural destructiveness to cultural incapacity to cultural blindness to cultural precompetence to cultural competence to cultural proficiency
	• Includes five essential elements: (1) Assess culture: name the differences, (2) Value diversity: claim the differences, (3) Manage the dynamics of difference: reframe the differences, (4) Adapt to diversity: train about differences, and (5) Institutionalize cultural knowledge: changing for differences.
Gay's Four Essential Actions for Culturally Responsive Teaching (2002 and 2013)	• Qualitative attributes include (1) validating and affirming, (2) comprehensive and inclusive, (3) multidimensional, (4) empowering, (5) transformative, (6) emancipatory, (7) humanistic, and (8) normative and ethical
	• Four foundational pillars of practice: (1) teacher attitudes and expectations, (2) cultural communication in the classroom, (3) culturally diverse content in the curriculum, and (4) culturally congruent instructional strategies
Paris & Alim's Culturally Sustaining Pedagogy Key Features (2017)	• Critical centering on dynamic community languages
	• Valued practices and knowledge
	• Student and community agency and input
	• Historicized content and instruction
	• Capacity to contend with internalized oppressions
	• Ability to curricularize all the above in learning settings

This figure, and the summary of Culturally Responsive Teaching research literature, can assist educators of dual language education with ensuring that they understand and are implementing pillar 3 sociocultural competence and pillar 4 critical consciousness, both in the classroom setting and when designing curriculum.

Conclusion: Key Take-Aways

This chapter serves as an introduction to the state of dual language education and was written to make the case for multilingualism, including a summary of the four pillars of dual language from the research literature, which includes sociocultural competence (or culturally sustaining practices, which is what we use in this book); high academic achievement, and bilingualism and biliteracy; the equal status of both languages within DLE; and the newly developed fourth pillar, critical consciousness. Also addressed in this chapter are a definition of multilingual learners and an overview of dual language immersion as a program model that leads to equity and does not promote subtractive schooling approaches.

Reflection Questions

1. In what other ways can bilingualism and biliteracy benefit the students you are teaching or the students in your DLI program?

2. How have the subtractive policies outlined in this chapter influenced you, your school, district, or community?

3. Which of the culturally responsive-sustaining research base can you use in your classroom or school site?

4. On a scale of 1–5 (1 being lowest and 5 being highest), where is your school with respect to implementing the four pillars of education? Why would you rate them that way?

   a. Bilingualism and Biliteracy

   b. High Academic Achievement

   c. Sociocultural Competence

   d. Critical Consciousness (fourth pillar)

5. Have you and your grade-level DLI teachers tried using the *Guiding Principles for Dual Language Education* self-reflection rubrics? If not, how do you see your team using them in the future?

6. How do you see yourself using the literature on Culturally Responsive-Sustaining Pedagogies in your classroom?

7. How will you address the Black Lives Matter movement as connected to critical consciousness?

References

Altman, C., Goldstein, T., & Armon-Lotem, S. (2018). Vocabulary, metalinguistic awareness and language dominance among bilingual preschool children. *Frontiers. in Psychology, 9*, 1953. https://doi.org/10.3389/fpsyg.2018.01953

August, D., & Shanahan, T. (Eds.). (2006). *Developing literacy in second-language learners: Report of the National Literacy Panel on Language-Minority Children and Youth.* Lawrence Erlbaum Associates Publishers.

Baker, C., & Wright, W. E. (2017). *Foundations of bilingual education and bilingualism.* Multilingual Matters.

Bialystok, E. (1991). *Language processing in bilingual children.* Cambridge University Press.

California Commission on Teacher Credentialing (CTC). (2018). *Approved programs and institutions.* Projections for future years. Retrieved May 1, 2018, from https://www.ctc.ca.gov/commission/reports/data/app-approved-program

California Department of Education. (2018). *Global California 2030: Speak. Learn. Lead.* https://www.cde.ca.gov/eo/in/documents/globalca2030report.pdf

Center for Applied Linguistics. (2004). *CAL dual language program dictionary.*

Diaz, R., & Klinger, C. (1991). Towards an explanatory model of the interaction between bilingualism and cognitive development (pp. 167–192). In E. Bialystok (Ed.), *Language processing in bilingual children.* Cambridge University Press. doi:10.1017/CBO9780511620652.010

Gay, G. (2002). *Culturally responsive teaching: Theory, research, and practice.* Teachers College Press.

Gay, G. (2010). *Culturally responsive teaching: Theory, research, and practice* (2nd ed.). Teachers College Press.

Gonazález, N., Moll, L.C., & Amanti, C. (2005). *Funds of knowledge: Theorizing practices in households, communities, and classrooms.* Lawrence Erlbaum Associates Publishers.

Hakuta, K. (1986). *Mirror of language.* Basic Books.

Howard, E. R., Lindholm-Leary, K. J., Rogers, D., Olague, N., Medina, J., Kennedy, B., Sugarman, J., & Christian, D. (2018). *Guiding principles for dual language education* (3rd ed.). Center for Applied Linguistics.

Ladson-Billings, G. (1995). Toward a theory of culturally relevant pedagogy. *American Educational Research Journal, 32*(3), 465–491.

Lyons, J. (1995). The past and future directions of federal bilingual education policy. In O. García & C. Baker (Eds.), *Policy and practice in bilingual education: Extending the foundations* (pp. 1–15). Multilingual Matters.

Menken, K. (2013). Emergent bilingual students in secondary school: Along the academic language and literacy continuum. *Language Teaching, 46*(4), 438–476.

Najarro, I. (2023). The equity question of dual language programs. *Education Week.* https://www.edweek.org/teaching-learning/the-equity-question-of-dual-language-programs/2023/05?utm_source=nl&utm_medium=eml&utm_campaign=eu&M=6875409&UUID=8d0638089bf51f7ffbe213c6d29fe6af&T=9194755

Nuri Robins, K., Lindsey, R., Lindsey, D., & Terrell, R. (2006). *Culturally proficient instruction (Multimedia Kit): A multimedia kit for professional development.* Corwin.

Palmer, D. K., Cervantes-Soon, C., Dorner, L., & Heiman, D. (2019). Bilingualism, biliteracy, biculturalism, and critical consciousness for all: Proposing a fourth fundamental goal for two-way dual language education. *Theory Into Practice, 58,* 121–133. https://doi.org/10.1080/00405841.2019.1569376

Paris, D., & Alim, H. S. (2017). *Culturally sustaining pedagogies: Teaching and learning for justice in a changing world.* Teachers College Press.

Pew Research Center. (2020). *Amid protest, majorities across racial and ethnic groups express support for the Black Lives Matter Movement.* https://www.pewresearch.org/social-trends/2020/06/12/amid-protests-majorities-across-racial-and-ethnic-groups-express-support-for-the-black-lives-matter-movement/

Rutherford-Quach, S., Torre Gibney, D., Kelly, H., Ballen Riccards, J., Garcia, E., Hsiao, M., Pellerin, E., & Parker, C. (2021). *Bilingual education across the United States.* CCNetwork.

Soto, I., Sagun, T, & Beiersdorf, M. (2023). *Equity moves to support multilingual learners in mathematics and science, grades K–8.* Corwin.

Storme, M., Çelik, P., Camargo, A., Forthmann, B., Holling, H., & Lubart, T. (2017). The effect of forced language switching during divergent thinking: A study on bilinguals' originality of ideas. *Frontiers in Psychology, 8,* 2086. https://doi.org/10.3389/fpsyg.2017.02086

Tabaku, L. (2021). *The guiding principles and the critical third pillar: Sociocultural competence.* https://www.cal.org/news/the-guiding-principles-and-the-critical-third-pillar-sociocultural-competence/

Thomas, W. P., & Collier, V. P. (2012). *Dual language education for a transformed world.* Dual Language Education of New Mexico – Fuente Press.

U.S. Department of Education, Office for Civil Rights, & U.S. Department of Justice. (2015, January). *Dear colleague letter: English learner students and limited English proficient parents* (p. 12). http://www2.ed.gov/about/offices/list/ocr/letters/colleague-el-201501.pdf

A PREVIEW OF SUBSEQUENT CHAPTERS

A brief chapter summary, as well as the title and author of each subsequent chapter, has been included below. We encourage you to first read the chapters that are specific to your job description, or chapters that connect most to your job description. We also encourage you to then select a few chapters that challenge you and that perhaps you have the least prior experience or background knowledge around. This will assist you with continuing to grow in your DLE depth of knowledge. The subsequent chapters and topics are as follows:

Chapter 2: "From Culturally and Linguistically Subtractive to Culturally and Linguistically Sustaining Pedagogy"

- Sydney Snyder
  - This chapter takes a deeper dive into what it means to develop culturally sustaining dual language programs, which integrates sociocultural competence and culturally sustaining practices throughout every aspect of the program, including the program structure, curriculum and instruction, professional development, and family and community.

Chapter 3: "From One Language to Biliteracy and Content in Two Languages"

- Margarita Calderon
  - This chapter addresses how biliteracy can be developed in multiple contexts with a focus on bilingual classroom settings and supporting bilingual teachers.
  - This chapter focuses on how biliteracy can be developed in a multilingual classroom with specific strategies for this context.

Chapter 4: "From Monolingual Assessment to Assessment in Multiple Languages"

- Margo Gottlieb
  - This chapter focuses on best practices for assessing multilingual learners.
  - A focus on teacher and student assessment, with specific application to the classroom.

Chapter 5: "From Educator Collaboration in a Monolingual Setting to Collaboration in a Dual Language Setting"

- Andrea Honingsfeld and Joan Lachance
  - This chapter focuses specifically on strategies for promoting collaboration in dual language settings.

Chapter 6: "From Leading a Monolingual Program to Leading a Dual Language Program"

- Marga Marshall and David Nungaray
  - This chapter focuses on what dual language leaders need to know about leading dual language programs.
  - The dos and don'ts of new programs, including the importance of having strong, effective, and knowledgeable leadership.

Chapter 7: "From 'One Size Fits All' Workshops to Job-Embedded Professional Learning for Dual Language Teachers"

- Rubí Flores
  - This chapter focuses on long-term professional development in DLE settings that is ongoing, comprehensive, inclusive, and differentiated. It also focuses on the essential elements of professional learning that dual language education teachers need.

Chapter 8: "From Monolingual Policies to Dual Language Policies"

- Lyn Scott
  - This chapter focuses on how to strategically create statewide policies for dual language education. This chapter also addresses California and other states as case studies for statewide dual language policy.

From Culturally and Linguistically Subtractive to Culturally and Linguistically Sustaining Pedagogy

SYDNEY SNYDER

PREMISE

Dual language programs are well positioned to be models of culturally and linguistically sustaining pedagogy that can inform instruction of multilingual learners (MLLs) at a national level. To meet this critical goal, dual language programs must support students in becoming multilingual and multicultural by using students' backgrounds, experiences, and cultural assets as foundations for all learning and placing equitable and strengths-based instruction of MLLs at the heart of their work. Supporting students in sustaining their cultural and linguistic assets must be a central goal of Dual Language Education (DLE).

VIGNETTE

It's the school year's first Parent Teacher Association (PTA) meeting at Ellen Ochoa Elementary (EOE), a K–5 elementary school with a two-way bilingual immersion program for Spanish and English. As described in chapter 1, a two-way program is a model that has the goal of students developing language proficiency in two languages by receiving instruction in English and another language. At EOE, the student body is approximately 35 percent native Spanish speakers and 65 percent native English speakers. The PTA meeting is held in the evening in the school cafeteria, and a local student service group offers free childcare for families during the event.

The meeting begins with an introduction of the officers and an apology from the PTA president, an English-only speaker. She explains that unfortunately the Spanish interpreter who was supposed to attend the event is unable to be there, and she asks the one PTA officer who speaks Spanish if she would be able to interpret highlights from each of the agenda items throughout the evening. However, as the evening progresses, the amount of the meeting being interpreted into Spanish decreases as the PTA officer notices that some of the non-Spanish speaking parents appear restless and impatient when information and discussions are interpreted into Spanish. Eventually, the interpretation stops entirely.

During the meeting, the PTA president highlights past fundraisers that have been held for the school including a golf tournament and a family bingo night. She asks for other ideas, and a Spanish-speaking mother suggests a possible 3-on-3 soccer tournament or a tamale sale. These ideas are quickly dismissed with the concern that they won't generate enough interest for the amount of work that will be required.

During the new business portion of the meeting, a group of English-only parents raise a concern that new math content is currently being introduced for all students in Spanish. These parents feel that even though the math skills are reinforced in English their children will be disadvantaged in math. They ask that the PTA leadership draft a letter to the administration to request that all new math concepts be first introduced in English. The Spanish-dominant families remain silent during this discussion.

After reading this scenario, reflect on these questions:

- Viewing this scenario through the lens of cultural and linguistic equity, what stands out to you?

- What are the norms and practices of the Ellen Ochoa Elementary PTA that need to be addressed to foster equity of voice in the organization?

- What role does the idea of discomfort play in this scenario? Who accepts experiences of discomfort, and who doesn't?

- What aspects of this scenario can you identify with related to your own teaching context?

THE URGENCY

Culturally responsive and sustaining pedagogy must be a priority for dual language programs and a central focus in school-based planning, educator professional development, and instruction. While urgent for many reasons, a commitment to culturally responsive teaching practices is needed to address the continued impact of the COVID-19 pandemic on MLLs and students of color, the discrepancy between teacher and student demographics in the field of education, and the current culture wars having a staggering impact on education.

Despite the efforts and creativity on the parts of school districts and educators to continue offering high-quality instruction throughout the pandemic, research demonstrates that the pandemic had a disproportionate impact on academic learning and social and emotional well-being for MLLs and students of color. A variety of factors such as inequitable access to in-person learning, technology, and conducive learning environments and decreased opportunities for English language growth and academic skills development further widened preexisting disparities in opportunities and achievement for these students (Sahakyan & Cook, 2021; U.S. Department of Education, Office for Civil Rights, 2021; Villegas & Garcia, 2022).

Additionally, while the number of teachers of color is on the rise, there is still a significant gap between the percentage of teachers of color and the percentage of students of color nationally (Ingersoll et al., 2018; Schaeffer, 2021). The National Center for Educational Statistics (NCES) data shows that 79 percent of public school teachers identified as non-Hispanic white during the 2017–2018 school year (Schaeffer, 2021). Additionally, 7 percent identified as Black, 9 percent as Hispanic or Latinx, 2 percent as Asian American, and fewer than 2 percent of teachers identified either as American Indian or Alaska Native, Pacific Islander, or of two or more races. In contrast, in the 2018–2019 school year, 47 percent of U.S. public school students identified as white, 27 percent as Hispanic or Latinx, 15 percent as Black, and 5 percent as Asian. Approximately 1 percent or fewer identified as Pacific Islander or American Indian or Alaska Native, and around 4 percent were of two or more races (Schaeffer, 2021).

Because public school educators remain a primarily white and middle-class workforce, many students of color in US schools lack adult role models and contact with teachers who understand their racial and cultural backgrounds (Ingersoll et al., 2018). While sharing cultural and linguistic backgrounds is not a requirement for advocacy of equitable education for MLLs, the demographic disparity between students and teachers does highlight the need for educators who understand the specific needs of MLLs and their families. To address educational inequities and strengthen educational opportunities for MLLs, students must have teachers who are committed to equity and who believe all children can succeed, who are trained to use multicultural materials and resources, and who value the use of home language varieties (Alanís & Rodríguez, 2008;

Banks & McGee Banks, 2019; de Jong, 2011; García et al., 2016; Gay, 2010; Howard et al., 2018; Ladson-Billings, 2004; Lindholm-Leary & Borsato, 2006).

Furthermore, the dramatic uptick in legislation aimed at limiting the discussions of culture, race, and racism in U.S. history highlights the urgent need for stakeholders in dual language programs to be advocates for education that is culturally and linguistically sustaining as well as vocal proponents of systemic change. For example, in 2022, six states passed bills limiting or specifying what schools can teach related to concepts of race, sex, color, and/or national origin (Young & Friedman, 2022). Professional development focused on culturally responsive teaching practices can support educators in understanding where resistance to discussions of multiculturalism, equity, and social justice come from and how to address opposition to instruction, resources, and policies that foster inclusion and equity for all students (Gay, 2010).

RESEARCH BASE

The title of this chapter is *From Culturally and Linguistically Subtractive to Culturally and Linguistically Sustaining Pedagogy*. Before exploring strategies for culturally responsive teaching, I would like us to have a shared understanding of the language used to frame this chapter and the research behind it. Additional information on the theoretical evolution of culturally responsive and sustaining pedagogies is provided in chapter 1.

Valenzuela (1999) in her ethnographic research of Mexican American and Mexican immigrant students in Houston described the concept of *subtractive schooling*, an institutionalized process in which students who are outside of the dominant culture have their linguistic, cultural, and historical identities stripped away by schools' curriculum and policies (for more on subtractive and additive policies and practices, see chapter 1). When students' cultural and linguistic backgrounds and experiences are seen as obstacles to be overcome rather than assets to be valued and built on, these students experience subtractive schooling.

To combat the systematic way that educational systems foster a loss of MLLs' linguistic and cultural identities through everyday education, researchers and educators have advocated education that is culturally responsive, culturally relevant, and culturally sustaining (Gay, 2002, 2010; Ladson-Billings, 1992, 1995; Paris & Alim, 2017). Ladson-Billings (1992, 1995) coined the term "culturally relevant pedagogy" to describe an instructional framework that seeks to empower MLLs intellectually, socially, emotionally, and politically. She emphasized the importance of incorporating MLLs' cultural references in all aspects of learning, having high expectations for students, and building students' sociocultural and critical consciousness. Palmer et al. (2019) argue that critical consciousness, an awareness that leads to the identification and struggle against inequitable social systems, should be a fundamental goal for DLE. Figure 2.1 includes definitions of critical consciousness and sociocultural consciousness, which were discussed in chapter 1 and are referred to in greater detail throughout this chapter.

FIGURE 2.1 Critical Consciousness and Sociocultural Consciousness Defined

Critical consciousness: the ability to analyze and identify inequity in social systems and to commit to taking action against these inequities (Freire, 1970)

Sociocultural consciousness: the awareness that your worldview is not universal and the belief that your worldview is not superior to the worldviews of others

In contrast to subtractive schooling, Paris and Alim (2017) describe the urgent need for *culturally sustaining pedagogies* in which schools are places for nurturing the cultural practices of students of color. Culturally sustaining practices are centered on systematically integrating students' languages and ways of being into classroom learning and across curricular units. These practices are about supporting students in making meaningful connections between their learning and the histories of racial, ethnic, and linguistic communities (Ferlazzo, 2017). To engage in this work, Paris and Alim (2017) also emphasize the necessity of collaboration with students and their communities to identify the aspects of culture and language they want to sustain through schooling.

IMPLICATIONS FOR PRACTICE AND IMPLEMENTATION

Based on a synthesis of research and discussion in the field related to culturally responsive and culturally sustaining teaching, Diane Staehr Fenner and I developed a framework of culturally responsive teaching centered on five guiding principles with classroom and school look-fors for each guiding principle (Snyder & Staehr Fenner, 2021). The goal of the look-fors is to help make culturally responsive teaching practices concrete and actionable and to help integrate these practices across all aspects of a school or district. I have adapted the guiding principles and identified new look-fors to ensure that these recommendations are relevant to and respond to the urgent needs of dual language programs. Through these changes, I have strengthened the focus on cultural and linguistic equity and culturally sustaining practices in dual language programs as well as addressed the need for the development of critical consciousness. I have also included concrete examples of activities or tools that support the guiding principle. The five guiding principles are as follows:

Guiding Principle 1: Culturally responsive teaching is assets-based and grounded in a framework of cultural and linguistic equity.

Guiding Principle 2: Culturally responsive teaching simultaneously supports and challenges students.

Guiding Principle 3: Culturally responsive teaching puts students at the center of the learning.

Guiding Principle 4: Culturally responsive teaching leverages and sustains students' cultural and linguistic backgrounds and fosters sociocultural competence.

Guiding Principle 5: Culturally responsive teaching unites students' schools, families, and communities.

Guiding Principle 1: Culturally Responsive Teaching Is Assets-Based and Grounded in a Framework of Cultural and Linguistic Equity.

Guiding Principle 1 is the foundation of culturally responsive teaching because it asks educators to recognize and value the assets that MLLs bring to the classroom and to build on these assets during instruction. MLLs benefit when they are members of caring school and classroom communities. A commitment from all staff to an assets-based view of students and their families is central to fostering such communities (Gay, 2010; U.S. Department of Education, Office of Planning, Evaluation and Policy Development, Policy and Program Studies Service, 2012). To use students' assets as a foundation for learning, educators must first understand their students' backgrounds, experiences, and goals. A dual language program that is committed to culturally sustaining pedagogy will incorporate opportunities and procedures for educators to learn about and cultivate relationships with students and their families. Without knowledge of MLLs and their families, it is impossible to value and sustain students' cultural and linguistic assets.

Language and culture portraits described in figure 2.2 is one strategy that can be used to learn about students' cultural and linguistic assets and to demonstrate support for these assets. This activity exemplifies the way in which language and culture are integral parts of our identity that connect us to our families and communities and ultimately shape how we see and interact with the world (Hamman-Ortiz, 2021b).

FIGURE 2.2   **Strategy: Language and Culture Portraits**

Language and Culture Portraits is an activity shared by Hamman-Ortiz (2021b) as a tool for supporting students in thinking about the languages and cultures to which they belong and reflecting on how these different aspects of themselves shape who they are and how they experience the world. Students map the languages and cultures that are part of them to a visual representation of their body. To lead this activity:

- Ask students to create a list of the languages and cultures to which they belong. This list can include any aspects of identity that students wish to include (ethnicity, race, gender/gender identity, nationality, and religion). It can include both languages they speak and languages that are part of their history.

- Students should individually assign a color to each aspect of identity on their list (e.g., Spanish - red; Muslim - blue, female - green).

- Give students a silhouette of a person to map the aspects of their identities to different parts of their body. This mapping can be literal (coloring the mouth the color of the language[s] you speak) or the mapping can be symbolic (coloring the torso a particular color because it is an aspect of identity you carry with you at your core but yet is often not seen by others).

- Ask students to share their language and culture portraits and celebrate the strength and joy that comes from being multilingual and multicultural. Language and culture portraits can be shared in whole groups, small groups, or in a gallery walk format. However, it is important that students feel they have a safe space to share, and all sharing should be optional for students.

In addition to an assets-based view of MLLs and their families, Guiding Principle 1 also speaks to the need to advocate cultural and linguistic equity in dual language programs and to identify areas of inequity. Culturally responsive educators must ask questions and collect evidence of areas of inequity in their schools and programs and then share this information with colleagues and administrators. Examples of questions to consider:

- Is one language valued more than another or integrated more frequently into instruction?
- Are students' home cultures equitably represented in the school curriculum and materials?
- Are racial and ethnic groups equally represented in gifted and talented programs, honors or AP classes, and extracurricular activities? If not, why not?
- Are students from any racial or ethnic group receiving punitive consequences (e.g., removal from class, detention, suspension) at higher rates than other students?

To take a closer look at possible areas of inequity in your context, use the *Exploring Inequity in My Context* (Snyder & Staehr Fenner, 2021) tool. This tool can be accessed on the companion website for this book. [online resources]

As you reflect on possible areas of inequity in your context, consider an area that you would like to prioritize, what data you can collect to support your analysis, and whom you might collaborate with to foster more equitable practices in your context. The work of addressing inequities requires strong advocacy skills, so having allies who support your work is important. Begin by collaborating with individuals you trust who have a shared understanding of the need for change. Then as a team consider the most effective way to approach individuals who are in positions of power who can support your efforts.

As you read the examples in figure 2.3. Guiding Principle 1 Look-Fors, reflect on which of these action items are already in place in your dual language school community, which have been started but could be strengthened, and which might be a priority in thinking about next steps.

> The Exploring Inequity in My Context tool is a helpful tool for self-reflection of inequities in our context. The list of inequities, area of focus, data needed, potential allies, and steps to take allow individuals, and perhaps learning communities, to truly explore one inequity in one's context at a time. The reflection questions allow participants to go deeper with the tool.
>
> **Ivannia**

FIGURE 2.3   ## Guiding Principle 1 Look-Fors

- The school mission espouses an assets-based perspective of all learners and a commitment to cultural and linguistic equity. All stakeholders (i.e., students, families, teachers, staff, administrators, and school partners) understand and embrace the mission.
- All teachers receive professional development on culturally sustaining teaching practices and anti-bias training when they are hired.
- Students learn about and discuss the benefits of being multilingual and multicultural (e.g., cognitive benefits, cultural benefits, and academic and professional benefits).
- There is space and a process to challenge inequities and inequitable practices within the school without fear of repercussions.
- There is time and space to support teachers in learning about their students' backgrounds, interests, families and communities, and goals.

Source: Adapted from Snyder and Staehr Fenner (2021)

Guiding Principle 2: Culturally Responsive Teaching Simultaneously Supports and Challenges Students.

Guiding Principle 2 is framed around the importance of having high expectations for all students, but at the same time recognizing the individual support that students may need to meet those expectations. Kleinfeld (1975) in her work with Inuit and Yupik students in Alaska coined the term "warm demander" to describe this balance of high expectations and scaffolded support. Hammond (2015) explains that the essential goal of being a warm demander is "to help students take over the reins of their learning" (p. 100). In our work on culturally responsive teaching, Diane and I expanded that term to become a "warm and informed demander." A warm and informed demander is an educator who believes that all students can learn and strives to foster student autonomy by understanding students' strengths and areas for growth and building on these during instruction. To be an informed demander means having a deep understanding of each student's background, including prior educational experiences, home language, culture, interests outside of school, and goals (Snyder & Staehr Fenner, 2021). Guiding Principle 2 asks educators to act as warm and informed demanders to both support and challenge MLLs in systematic and ongoing ways.

Supporting MLLs

Educators can foster MLLs' autonomy in their learning through the instructional scaffolds and routines that they build into their daily teaching (e.g., use of visuals, think-alouds to model metacognitive skills). However, in addition to using these types of scaffolds, it is essential to support students in understanding and using the unique resources that they carry with them as MLLs.

> Thank you for including explicit ways in which MLLs might transfer their vocabulary from one language to another by being explicit about cognates.
>
> **Ivannia**

As MLLs acquire new languages, we must explicitly teach them to integrate the knowledge and skills that they already have in their home languages and be strategic in pointing out differences. MLLs should have an opportunity to *leverage their dual language brain* and explore the rules and patterns that are the same across languages and those that are distinct.

Drs. Escamilla et al. (2022) in their work on literacy instruction for MLLs advocate the explicit teaching of strategies that support MLLs in learning to integrate their home languages with English during literacy instruction and build cross language connections (Escamilla et al., 2022; U.S. Department of Education, Office of English Language Acquisition, 2022). For example, teachers might color code print in the classroom to identify patterns that differ between English and the partner language. Similarly, students might engage in an activity in which they analyze sets of cognates and circle differences between the words. Figure 2.4 is an example of how you might ask students to compare and identify similarities and differences in cognates.

FIGURE 2.4 **Cognate Comparison**

action and ac**ción**

celebra**tion** and celebra**ción**

na**tion** and na**ción**

The explicit instruction around language integration will not only support students in developing language and literacy skills at a faster rate, but it will also free up important teaching time and cognitive space for students (Escamilla et al., 2022; U.S. Department of Education, Office of English Language Acquisition, 2022). For example, rather than spending time teaching both the English alphabet and the Spanish alphabet, teachers can identify the similarities between the two alphabets and focus instruction on teaching what is different about the two alphabets (Escamilla et al., 2022; U.S. Department of Education, Office of English Language Acquisition, 2022).

Challenging MLLs

Often when we talk about teaching MLLs, the instructional focus is on the need for scaffolded support. However, equally important are the steps that we take to challenge students. The challenge is where we guide students in being researchers, inventors, and activists, where students have space to question and explore. In challenging students, we ask them to think critically and make cross-curricular connections (Snyder & Staehr Fenner, 2021). We give them opportunities to take part in projects that build critical consciousness (our fourth pillar in dual language instruction) and foster social action. By embedding within these units, the academic language and skills that students are already working on, these types of projects can be integrated into your curriculum. A classroom library inventory, described in figure 2.5, is one example of a project-based learning opportunity that will challenge students. It also could be integrated into a unit you are already working on related to opinion writing.

FIGURE 2.5 **Classroom Library Inventory**

Purpose: A classroom library inventory is one way to begin discussions with students about representation in books and other curricular materials.

Getting started: To begin a library inventory unit, define key terms that will be used during the unit. You can share with students the concept of mirrors, windows, and sliding glass doors, explained below (Bishop, 1990; Style, 1988). Through read-alouds and discussion, model the concepts of mirror and window books and talk with students about why it is important for all students to have access to books that are both mirrors and windows.

(Continued)

(Continued)

> **Mirror resources:** Resources that represent the identities, backgrounds, and experiences of the learner (Bishop, 1990; Style, 1988).
>
> **Window resources:** Resources that give the learner an opportunity to learn about the experiences and backgrounds of people who don't share their cultural and linguistic background (Bishop, 1990; Style, 1988).
>
> **Sliding glass doors:** The way in which window resources can allow us to immerse ourselves briefly in the experiences and worlds of others who may be different from us and help us build empathy and understanding for other ways of being (Bishop, 1990).

During the read-alouds, students can take note of characters, authors, and languages in the books that fill their classrooms or school libraries. They should be prompted to ask questions and answer questions such as:

- Does this book have characters who look like me and who have similar experiences to me? How?
- Does this book have characters who look different from me or have different experiences from mine? How?
- Does the author of this book share my cultural and linguistic background? How?
- Does the author of this book have cultural and linguistic backgrounds that are different from mine? How?
- Does this book help me understand a different viewpoint or a different way to live? How?
- Are there an equal number of books in the library in English and my home language? Why or why not?

Next steps: Once students understand and can talk about books and resources through the lens of mirrors, windows, and sliding glass doors during class discussions, have them begin to explore their own classroom and school libraries. New York City educator Stephanie Reyes created a tracking tool in which students could note the characteristics that they were looking for in books in their library and the number of books that they found. She also had students write letters to authors and publishers asking for stronger representation in the books that they write and publish (Reyes, n.d.; Snyder & Staehr Fenner, 2021).

Projects such as a library inventory encourage students to think critically about inequitable systems and their role in working for change. As you reflect on Guiding Principle 2, consider the look-fors in figure 2.6.

FIGURE 2.6 Guiding Principle 2 Look-Fors

- MLLs are provided with consistent instructional scaffolding (e.g., modeling, visuals, formulaic expressions, multimodal representation) across content areas to support them in engaging with challenging grade-level content and in developing academic language.
- Students are provided instructional supports that foster opportunities for language integration (e.g., multilingual word walls, student-generated bilingual dictionaries).
- Instruction includes activities that foster critical thinking and reflection (e.g., open-ended discussion prompts, students monitoring of their learning).
- Instruction includes activities that require students to make connections to their prior experiences and learning.
- Instruction includes activities that require students to consider alternative ways of understanding information and engages students in developing a critical consciousness (e.g., analyzing the shift from celebrating Columbus Day to celebrating Indigenous People's Day).

Source: Adapted from Snyder and Staehr Fenner (2021)

Guiding Principle 3: Culturally Responsive Teaching Puts Students at the Center of the Learning.

Student-centered learning prioritizes student involvement and student choice in their learning. It is a shift away from a lecture-style model in which the teacher does a significant amount of the talking. In a student-centered classroom, students play an active role in determining classroom norms. They have daily opportunities for informal and structured peer learning activities. In addition, they set goals for their learning and engage in ongoing self-assessment and reflection related to their learning.

Informal and Structured Opportunities for Peer Learning

To examine student-centered learning in a dual language classroom, it is essential to consider what opportunities are available to support equity of voice and engagement. Consider these questions:

- What policies and norms do you have in your classroom or school related to language use? How were these norms created?

- Are there separate planned times for whole-class discussions to be conducted in English and the partner language? Is there language equity regarding how these discussions are planned that are consistent with the program model and the policies for language use?

- Are there expectations around language use in small-group discussions that foster equity of voice and are consistent with the program model and the policies for language use?

- Is there equity of voice between students coming from English-dominant homes and students coming from homes in which a language other than or in addition to English is spoken? Which students tend to speak the most in both whole-group and small-group discussions?

As you reflect on these questions, what do you notice about potential areas for growth in planning informal and structured peer learning opportunities?

In designing effective peer learning opportunities in dual language classrooms and ensuring that MLLs are well-supported to take part, it is important to be intentional about student groupings, pair and group work routines and scaffolds, and the inclusion of structured opportunities for language development. Use a variety of student grouping strategies that are intentionally selected to support the goals of the activity. For example, you might intentionally group students in heterogeneous home language groups to be able to provide opportunities for language modeling or group students in homogenous home language groups to provide opportunities for content discussions in students' dominant language. Expectations for language use during small-group discussions should be aligned with the program model and school policies for language use.

Further, you can implement peer learning routines that require all students to take an active role and be accountable for the discussion. The strategy described in figure 2.7 is one example of a peer learning routine to support group accountability. In addition, giving students structured independent thinking or practice time with needed scaffolds (e.g., sentence stems, visuals, glossary of key vocabulary) prior to the peer discussion will help students come to the discussion better prepared to take part. The *Peer Learning Activity Checklist* (Snyder & Staehr Fenner, 2021) is a tool to support you as you develop effective and engaging peer learning opportunities. This tool can be found on the companion website for this book. [online resources]

FIGURE 2.7   ## Strategy: Prep the Reporter

Prep the reporter is a strategy that can be used to support accountability for group work. One student is selected to be the reporter for the group, but prior to the whole-group share out, all students are responsible for helping the reporter prepare to share. Model for the class what it looks like to "prep the reporter" and provide the opportunity for students to practice this skill. Emphasize to students that the reporter is representing the group's ideas and getting the reporter ready to share is a team responsibility. The reporter can be randomly selected or selected strategically by the teacher to foster equity of voice within a classroom. Depending on the language proficiency levels of the reporter and the language of the discussion, students may benefit from sentence stems or frames to support them in sharing the group ideas.

Source: Adapted from Motley (2022)

Engaging Students in Self-Assessment and Goal Setting

Engaging students in self-assessment and goal setting is an important step in building student autonomy and strengthening student motivation. An important component of having students self-assess is helping them build their understanding of the success criteria (Brookhart, 2020). To begin, you can ask students to analyze strong and weak models of academic learning tasks in the language in which students will be completing the academic task. For example, if students are going to be asked to write an explanation for the steps that they took to solve a math problem in Arabic, you might provide two models that share the same final answer but differ regarding the use of academic language, cohesiveness of ideas, and use of sequencing words. During these discussions, have students share what they notice about the different models. These discussions will support students in understanding and being able to describe success criteria in student-friendly terms. These success criteria can be used to develop anchor charts, student checklists, and student-friendly rubrics. When asking students to use student checklists or rubrics for self-assessment, only use select criteria that you have discussed and practiced.

As students gain skills at self-assessment, you can add additional criteria and have students take greater agency in the assessment process. For example, you might have students select completed learning tasks for a portfolio. They can reflect on their work and use it to demonstrate their learning and language development in both languages over time (for more on equitable assessment practices, refer to chapter 4). As students self-assess, you can also ask them to set goals for further learning. For example, if students are rating their ability to use academic vocabulary to explain how they solved a math problem, you might ask them to reflect on one step they can take next to strengthen their use of this language. Students can also be asked to compare their academic language use and development in both languages.

Figures 2.8 and 2.9 are two examples of tools to support students with self-assessment and goal setting. Figure 2.8 is a student self-reflection tool that asks students to set goals for their language development in a particular language. The data table can be adjusted based on the type of language assessments used in your school. Students can shade in their score and then reflect on language domains in which they are strong as well as areas for growth. Rebecca Thomas, the educator who uses this self-assessment, has a modified version for students in lower grade levels that asks students to circle a picture to indicate in which language domain they are strongest and in which domain they most want to improve. Students can also be asked to share these self-assessments with their families so that families are aware of their child's language goals.

Figure 2.9 is a set of sentence stems that you might share with students during student-led conferences. During a student-led conference, students can reflect on a piece of work that they completed, think about what might have been challenging about the task, and/or something that they might do differently next time. The stems provided in this example can be adapted depending on students' grade levels and translated into other languages.

As you reflect on Guiding Principle 3, consider the look-fors in figure 2.10.

Guiding Principle 4: Culturally Responsive Teaching Leverages and Sustains Students' Cultural and Linguistic Backgrounds and Fosters Sociocultural Competence.

Guiding Principle 4 builds on Guiding Principle 1 in that it asks educators to use MLLs' assets including their prior knowledge, languages, cultures, and experiences as foundations for all learning. Guiding Principle 4 also highlights the importance of using curricular materials and resources that offer multilingual and multiethnic perspectives in dual language settings. Palmer et al. (2019) describe the need for students to have opportunities to study the histories of the different communities that are represented in their classroom and to build an understanding of their identities and the identities of others as they have been shaped by these histories. Providing opportunities for MLLs to explore and express their multifaceted identities fosters the development of sociocultural competence in all students.

FIGURE 2.8 Student Language Development Goal Setting Tool

Name _____ Date_____ Language _____

My Score	1.0	2.0	3.0	4.0	5.0	6.0
Listening						
Reading						
Speaking						
Writing						

From the data, I know that I am strong in _____.

From the data, I know I need to improve in _____.

I can improve my _____ by _____.

Source: Rebecca Thomas

Image Sources: istock.com/Yana Momchilova, istock.com/Ivan Zakalevych, istock.com/Avector, istock.com/Pavlo Stavnichuk

FIGURE 2.9 Sentence Stems for Student-Led Conferences

The learning objective for this task was to . . .

In this work, I wanted to demonstrate . . .

To demonstrate . . . I . . .

Something I think I did well was . . .

Something that was challenging for me was . . .

Something I might do differently next time is . . .

Something I have a question about is . . .

I enjoyed . . .

Source: Snyder and Staehr Fenner (2021, p. 168)

FIGURE 2.10 Guiding Principle 3 Look-Fors

- MLLs and non-MLLs participate equally in whole-group and small-group or pair-learning discussions.
- There are school policies and/or clear expectations around language use for whole-group and small-group discussions that allow for equity of voice for MLLs.
- Students have an opportunity to practice routines and language to support engagement in peer learning activities and ways of making connections to their peers' ideas.
- MLLs are given opportunities to speak and write about their lives, including people and events that are important to them.
- MLLs are involved in goal setting and self-assessment through the use of student goal sheets, checklists, student-friendly rubrics, and teacher-student or student-student conferencing related to content learning and language development.

Source: Adapted from Snyder and Staehr Fenner (2021)

A concrete example of what this concept might look like is a project-based unit shared in the California Department of Education's English Language Arts/English Language Development Framework called *Linguistic Autobiographies* (2015). During this unit, students engage in collaborative conversations and learning tasks to explore how the use of languages other than English, "nonstandard" varieties of English, and slang are perceived and responded to in the media. The unit includes an exploration of film, essays, and poetry that all touch on the theme of perceptions of language use, and the unit activities provide students an opportunity to reflect on the intersection of language and culture and the power dynamics that are embedded in how language is used and responded to.

Students in younger grade levels could be given opportunities to explore their own decisions, feelings, and beliefs about language and ways to respond to negative comments that they might hear related to the languages they use. During these conversations, educators can validate students' feelings while at the same time emphasizing the value of being multilingual and multicultural. Educators can also share resources and stories of individuals who are strong models of multilingualism and multiculturalism and invite former students into the classroom to share their experiences about the benefit of being multilingual.

Opportunities for translanguaging, the use of more than one language to communicate as a way to encourage the full use of students' linguistic resources, can also be intentionally integrated into instruction (Creese & Blackledge, 2010; Garcia et al., 2016). For example, MLLs might be given the opportunity to annotate an English text using notes in their home language or build background knowledge through a home language text or video. For more on translanguaging practices, see chapter 4. The one caveat to supporting translanguaging practices in a dual language program is the potential for it to open a door for the overuse of English (or the dominant language) and create a subtractive learning environment for students who have the nondominant language background (Howard et al., 2018).

Student creation of identity texts (multilingual, multimodal texts in which students independently or collaborative explore an aspect of their identity) can be a wonderful way to foster translanguaging practices and develop sociocultural competence (Cummins et al., 2005; Hamman-Ortiz, 2021a). Identity texts can be written, spoken, visual, musical, dramatic, or a combination of any of these modalities, and students can be given the freedom to use any of the languages in their linguistic repertoires. The structure and prompt used for identity texts can vary depending on the age of the students and the priorities for the activity. Here are two sample projects ideas:

> Read *The Best Part of Me* by Wendy Ewald. Ask students to develop their own images and writing to describe a part of themselves that they appreciate and what it means to their identity.

> Have students work in groups to showcase an aspect of their town, city, or community that is important to them. A project such as this can highlight the ways that different aspects of a community are important to different group members. The project could also be developed and presented multilingually (Hamman-Ortiz, 2021a).

As you reflect on Guiding Principle 4 and strategies that you use to leverage students' cultural and linguistic backgrounds and provide access to models of multilingualism and multiculturalism that students can relate to, consider the look-fors in figure 2.11.

FIGURE 2.11 **Guiding Principle 4 Look-Fors**

- High-quality instructional materials and texts in both languages are available and used consistently.

- Lessons and units include perspectives of individuals that come from students' home cultures, and culturally authentic resources (e.g., art, video, and audio-video materials) are representative of students' home cultures.

- Students becoming multilingual and multicultural is a clearly articulated and supported goal within the school community.

- Students are explicitly taught patterns of language and how to integrate their knowledge of their home language into their acquisition of the partner language.

- Leaders and role models from the communities are included in the learning (e.g., community members are invited to speak in class).

Source: Adapted from Snyder and Staehr Fenner (2021)

Guiding Principle 5: Culturally Responsive Teaching Unites Students' Schools, Families, and Communities.

Collaboration with all families and communities in a dual language program is critical to supporting MLLs' academic and social and emotional needs, particularly those from the non-English dominant group. Research has shown a strong positive correlation between family engagement and student outcomes such as higher rates of high school graduation and enrollment in higher education, higher grades and test scores, and higher levels of language proficiency (Ferguson, 2008; Henderson & Mapp, 2002; Lindholm-Leary, 2015; National Academies of Sciences, Engineering, and Medicine, 2017). In addition to these academic outcomes, the effective inclusion and valuing of all students' families and communities creates a richer and more caring learning space for MLLs.

This chapter began with a scenario that emphasized the ways in which English-dominant families frequently have greater voice and greater power in dual language school communities. Palmer et al. (2019) emphasize that in spaces where dominant norms prevail, those who do not share those norms may have feelings of discomfort, but that discomfort is ignored or overlooked because it is outside what is considered the standard way of being or doing. In the opening scenario, the voice of the Spanish-speaking families has been overpowered, and as a result, they weren't able to speak about any discomfort that they may have had with the language in which the meeting was conducted, the choice of fundraisers for the school, and proposed recommendations related to instruction. Instead, the English-dominant families controlled the language, the topics, and the outcomes of the meetings.

Thus, to foster strong partnerships with all families and communities in a dual language program, it is essential for schools and educators to create a safe space for MLLs' families to share their experiences and concerns and demonstrate a commitment to making sure that their voices are heard. In doing so, the English-dominant, often white families, may experience discomfort and push back against policies and procedures that lead to this discomfort. As a result, it is important to be able to clearly articulate a schoolwide commitment to MLL family engagement and equity of voice, especially for those who do not speak the dominant language. To support English-dominant families in understanding why this commitment to equity of voice and culturally and linguistically sustaining practices is so critical, administrators and school leaders can share examples that highlight the urgent need to address inequitable education and educational opportunity gaps that exist for certain MLLs. In addition, school leaders can also share the ways in which culturally and linguistically sustaining practices that create space for MLLs and their families to share their experiences and ideas benefit all members of a school community.

To develop a welcoming and safe space for MLL families and demonstrate the value that you place on their membership in the community, examine areas of inequity for non-English–dominant MLL families, engage in critical listening campaigns, build relationships with these families, and remove barriers that may be standing in the way of their family engagement.

> It is so essential to ask ourselves these questions (and often) when exploring the school environment and procedures for inequities for MLL families. Then, it is essential to create a common plan around each of the bullet points so that everyone is on the same page regarding how MLL family members can truly be a part of the school community.
>
> **Ivannia**

Examine your school environment and school procedures to determine areas of inequity for MLL families.

Consider what it is like for an MLL family member to be a part of the school community and consider the ways in which the school and families communicate by asking yourself these questions:

- Can all MLL families see themselves, their children, and their communities represented visually around the school?

- Are they greeted in their home languages when they come to the school or when they call the school?

- Is school information that all MLL families need readily accessible in a language and format that they can understand as required by federal law?

- Is family communication a two-way process in which families have a straightforward way to ask questions and raise concerns with school administrators and teachers?

If you answered no to any of these questions, consider the strategies (discussed next) and identify whom to partner with to address the issue.

Engage in critical listening through listening campaigns.

Critical listening is essential if we want to learn about MLL families. Safir and Dugan (2021) describe the importance of collecting "street data" to gain a greater understanding of the strengths of students and families and to identify what may be getting in the way of student learning. Palmer et al. (2019) explain that critical listening is not just about "offering simultaneous translation at meetings but providing opportunities for these parents to be *listened to*: to share their experiences, interrogate school leaders, or talk about issues they wish to see addressed" (p. 7). Schools need to move beyond written family surveys and reach out personally to MLL families, especially those who are non-English dominant, to ask them to take part in listening sessions and/or focus group discussions during which they can prioritize the issues that they would like to discuss. These listening sessions and focus groups should be offered in families' home languages in places where they feel comfortable (perhaps at a location in their communities) and at a time that is convenient for families to attend.

Build relationships with MLL families by learning about their communities and taking part in community events.

Spending time in MLL family communities will strengthen understanding of the assets that MLL students bring to your school and classroom and provide valuable information that can be used when tapping into students' backgrounds and experiences. One way to learn more about the communities of MLL families is through family or student-led community walks (L. Markham, personal communications November 25, 2019, as cited in Snyder & Staehr Fenner, 2021; Safir & Dugan, 2021). Student-led community walks can provide an opportunity for educators to learn about important sites and people in these communities. Community walks can also provide opportunities for critical listening and for building school, family, and community partnerships in support of students.

Remove barriers that might be standing in the way of family engagement.

When planning family engagement events or thinking about expectations around day-to-day family engagement, consider barriers (e.g., language in which the event is conducted, childcare, transportation, location or time of the event, comfort level) that might be preventing MLL family engagement. Then problem-solve strategies for eliminating those barriers (Staehr Fenner, 2014; Snyder & Staehr Fenner, 2021). It is critical to offer families a safe space and opportunity to share what these barriers might be rather than make assumptions about potential barriers.

As you reflect on Guiding Principle 5, consider the look-fors in figure 2.12.

FIGURE 2.12 **Guiding Principle 5 Look-Fors**

- The school visually demonstrates a commitment to multicultural families and students (e.g., flags from students' home countries, signs posted in multiple languages, and student work displayed on walls).

- The school offers space and time for the questions and concerns of non-dominant language families to be heard.

- Educators build relationships with and understanding of MLL families by spending time in their communities, meeting community leaders, and attending community events.

- The school demonstrates a commitment to MLL family engagement by asking about and eliminating barriers (e.g., language in which events are conducted, childcare, transportation, location or time of the event, comfort level) that may stand in the way of their participation.

- MLL family members are actively involved with school committees or organizations that are open to parents (e.g., PTA). It is essential to invite MLL family members to join and to create a space in which they feel comfortable and supported.

Source: Adapted from Snyder and Staehr Fenner (2021)

Collaborate to Determine Priorities

I have shared many ideas to integrate culturally responsive and sustaining teaching into dual language programs, and it can feel daunting to know what to prioritize. Collaborating with a school-based team and including MLL families and students in these discussions can be a unifying way to determine your needs and set goals for next steps. Figure 2.13. The Culturally Responsive School Checklist and Goal Setting for Dual Language Programs can be a helpful collaboration tool. It includes all the look-fors provided in this chapter and also includes space for you to determine your own look-fors related to each guiding principle. A downloadable copy of this checklist is available on the companion website.

FIGURE 2.13 Culturally Responsive School Checklist and Goal Setting for Dual Language Programs

Directions: Individually or collaboratively, reflect on the presence of each of these look-fors, grouped by guiding principle, in your context. In cases in which the look-for is not present, brainstorm what you will do to improve how the look-for is incorporated in your classroom or school. Then, based on your responses in the checklist, choose one guiding principle to focus on. List three steps you can take to strengthen that guiding principle in your context.

Look-Fors	Yes	Sometimes	No	To improve on how this look-for is incorporated in my classroom or school, I will . . .
Guiding Principle 1: Culturally responsive teaching is assets-based and grounded in a framework of cultural and linguistic equity.				
A. The school mission espouses an assets-based perspective of all learners and a commitment to cultural and linguistic equity. All stakeholders (i.e., students, families, teachers, staff, administrators, and school partners) understand and embrace the mission.				
B. All teachers receive professional development on culturally sustaining teaching practices and anti-bias training when they are hired.				
C. Students learn about and discuss the benefits of being multilingual and multicultural (e.g., cognitive benefits, cultural benefits, and academic and professional benefits).				
D. There is space and a process to challenge inequities and inequitable practices within the school without fear of repercussions.				
E. There is time and space to support teachers in learning about their students' backgrounds, interests, families and communities, and goals.				
Additional look-for:				
Additional look-for:				

(Continued)

(Continued)

Look-Fors	Yes	Sometimes	No	To improve on how this look-for is incorporated in my classroom or school, I will . . .
Guiding Principle 2: Culturally responsive instruction simultaneously supports and challenges students.				
F. MLLs are provided with consistent instructional scaffolding (e.g., modeling, visuals, formulaic expressions, multimodal representation) across content areas to support them in engaging with challenging grade-level content and in developing language.				
G. Students are provided instructional supports that foster opportunities for language integration (e.g., multilingual word walls, student-generated bilingual dictionaries).				
H. Instruction includes activities that foster critical thinking and reflection (e.g., open-ended discussion prompts, students monitoring of their learning).				
I. Instruction includes activities that require students to make connections to their prior experiences and learning.				
J. Instruction includes activities that require students to consider alternative ways of understanding information and engages students in developing a critical consciousness (e.g., analyzing the shift from celebrating Columbus Day to celebrating Indigenous People's Day).				
Additional look-for:				
Additional look-for:				

Look-Fors	Yes	Sometimes	No	To improve on how this look-for is incorporated in my classroom or school, I will . . .
🎯 **Guiding Principle 3:** Culturally responsive teaching places students at the center of the learning.				
K. MLLs and non-MLLs participate equally in whole-group and small-group or pair-learning discussions.				
L. There are school policies and/or clear expectations around language use for whole-group and small-group discussions that allow for equity of voice for MLLs.				
M. Students have an opportunity to practice routines and language to support engagement in peer learning activities and ways of making connections to their peers' ideas.				
N. MLLs are given opportunities to speak and write about their lives, including people and events that are important to them.				
O. MLLs are involved in goal setting and assessment through the use of student goal sheets, checklists, peer-editing activities, and teacher-student or student-student conferencing related to content learning and language development.				
Additional look-for:				
💬 **Guiding Principle 4:** Culturally responsive teaching leverages and sustains students' cultural and linguistic backgrounds and fosters sociocultural competence.				
P. High-quality instructional materials and texts in both languages are available and used consistently.				

(Continued)

(Continued)

Look-Fors	Yes	Sometimes	No	To improve on how this look-for is incorporated in my classroom or school, I will . . .
Q. Lessons and units include perspectives of individuals that come from students' home cultures, and culturally authentic resources (e.g., art, video, and audio-visual materials) are representative of students' home cultures.				
R. Students becoming multilingual and multicultural is a clearly articulated and supported goal within the school community.				
S. Students are explicitly taught patterns of language and how to integrate their knowledge of their home language into their acquisition of the partner language.				
T. Leaders and role models from MLL communities are included in the learning (e.g., community members are invited to speak in class).				
Additional look-for:				
Additional look-for:				
👥 **Guiding Principle 5:** Culturally responsive teaching unites students' schools, families, and communities.				
U. The school visually demonstrates a commitment to multicultural families and students (e.g., flags from students' home countries, signs posted in multiple languages, and student work displayed on walls).				
V. The school offers space and time for the questions and concerns of non-dominant language families to be heard.				

Look-Fors	Yes	Sometimes	No	To improve on how this look-for is incorporated in my classroom or school, I will . . .
W. Educators build relationships with and understanding of MLL families by spending time in their communities, meeting community leaders, and attending community events.				
X. The school demonstrates a commitment to MLL family engagement by asking about and eliminating barriers (e.g., language in which the event is conducted, childcare, transportation, location or time of the event, comfort level) that may stand in the way of their participation.				
Y. MLL family members are actively involved with school committees or organizations that are open to parents (e.g., PTA). It is essential to invite MLL family members to join and to create a space in which they feel comfortable and supported.				
Additional look-for:				
Additional look-for:				

Goal Setting

Based on my responses to the checklist, the guiding principle I prioritize to focus on is:

I will take the following three steps to strengthen this guiding principle:

1.

2.

3.

Source: Adapted from Snyder and Staehr Fenner (2021)

Conclusion: Key Take-Aways

It is often assumed that dual language programs are committed to equitable education and equitable educational outcomes for all students. However, culturally sustaining practices are not systematically integrated into all dual language programs. A shift from culturally and linguistically subtractive to culturally and linguistically sustaining pedagogy requires a schoolwide commitment to and professional development on understanding, valuing, and using MLLs' assets as foundations for learning. It asks educators to examine inequities of voice, representation, and opportunities in the classroom, in the curriculum, in school programs, and in family engagement and to build critical consciousness in all stakeholders. When we create a space for all voices to be heard and MLLs to thrive, the whole community will benefit and be strengthened.

Reflection Questions

1. What is the connection between culturally sustaining instructional practices and equity for MLLs?

2. Where might there be issues of inequity for MLLs in your context? What steps could you take to collect data about possible inequities?

3. Which of the five guiding principles stood out to you as a priority for your school or context? Why?

4. What is one step that you can take to support your school in strengthening its commitment to culturally and linguistically sustaining practices for MLLs?

5. What is one step you would like to take to build stronger partnerships with MLL families?

References

Alanís, I., & Rodríguez, M. A. (2008). Sustaining a dual language immersion program: Features of success. *Journal of Latinos and Education, 7*(4), 305–319. https://doi.org/10.1080/15348430802143378

Banks, J. A., & McGee Banks, C. A. M. (Eds.). (2019). *Multicultural education: Issues and perspectives* (10th ed.). Wiley & Sons.

Bishop, R. S. (1990). Mirrors, windows, and sliding glass doors. *Perspectives, 6*(3), ix–xi.

Brookhart, S. (2020, May). *Five formative assessment strategies to improve distance learning outcomes for students with disabilities.* (NCEO Brief #20). National Center on Educational Outcomes.

California Department of Education's English Language Arts/English Language Development Framework. (2015). *Snapshot 7.1. Investigating language, culture, and society: Linguistic autobiographies* (pp. 726–727). http://www.cde.ca.gov/ci/rl/cf/documents/elaeldfwchapter7.pdf

Creese, A., & Blackledge, A. (2010, February). Translanguaging in the bilingual classroom: A pedagogy for learning and teaching? *Modern Language Journal, 94*(1), 103–115.

Cummins, J., Bismilla, V., Chow, P., Cohen, S., Giampapa, F., Leoni, L., Sandhu, P., & Sastri, P. (2005). Affirming identity in multilingual classrooms. *Educational Leadership, 63*(1), 38–43.

de Jong, E. J. (2011). *Foundations for multilingualism in education: From principles to practice*. Caslon.

Escamilla, K., Olsen, L., & Slavik, J. (2022). *Towards comprehensive, effective literacy policy and instruction for English learner/emergent bilingual students*. National Committee for Effective Literacy.

Ferguson, C. (2008). *The school–family connection: Looking at the larger picture: A review of current literature*. National Center for Family and Community Connections With Schools.

Ferlazzo, L. (2017, July 6). Author interview: "Culturally sustaining pedagogies." *Education Week*. https://www.edweek.org/teaching-learning/opinion-author-interview-culturally-sustaining-pedagogies/2017/07

Freire, P. (1970). *Pedagogy of the oppressed*. Continuum.

García, O., Johnson, S. I., & Seltzer, K. (2016). *The translanguaging classroom: Leveraging student bilingualism for learning*. Caslon.

Gay, G. (2002, March/April). Preparing for culturally responsive teaching. *Journal of Teacher Education, 53*(2), 106–116.

Gay, G. (2010). *Culturally responsive teaching: Theory, research, and practice* (2nd ed.). Teachers College Press.

Hamman-Ortiz, L. (2021a, October). *Identity texts*. Notre Dame Center for Literacy Education. https://iei.nd.edu/initiatives/notre-dame-center-for-literacy-education/news/identity-texts

Hamman-Ortiz, L. (2021b, September). *Language and culture portraits*. Notre Dame Center for Literacy Education. https://iei.nd.edu/initiatives/notre-dame-center-for-literacy-education/news/language-and-culture-portraits

Hammond, Z. (2015). *Culturally responsive teaching and the brain*. Corwin.

Henderson, A. T., & Mapp, K. L. (2002). *A new wave of evidence: The impact of school, family, and community connections on student achievement*. National Center for Family and Community Connections With Schools.

Howard, E. R., Lindholm-Leary, K. J., Rogers, D., Olague, N., Medina, J., Kennedy, B., Sugarman, J., & Christian, D. (2018). *Guiding principles for dual language education* (3rd ed.). Center for Applied Linguistics.

Ingersoll, R. M., Merrill, E., Stuckey, D., & Collins, G. (2018). *Seven trends: The transformation of the teaching force*. CPRE Research Reports.

Kleinfeld, J. (1975). Effective teachers of Eskimo and Indian students. *School Review, 83*(2), 301–344.

Ladson-Billings, G. (1992). Reading between the lines and beyond the pages: A culturally relevant approach to literacy teaching. *Theory Into Practice, 31*(4), 312–320.

Ladson-Billings, G. (1995). Toward a theory of culturally relevant pedagogy. *American Research Journal, 32*(3), 465–491.

Ladson-Billings, G. (2004). New directions in multicultural education: Complexities, boundaries, and critical race theory. In J. A. Banks & C. A. M. Banks (Eds.), *Handbook of research on multicultural education* (2nd ed., pp. 50–65). Jossey Bass.

Lindholm-Leary, K. J. (2015). *Sobrato family foundation early academic and literacy project after five full years of implementation: Final research report*. Sobrato Family Foundation.

Lindholm-Leary, K. J., & Borsato, G. (2006). Academic achievement. In F. Genesee, K. Lindholm-Leary, W. Saunders, & D. Christian (Eds.), *Educating English language learners* (pp. 157–179). Cambridge University Press.

Motley, N. (2022). *Small moves big gains.* Seidlitz Education.

National Academies of Sciences, Engineering, and Medicine. (2017). *Promoting the educational success of children and youth learning English: Promising futures, Box 7.5.* National Academies Press. https://doi.org/10.17226/24677

Palmer, D., Cervantes-Soon., Dorner, L., & Heiman, D. (2019). Bilingualism, biliteracy, biculturalism, and critical consciousness for all: Proposing a fourth fundamental goal for two-way dual language education. *Theory Into Practice, 58*(2), 121–133. doi:10.1080/00405841.2019.1569376

Paris, D., & Alim, H. S. (2017). *Culturally sustaining pedagogies: Teaching and learning for justice in a changing world.* Teachers College Press.

Reyes, S. (n.d.). *Diversity in your classroom library: Mirrors and windows projects.* Teachers Pay Teachers.

Safir, S., & Dugan, J. (2021). *Street data: A next-generation model for equity, pedagogy, and school transformation.* Corwin.

Sahakyan, N., & Cook, H. G. (2021). *Examining English learner testing, proficiency, and growth: Before and throughout the COVID-19 pandemic.* Wisconsin Center for Education Research, University of Wisconsin–Madison.

Schaeffer, K. (2021). *America's public school teachers are far less racially and ethnically diverse than their students.* Pew Research Center.

Snyder, S., & Staehr Fenner, D. (2021). *Culturally responsive teaching for multilingual learners: Tools for equity.* Corwin.

Staehr Fenner, D. (2014). *Advocating for English Learners: A guide for educators.* Corwin.

Style, E. (1988). Curriculum as window and mirror. *Listening for all voices.* Oak Knoll School Monograph. https://www.nationalseedproject.org/itemid-fix/entry/curriculum-as-window-and-mirror

U.S. Department of Education, Office for Civil Rights. (2021). *Education in a pandemic: The disparate impact of COVID-19 on America's students.* Author. https://www2.ed.gov/about/offices/list/ocr/docs/20210608-impacts-of-covid19.pdf

U.S. Department of Education, Office of English Language Acquisition. (2022, September 21). *Effective literacy instruction for multilingual learners: What it is and what it looks like* [webinar]. https://ncela.ed.gov/events/2022-09-21-webinar-effective-literacy-instruction-for-multilingual-learners-what-it-is-and

U.S. Department of Education; Office of Planning, Evaluation and Policy Development; Policy and Program Studies Service. (2012). *Language instruction educational programs (LIEPs): A review of the foundational literature.* Author. https://www2.ed.gov/rschstat/eval/title-iii/language-instruction-ed-programs-report.pdf

Valenzuela, A. (1999). *Subtractive schooling: Issues of caring in education of US-Mexican youth.* State University of New York Press.

Villegas, L., & Garcia, A. (2022). *Educating English learners during the pandemic: Insights from experts, advocates, and practitioners.* New America.

Young, J., & Friedman, J. (2022). *America's censored classrooms.* Pen America.

chapter three

From One Language to Biliteracy and Content in Two Languages

MARGARITA CALDERÓN

PREMISE

Studies of effective schools consistently and conclusively demonstrate that high-quality programs have a cohesive schoolwide shared vision; a set of goals that define their expectations for achievement; and an instructional focus and commitment to achievement and high expectations that are shared by students, parents, teachers, and administrators (Berman et al., 1995; Slavin & Calderón, 2001). The importance of these shared values is reinforced in studies of mainstream schools, low-performing schools, dual language schools, and other bilingual programs serving multilingual learners (MLLs) (Howard et al., 2018).

High-quality biliteracy can be developed in a variety of contexts when curriculum, instruction, and professional development implementation are carefully crafted and implemented. That means implementing schoolwide bilingual or dual language programs that involve everyone in the school. Sometimes schools struggle to have a dual language program beyond a few classes or grades. A track with only one grade level lacks school and community support. Yet all programs can grow when the integration of language, literacy, content, and commitment is the goal.

In Bilingual and Dual Language Programs

- There is a balance of time devoted to two languages.

- Academic language, foundational reading, reading comprehension, and writing skills are taught in both languages.

- Math, science, social studies, and language arts are taught at high levels of achievement in both languages.

- Speakers dominant in one language are given timely equal opportunities or enhanced opportunities to become dominant in two languages.

- Students are afforded opportunities to participate in art, music, sports, and clubs.

- All English as a Second Language (ESL) and English Language Development (ELD; ESL/ELD), special education, core content teachers, coaches, counselors, equity directors, and administrators participate in comprehensive yearlong professional development and school-site collaborative learning.

- There is an understanding of cultural and linguistic diversity and equitable instruction.

- School leaders value and understand immigrant students, use data to measure progress, and engage families and community.

> While evidence-based instructional features may be applicable across a variety of contexts, it is equally noteworthy to mention that both bilingual and monolingual teachers can foster MLLs' bilingual and biliteracy development. With teachers as facilitators, MLLs of the same partner language can readily interact with each other in multiple languages. In a literacy block, for example, MLLs can exchange different perspectives, brainstorm ideas, or offer feedback on draft projects.
>
> **Marga**

While this book advocates dual language programming, it is worth noting that in monolingual settings or ESL/ELD or middle and high school classrooms, many of the evidence-based features are the same.

As we can see below, the same features for ESL, ELD, or general education classrooms apply. The type of program selected by a school requires the same features. The only difference is the first item where students are taught literacy in English but with respect to their primary language.

- Academic language, foundational reading, reading comprehension, and writing skills are taught in English, but teachers can use the students' primary language if possible, and students are afforded opportunities to use translanguaging for processing information.

- Math, science, social studies, and language arts are taught at high levels of achievement.

- Speakers dominant in their primary language are given timely equal opportunities or enhanced opportunities to become dominant in English.

- Students are afforded opportunities to participate in art, music, sports, and clubs, which are sometimes traded in for pulloutl ESL sessions.

- All ESL/ELD, special education, core content teachers, coaches, counselors, equity directors, and administrators participate in comprehensive yearlong professional development and school-site collaborative learning.

- There is an understanding of cultural and linguistic diversity and equitable instruction.

- School leaders value understanding immigrant students, use data to measure progress, and engage families and community.

FIGURE 3.1 Key Biliteracy Components

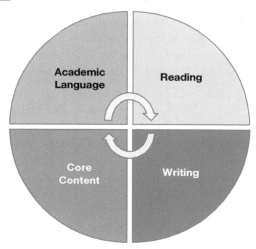

**Social-Emotional Learning and
Discourse Undergird All**

WHY A WHOLE SCHOOL APPROACH?

As the saying goes, build it and they will come. Many parents are waiting for a dual language program to be established. Despite teacher shortages, if a whole school builds the infrastructure for quality dual language learning, it will materialize.

This chapter focuses on how biliteracy can be developed in both multilingual and monolingual classrooms in secondary schools with specific strategies and best practices for each context. Nevertheless, the process of language development, reading, and writing described here applies to K–12 instruction.

We take the position that schoolwide dual language programming provides maximum benefits to MLLs; however, we wish to reinforce that educators

Notice how effective research-based ESL/ELD, sheltered, bilingual, and dual language programs encompass the integration of four essential components (Calderón, 2007).

The strength of biliteracy development for MLLs rests on the interaction among these components as one builds on and reinforces the others.

Margo

working in less ideal circumstances (i.e., monolingual settings) can still promote the attainment of biliteracy. The chapter describes some of the features of quality instruction that can move a whole school from monolingualism to bilingualism. For this purpose, instructional strategies that transfer between languages and cut across school contexts, core content classes, grade levels, and existing programs are described.

The features described here are from national experimental and quasi-experimental studies of (1) reading for MLLs in Chicago, Boston, and Socorro, Texas, funded by the Institutes of Children's Health and Development (NIH) conducted by Harvard, Center for Applied Linguistics, University of Houston, and Johns Hopkins University on reading in Spanish and transfer between languages (August et al., 2005); (2) empirically tested programs from the five boroughs of New York, El Paso, Texas, and Hawaii (Calderón, 2007; Calderón & Carreón, 1994; Calderón et al.,1998); and (3) other longitudinal experimental studies funded by the U.S. Department Institute of Educational Science focused on developing reading comprehension for English language learners (ELLs) (Slavin et al., 2011) and messages from the National Literacy Panel for Language Minority Children and Youth (August & Shanahan, 2006, 2008).

These studies demonstrated that a whole school approach to professional development serves to move everyone in the same direction and grow a positive mindset toward biliteracy in elementary grades and in all subject areas in secondary schools. An instructional path to this journey is mapped out in this chapter.

VIGNETTES

Imagine These Students!

Marta is a newcomer from Chihuahua entering third grade. Her native language is Spanish, and she speaks very little English. Martha came to this school because her mother wanted her to attend a bilingual school. Luckily the third-grade English and Spanish bilingual teachers have plans for addressing this newcomer's situation. In Martha's classroom, students sit in teams of four; two are dominant English, and two are dominant Spanish speakers. They learn social norms of interaction, how to work collaboratively, and how to sustain their daily learning. By the end of the year, they will have developed both languages exponentially while learning math, science, social studies, and literature from around the world. Moreover, they will have learned to appreciate, respect, and interact with students from different cultures, levels of English proficiency, and diverse views.

Imagine This Program!

This week, the teams of fifth-grade Spanish-English speakers will receive their instruction in Spanish in the morning and English in the afternoon. They have a reading selection that the teacher parsed to select vocabulary for preteaching, words for practicing phonemic awareness and decoding, and a sentence structure to highlight and use in their compositions. In the afternoon, the students will experience similar instruction but in English, using a different text. Both texts use climate change as the topic to branch off into science, look into the social impact, and use math to predict hurricanes. Each language teacher uses different texts, not translations, as they approach different subtopics of climate change from different sources.

The middle and high school teachers who will be receiving the students from this exemplary elementary school are preparing by retooling their practices of integrating vocabulary, reading comprehension, and writing skills development to match the elementary success. After all, they will be inheriting these great-thinking, world-savvy, multilingual children. They also know that more newcomers will be arriving in the fall from different parts of the world and that the traditional ways of teaching will no longer work.

Imagine This School!

The whole faculty, leadership, instructional coaches, and counselors or health specialists attend the same professional development series of workshops at the school. Each workshop is delivered in English or in Spanish. Teachers get to choose which language to engage in. After each workshop, the onsite coaches and principals shadow the expert coaches as they observe, give feedback, and plan next steps with the teachers because they are shifting coaching and evaluation practices to fit the new instructional approaches. A monthly session on assessment helps everyone gauge the progress of the students. Teachers study student performance data and their own coaching summaries. Next steps are revised accordingly. Co-teachers work together on the next steps.

THE URGENCY FOR CHANGE: SUPPORTED BY FEDERAL GUIDELINES

The historic decline in reading and math scores on the National Assessment of Educational Progress (NAEP) for all students became our main urgency in 2022. While some MLLs saw small increases in reading scores, the gap between white and Latinx students has hardly moved, albeit the gap has always been there. This is disappointing indeed, and it shows a misunderstanding or disregard of equity as it applies to instructional programs for students of color. Federal regulations highlight two important matters that can no longer be ignored: the underprepared teachers and measuring student progress (or lack thereof).

". . . [D]istricts must ensure that low-income students and students of color are not taught at disproportionate rates by ineffective, out-of-field, or inexperienced teachers, and must measure and report on progress toward eliminating inequities." (Every Student Succeeds Act [ESSA], 2015)

This is the time to make necessary shifts to enhance multilingual and bilingual programs. Moreover, these are the times to start successful programs from scratch to meet the specific needs of MLLs. Many federal regulations support these enhancements and even provide different sources of funding. Most important, federal regulations call for high-quality education for all MLLs to close the achievement gap that has remained stagnant.

"The purpose of Every Student Succeeds Act [ESSA] is to provide all children significant opportunity to receive a fair, equitable, and high-quality education, and to close educational achievement gaps." (ESSA, 2015)

To begin to close the gap, regardless of the program and language(s) of instruction, MLLs must have quality instruction in all core content areas (math, science, social studies, language arts). In a dual language program, core content teachers would use English and the home language to address all subjects in both languages at all grade levels. Literacy must be developed in both languages from PK forward, and/or when a child enters the school.

In secondary schools, all core content teachers who have or will have multilingual students must be prepared to integrate academic language, reading comprehension, and writing skills into their math, science, social studies, language arts, advanced placement, and STEM classes. In secondary dual language settings, these skills are addressed in both the program language and English.

Quality bilingual teachers and general education teachers must be hired or prepared on the job through intensive and comprehensive professional development. They must be monitored and their progress measured based on the impact they have on their students. Archaic ways of observing or evaluating teachers with MLLs should be replaced with more up-to-date tools and training. In addition to general education teachers with MLLs in their classroom, credentialed or certified ESL/ELD and/or bilingual teachers need to fine-tune and update skills to have the whole school move forward on the same page.

"An equity-focused school system—one that sets high expectations for all students, provides resources necessary for meeting those expectations, measures and reports progress toward them, and ensures action when any school—or any group of students—falls off track." (ESSA, 2015)

If any ML "falls off track," an effective intervention must be available based on the specific need of the student. Each student must be meticulously assessed to determine the best intervention for that student. One-size intervention does not fit all. Some might need more vocabulary, others decoding or reading comprehension or how to read math problems or apply writing conventions. The school must be unambiguous about identifying the specific need. The days of grouping all "underachieving" MLLs into a generic

---

So excited to see this powerful call for advocacy! It is well aligned to Secretary Cardona's vision and call to action to Raise the Bar: Lead the World:

"Let's look at our students in bilingual programs as gifted with assets that we want other students to have. Being bilingual and bicultural is a superpower!

"Let's place a high value on having graduates be multilingual. Recognition for that, such as earning a Seal of Biliteracy, which many states have, should be celebrated at graduation as much as an honors cord. Let's face it: you will have more options in life being bilingual.

"Let's improve multilingual education to give our students opportunities to excel in global markets where multilingualism and cultural differences are embraced and valued."

Excerpts from the Remarks delivered by U.S. Secretary of Education Miguel Cardona on January 24, 2023

Andrea

class with one ESL or "sheltered" teacher should be long past. (For more on Assessing in two languages, see chapter 4.)

Under ESSA (2015), states are responsible for holding schools accountable for serving the needs of MLLs according to guidelines by the Offices of Civil Rights from the U.S. Department of Education and the U.S. Department of Justice. Concomitantly, the state should allocate funding for addressing the guidelines. Some states are highly involved in the development of standards and curriculum guides for English development. Moreover, for continuous professional learning, states need to bring together experts in the field to learn and stay informed of best practices. Such successful efforts plus positive messaging are disseminated to all districts. We urge school committees to become reacquainted with the services and funding that state offices can provide as they plan to implement their dual language programs.

ESSA places emphasis on equity as situated in the classroom, school, and community. The school might want to revisit its plans or mission on equity with a focus on the following questions:

- Is our definition of equity too broad?

- Is it helping connect with parents?

- Is it often misinterpreted, watered down, or in need of clarification?

- Are our instruction and professional development only a set of disjointed efforts?

For MLLs equity begins with being provided with quality instruction in language, literacy, and core content. It also means providing more access and opportunities for family education. Additionally, for educators, the comprehensive professional development sustains a focus on multilingual successful instructional practices and support structures throughout the year.

RESEARCH BASE

Dual language instruction has empirical research grounded in some experimental-control comparative studies. Nevertheless, the focus of research and policy in bilingual education has typically slanted toward descriptive studies on effective strategies for educating MLLs (August & Hakuta, 1997; Christian & Genesee, 2001; Takanishi & Le Menestrel, 2017).

National researchers' panels have been convened in the past 20 years to review the literature on bilingual education and ELLs (whom we refer to as MLLs in this book). These reviews focused on the development of language and literacy. Some of the major syntheses of research have published their results and produced guidelines for the field.

Literature Reviews

- Synthesis of research from the National Literacy Panel on Language-Minority Children and Youth (August & Shanahan, 2006).

- *Developing reading and writing in second language learners. Lessons from the Report of the National Literacy Panel on Language-Minority Children and Youth* (August et al., 2008).

- Synthesis of research from the National Academies of Science titled *Promoting the Educational Success of Children and Youth Learning English: Promising Futures* (Takanishi & Le Menestrel, 2017).

- Synthesis of research compendium on teaching vocabulary titled *Research and Development on Vocabulary* (Hiebert & Kamil, 2005).

- Reviews have also been conducted under the auspices of educational centers or universities (Genesee et al., 2006; Lindholm-Leary & Genesee, 2010; Slavin & Cheung, 2005).

- Independent reviews have been conducted by Escamilla & colleagues (2022), Thomas & Collier (1997), and those mentioned in other chapters in this book.

- An early review of the literature Slavin and Cheung (2005) found a positive effect of bilingual programs, especially paired bilingual programs (which we know as 50/50 dual language programs), on English reading achievement, with an overall effect size of +0.31. Students in these paired bilingual programs were taught reading in both English and Spanish at different times of the day.

- The review by a panel convened by the Center for Applied Linguistics put together the *Guiding Principles for Dual Language Education for Effective Program Design and Evaluation* (Howard et al., 2018).

The reviews of the literature have served to develop guidelines for program implementation and instructional practices for developing literacy or biliteracy in dual language and monolingual classroom contexts.

Concomitantly, there have been different types of empirical and descriptive studies to validate the panels' findings. Some studies focused on describing teacher practices, others studied student outcomes after the fact to compare types of programs, and a handful implemented 5- to 6-year experimental or quasi-experimental studies where students were matched, assigned to experimental control groups, and tested on a yearly basis to measure the effects of instructional strategies and program designs. These empirical studies align with the *Guiding Principles for Dual Language Education*.

LONGITUDINAL STUDIES USED TO DESCRIBE CURRICULUM AND INSTRUCTIONAL FEATURES IN THIS CHAPTER

Study #1. One 5-year experimental study by Calderón et al. (1998) evaluated a reading program called *Bilingual Cooperative Integrated Reading and*

Composition (BCIRC). Participants were 222 Latinx children in the Ysleta Independent School District in El Paso, Texas. Seven of the highest-poverty schools with dual language programs in the district were assigned to experimental (3 schools) or control (2 schools) conditions. The experimental and control groups were well matched on pretest and demographics. Analyses of covariance controlling for Bilingual Syntax Measure scores found significantly higher scores for students in BCIRC classes with a median effect size of +0.54. This study qualified to be included in the U.S. Department of Education What Works Clearinghouse (WWC). Many programs currently used in schools do not qualify for the WWC or are showing no or negative effects on MLLs.

Study #2. A study of *Two-Way Bilingual Cooperative Learning* set out to describe the interaction structures that benefit diverse linguistic and cultural backgrounds of students during dual language learning. The 5-year descriptive study took place in a K–5 dual language school in El Paso, Texas (Calderón & Carreón, 2001). This school was selected due to its premise that linguistic differences children bring to a school must be viewed as positive contributions and pathways to accelerate learning. English and Spanish language K–5 teachers co-taught throughout the day in each classroom. Two English-dominant and two Spanish-dominant students sat and worked together in a team throughout each class. As the Spanish teacher taught, the English teacher monitored the teams. They switched roles when they switched languages. Although some students were English dominant and others Spanish dominant in year one of the study, all met district testing criteria in both languages by fifth grade.

Study #3. Another 2-year matched control experiment was carried out by researchers from Harvard, Johns Hopkins, and the Center for Applied Linguistics to measure and describe the *Transfer from Spanish into English Reading* evaluating an enriched transition program for children who had been taught in Spanish using Success for All and were moving to the English program in third grade. The enriched transition program was a modified version of BCIRC vocabulary instruction and the Success for All beginning reading (Reading Roots). Participants were 238 Spanish-dominant students in eight schools in Boston, Chicago, and El Paso, Texas. The study compared students who received the full program to matched students in similar control schools. After controlling for Spanish and English Woodcock Scales, treatment students scored higher than control students on Woodcock Word Attack (ES=+0.21), Passage Comprehension (ES=+0.16), and Picture Vocabulary (ES=+0.11), with a median effect size of +0.16. The effects of Success for All on the achievement of Spanish-dominant MLLs were generally positive. Across all three studies, the overall weighted effect size was +0.36 (August et al., 2001; August et al., 2005; Calderón et al., 2005;). The students continued to be at grade level into middle school. The importance of this study was that it showed the features and structures that help students transfer from Spanish reading to English reading and the strategies that help bridge both languages.

Study #4. A 5-year study in middle and high schools was commissioned by the Carnegie Corporation of New York to focus on core content instruction in secondary schools with high multilingual student populations in four experimental middle and high schools and four comparison schools in Kauai, Hawaii, and four in Washington Heights, New York City. All core content teachers in the experimental schools participated in whole-school professional development workshops and coaching. An adaptation of BCIRC for integrating language and literacy into math, science, social studies, and language arts in middle and high schools became *Expediting Comprehension for English Language Learners/Acelerando la comprensión en Español: Lectura, escritura y razonamiento académico (ExC-ELL/ACE-LERA).* In addition to the overall effect sizes (+0.36 to +0.42), the ExC-ELL/ACE-LERA schools that were originally identified as low-performing became the highest-performing schools in those districts after 2 years of implementation (Calderón, 2007). Results of these longitudinal studies have been replicated, and their positive effects have been sustained in the past 10 years where the whole school was involved and not just a few designated teachers (Calderón & Minaya-Rowe, 2011; Calderón et al., 2023).

These quantitative studies, as well as syntheses from literature reviews, and qualitative studies, affirm the benefits of dual language instruction and whole-school approaches. The *Two-Way Bilingual Cooperative Learning, BCIRC, Transfer from Spanish into English Reading,* and *ExC-ELL/ACE-LERA* studies provide evidence-based instructional strategies that align with the principles of dual language education. Those instructional strategies that cut across the four studies are shared in this chapter.

> It would be remiss of me if I didn't mention that infused within bilingual or dual language programs along with comprehensive curriculum, instructional strategies and professional learning are also sound assessment practices (you may wish to keep on reading into chapter 4). Whatever is addressed programmatically, from translanguaging in oral and written discourse to content-driven language and literacy, should also be represented in classroom assessment.
>
> **Margo**

IMPLICATIONS FOR PRACTICE AND IMPLEMENTATION

Cross-Disciplinary Approaches to Curriculum and Instruction in Both Languages

A quality dual language program begins with a comprehensive curriculum, instructional strategies, and assessment practices that cut across all subjects and both languages, and a professional development program with coaching as follow-up transfer into the classroom to support continuous implementation of those components. See the chapter on assessment.

Features of Cross-Disciplinary Approaches to Curriculum and Instruction

- Integrated language and literacy with core content instruction
- Academic language and/or vocabulary and discourse strategies
- Reading foundational skills in both languages
- Slow reading and close reading with peers for comprehension

- Structured cooperative learning to actuate ample verbal discourse

- Writing in two languages and between languages

- Application of cross-linguistic transfer and translanguaging in discourse, reading, and writing (knowing and applying what transfers and what doesn't)

- Assessments in two languages

- An effective model for co-teaching

- An effective model for coaching with a specific observation protocol for vocabulary, reading, and writing

Points to Consider for Teaching Vocabulary in Both Languages

1. **Teaching vocabulary is a precursor to reading.** Vocabulary is not a long list of words to be taught in isolation. Vocabulary is not spending 15 or more minutes per word as students copy definitions, write easy examples and non-examples, and draw pictures of the word. This takes up too much student time, and the teacher usually has to reteach the word the following day. With this approach, students go through the motions but do not actually master the word. Moreover, not all words can be represented with drawings, especially the more academic processing words. See the section on vocabulary instruction below for an effective and efficient strategy for preteaching vocabulary before reading to help students comprehend what they are about to read.

2. **Word knowledge is key for phonemic awareness and decoding in each language**. Vocabulary can be taught in early childhood grades when students are practicing phonemic and/or phonological awareness. Vocabulary is also taught in decodable books and books that are at grade level, including basal readers, science and social studies texts, descriptions, and math problems. Adapted texts and adapted phonics also apply to newcomers in the upper grades who need decoding in their home language as well as in English. To decode well, students must know the meaning of the words in phonics lessons.

3. **Word knowledge is key for reading comprehension in each language**. Vocabulary is selected from the text the students are about to read. A text can be a trade book, novel, science lab instructions and inquiry questions or processes, a newspaper, math problems, and history or current events. STEM projects and STEM classes are ideal because students are pretaught words to read and use many words repeatedly and are introduced to more as they continue to read. In STEM inquiry students can use the language of their choice and translanguaging to facilitate discussions, concept clarification, and anchor concepts.

4. **New vocabulary is anchored in discourse opportunities**. The proverbial "ELs need to talk more" is often heard but rarely enacted throughout a lesson. Teachers can provide opportunities for partner and team practice of discourse skills during reading and writing. Techniques that enhance reading comprehension and discourse development include verbal summarization after reading each paragraph, formulating questions with peers about the text, discussing characteristics and text structure, written summaries, and verbal retelling or enacting (August et al., 2008; Calderón, 2007).

5. **Reading anchors word knowledge in any language.** Most textbooks and basal readers select core content words and define them in the glossary. Even so, teachers know that there are more important words to select. Textbooks mostly select what are called *Tier 3 words*—content-specific words, whereas the words that affect comprehension for MLLs are those that nest content-specific words. These are the words in long sentences, typically called *Tier 2 words*, and consist of information processing, polysemous, transition, cognates, false cognates, idioms, and words for specificity. *Tier 1 words* are those simple, easy, everyday words that most non-English learners know by second grade. However, many MLLs might not know them.

Teachers use organizers such as the ones in figure 3.2 to select words to teach from a text the students are about to read.

FIGURE 3.2 **Types of Words and Phrases to Choose From a Text**

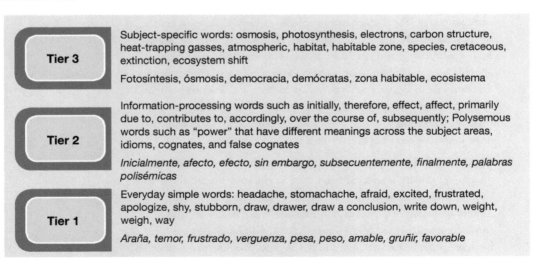

Tier 3	Subject-specific words: osmosis, photosynthesis, electrons, carbon structure, heat-trapping gasses, atmospheric, habitat, habitable zone, species, cretaceous, extinction, ecosystem shift
	Fotosíntesis, ósmosis, democracia, demócratas, zona habitable, ecosistema
Tier 2	Information-processing words such as initially, therefore, effect, affect, primarily due to, contributes to, accordingly, over the course of, subsequently; Polysemous words such as "power" that have different meanings across the subject areas, idioms, cognates, and false cognates
	Inicialmente, afecto, efecto, sin embargo, subsecuentemente, finalmente, palabras polisémicas
Tier 1	Everyday simple words: headache, stomachache, afraid, excited, frustrated, apologize, shy, stubborn, draw, drawer, draw a conclusion, write down, weight, weigh, way
	Araña, temor, frustrado, verguenza, pesa, peso, amable, gruñir, favorable

Subject-specific words (Tier 3 words) are sometimes called technical words, academic words, or academic language. In essence, all words used as soon as students enter a classroom are academic words. Textbooks highlight mainly Tier 3 words and define them in the glossary. Nevertheless, without knowing all those Tier 2 words in each sentence, students won't be able to understand or learn the Tier 3 concepts.

After selecting five mainly Tier 2 words from the text that students are about to read, the teacher preteaches those words using the following seven steps. The teacher spends 1 minute teaching steps 1 to 5 providing the sentence with the word as found in the text, the dictionary definition, a teacher example, and a grammatical aspect of the word within a sentence frame for step 6. In step 1 the students say the word after the teacher 3 times to practice pronunciation. In step 6, the students practice the word verbally in pairs using the sentence frame for 1 minute. They take turns providing four or five examples each. In step 7, the teacher reminds students when they are to use this word.

FIGURE 3.3 Preteaching a Word or Phrase in English

1. Say, *prevail* three times after me.
2. The book says: We will *prevail*, no matter how difficult the task.
3. Dictionary definition: To prove more powerful than opposing forces.
4. Example: It is hard for me to stop using my phone late at night, but I will prevail.
5. Prevail is a verb.
6. Use this frame: ___ is hard for me, but I will *prevail* because ___.
7. Be sure to use *prevail* in your self-assessment summary today.

Source: Calderón et al. (2023)

FIGURE 3.4 Preteaching a Word or Phrase in Spanish

1. Pida a los alumnos que repitan después de usted tres veces: *causa*.
2. La *causa* del calentamiento es el aumento de gases de efecto invernadero.
3. *Causa* es el origen de algo.
4. Ejemplo: Jennifer faltó a clase a *causa* de un fuerte resfriado.
5. *Causa* es cognado con "cause."
6. Use *causa* con este marco: __ me causa temor porque _____.
7. Use *causa* en tu resumen verbal de la lectura.

Source: Calderón and Espino (2019)

LESSON DESIGN AND ASSESSMENT TOOL

In addition to preteaching key words before students read, other features can be considered for assessing what is in place and what needs to be included in the school's curriculum plan to improve student outcomes. Figure 3.5 lists some of those implementation requisites. Use this chart to assess your curriculum framework.

FIGURE 3.5 What It Looks Like in My Classroom, School, and District

Implementation Features	My Class	All Other Classrooms	Some Classrooms
1. Language and literacy are integrated into all core content instruction.			
2. Academic language/ vocabulary and discourse strategies in both languages are used in every class to build reading comprehension and content learning.			
3. Reading foundational skills in both languages: phonemic awareness, phonics, to build decoding skills and fluency are taught.			
4. Reading comprehension skills in both languages are taught, highlighting background knowledge and using close reading with peers.			
5. Structured cooperative learning is designed to actuate ample verbal discourse.			
6. Writing in two languages and between languages across the subject areas is part of subject-specific lessons.			
7. Cross-linguistic transfer and translanguaging during discourse, reading, and writing are used.			
8. All teachers are aware of what transfers and what doesn't transfer across languages.			
9. Early screening and assessments as described in chapter 4 are used.			
10. Effective co-teaching practices as described in chapter 5 are used.			
11. Whole-school comprehensive professional development and coaching are focused on effective evidence-based instructional strategies as described in this chapter.			

online resources

LANGUAGE AS THE PROMOTER OF MULTICULTURALISM, DIVERSITY, AND EQUITY

When dual language programs implement the eleven features in figure 3.5, they create an environment where multicultural diversity and equity thrive. The structural features in a classroom where students from different language and cultural backgrounds work together help construct student-centered learning and accountability.

Appreciation for differences, as well as sociocultural and social-emotional competencies develop as students get to know each other through interactions around interesting projects, challenging roles, individual accountability, and reminders of social norms of interaction. In teamwork, students can use their own discourse as they teach and learn from their peers a new language. The high expectations through messaging and criteria call for constant rigorous production in both languages.

CROSS-LINGUISTIC TRANSFER AND TRANSLANGUAGING IN DISCOURSE, READING, AND WRITING

Most research on cross-linguistic transfer discusses cognates and some syntactical features of the languages as features that transfer.

However, we need to look at transfer from a more rigorous and challenging perspective. Beyond text features, instruction can add *critical thinking, literary analysis, depth of reading comprehension strategies, and the development of composition skills for text-based writing*. Those protocols and routines transfer across languages.

FIGURE 3.6   ## Examples of Macro Features That Transfer Between Languages

- Critical thinking (generating and testing ideas) as students interact with others and/or write compositions.

- Effective strategies for learning vocabulary and applying it in discourse with peers.

- Reading a text for learning content; text structures (narrative, informational, sequential, cause and effect, problem-solution, compare-contrast); higher order thinking (comprehending nuances, discussing depth of content, analyzing author's craft, stating claims or counterclaims).

- The writing process (organizing, drafting, editing, revising, proofing, writing powerful conclusions and titles) and writing conventions (academic vocabulary, syntax, voice, text features, text structures, literary devices, word choice) also transfer, but grammatical features need more attention.

FIGURE 3.7 Examples of Micro Features That Transfer at the Word Level

Cognates	
Analizar	Analyze
Clasificar	Classify
Comunicar	Communicate
Hipnotizar	Hypnotize
Ósmosis	Osmosis
Congreso	Congress
Prefixes and Suffixes	
Pre-	pre-
Su-	su-
Anti-	anti-
-ción	-tion
-logia	-logy
-encia	-ence

> The "zoom-out" and "zoom-in" from the macro and micro perspectives will be so helpful for educators as they implement these via their multilingual pedagogies—especially the macro features. These emphases are so supportive of discourse development.
>
> **Joan**

Features That Do Not Easily Transfer Unless Explicitly Taught in Both Languages

Just as English learners struggle with pronunciation, decoding, spelling, and word meaning, Spanish as a second language learners will struggle with some features of Spanish or translation hurdles. Here are some examples:

- The false cognates

Éxito	success
Atender	assist, serve, nurse
Asistir	attend
Personaje	character
Caracter	personality, nature, guts

- Words that are polysemous in Spanish and confusing to second-language learners

  Falda (skirt, slope, brisket)
  Frente (a front, in front, forehead)
  Media (stocking, sock, mean, median, average, half)
  Planta (plant, floor, sole, tier)
  Araña (spider, chandelier, to scratch)

- Words that look alike but have different meaning depending on the article

  La capital (capital city)   El capital (money, capital)
  La corte (law court)   el corte (haircut, cutting)
  La cura (treatment)   el cura (priest)
  La pendiente (slope, incline)   el pendiente (pending, unsettled)

- Words look alike but have different meaning depending on the accent

  Amo (owner)   amó (loved)
  Lastima (hurt)   lástima (too bad)
  Libro (book)   libró (free, rid, made it)
  Buque (ship)   buqué (flowers bouque, aroma)

USING NEW VOCABULARY IN VERBAL DISCOURSE

The purpose of teaching vocabulary is to develop speaking abilities. Fluid discourse comes from having a large pool of words to choose from and rich content from books students read. Another proverbial "if you want to learn something, teach it" illustrates how important verbal interaction is for MLLs.

FIGURE 3.8   Discourse

Discourse is written or spoken communication. A formal discussion of a topic in speech or writing. Engagement in conversation. To debate. A connected series of utterances. A conversation around a text.

For MLLs, Discourse is

- one instructional component that is a must to help them succeed;

- one instructional component that can be integrated into math, science, social studies, and all subjects in addition to ESL/SSL/language arts; and

- the component that is frequently left out because there is too much content material that must be "covered."

Ample Interaction Opportunities to Anchor Vocabulary

Anchoring content knowledge is accomplished through ample time for peer interaction in cooperative learning/collaborative learning structures.

Cooperative learning strategies set a safe context for language practice for MLLs. Management of student interaction helps students gain a deeper understanding of word meanings as they discuss concepts across content area lessons. Teachers should use these interaction strategies to consolidate knowledge with language and literacy and continuously assess individual student progress (Calderón & Minaya-Rowe, 2003).

The following examples can be used for integrating more student oral discourse in multiple languages across math, science, social studies, and language arts.

> Absolutely! Multilingual learners should have dedicated time to interact with each other in the language(s) of their choice. Having different patterns or structures for presenting information or engaging in inquiry heightens the students' opportunities to simultaneously develop oral language within the content areas.
>
> **Margo**

Integrating Discourse Into Every Lesson, Home Language, and Translanguaging

(See more examples of translanguaging in chapters 4 and 7)

1. Reducing teacher presentation to no more than 5 minutes and stopping to ask students to "Teach Your Buddy what I just said and use my words."
   a. after writing a part of a **math** equation on the board, stop and let them teach each other;
   b. during the inquiry part of **science,** let students discuss at every step; and
   c. as you relate a historical event or a **social studies** issue, chunk the content and ask students to summarize what happened so far or share your ideas.

2. Building content ideas by explicitly saying
   a. this is the concept,
   b. these are some facts,
   c. these are some claims, and
   d. let's explore.

3. Working in teams of four with a mix of English-speaking students and MLLs, ask them to talk about
   a. different types of graphic organizers for graphing scientific concepts,
   b. key information from each paragraph,
   c. solving the math problem, and
   d. team presentations to the class.

4. Using their own background knowledge, culture, personal history, and home language to
   a. design a path for the character who must solve a dilemma;
   b. set a goal;
   c. come up with a different ending of a story; and
   d. build a better community.

5. Bringing closure to the learning during each class period by

   a.   debriefing with open-ended questions and

   b.   having partners summarize for each other what they learned in both languages.

Caveat: For quality discourse to occur a teacher must

- Preteach the words, sentence frames, and sentence starters in both languages that you want to hear in their discourse.

- Provide interesting content to read in both languages.

- Have students do Partner Reading and Summarization after each paragraph in both languages.

- Teach social-emotional norms and protocols for working together, respecting each other's discourse and ideas, and learning from a task.

DEVELOPING LITERACY AND BILITERACY

Structuring Reading in Two Languages Simultaneously

Schools must capitalize on the linguistic and cultural differences that children bring with them.

When two English-dominant and two Spanish-dominant students sit and work together in teams, they are challenged and supported by their peers. During Spanish instruction, the English teacher monitors the teams as the Spanish teacher conducts a lesson. They switch roles when they switch languages. Spanish-dominant speakers become the more capable peers during Spanish, and English-dominant speakers become the more capable peers during English instruction. They quickly learn to be helpers and to accept help (Calderón & Carreón, 2001; Vygotsky, 1978).

Thank you, Margarita, for this emphasis. It's a place for peers to increase interaction as they collaborate while editing, which is also a space for them to translanguage while they communicate with each other about their writing.

Andrea

FIGURE 3.9 | Reading

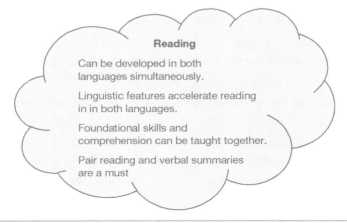

Reading

Can be developed in both languages simultaneously.

Linguistic features accelerate reading in in both languages.

Foundational skills and comprehension can be taught together.

Pair reading and verbal summaries are a must

Points to Consider for Developing Literacy or Biliteracy

1. **Literacy for second-language learners**. Literacy for MLLs is a comprehensive, multidimensional, approach that integrates the speaking, listening, reading, and writing domains. Language and literacy are connected. Moreover, language and literacy are a link with academic content learning in one or more languages.

2. **Language and literacy development for MLLs are different** from the development for monolinguals (August et al., 2001, August & Shanahan, 2006; August et al., 2008). The National Literacy Panel (1998) concurred with the National Reading Panel (2001) that reading entails *five foundational components: phonemic awareness, phonological awareness, vocabulary, fluency, and comprehension. These are typically known as "the five" but must be addressed differently for MLLs.*

3. **The science of reading.** Since school districts are moving toward the *science of reading*, the foundational skills must be addressed in their plans. Reading comprehension is one of the five. All should be addressed in both languages to create a strong biliteracy program.

   The Reading League (2022) emphasizes that **the science of reading is not:**
   - An ideology
   - A fad, a trend, a new idea, or a pendulum swing
   - A political agenda
   - A one-size-fits-all approach
   - A program of instruction
   - A single, specific component of instruction, such as phonics

4. **The foundational skills for decoding**. Phonemic and phonological awareness, fluency, vocabulary, spelling, decoding, syntax, background knowledge, and other attributes are often listed as the foundational skills. Whereas reading comprehension is also one of the five, it is often assumed that after teaching phonics the students automatically develop comprehension.

5. **The foundational skills for reading comprehension**. Reading comprehension is based on knowing how to decode but has its own strategies and components. Partner Reading with Summarization has been shown to be the most effective reading approach for integrating all five foundational skills. When students read aloud in pairs alternating sentences, they anchor decoding, develop prosody, and understand sentence structure and punctuation. When they stop after each paragraph and summarize, students practice the new vocabulary, discourse protocols, comprehend at a deeper level, and learn the content. Other types of reading are not as effective for comprehension (e.g., round-robin, calling on one student at a time, choral reading). Some approaches have negative effects for MLLs such as silent reading. For depth of comprehension, students need to talk with peers to clarify their thinking, learn new ideas, and build knowledge together.

6. **The science of reading in two languages.** For second language learners, the lessons are amplified to include word meaning for all

words being introduced, followed by ample oral practice with new words. While phonemic and phonological awareness are different between English and Spanish, the process or strategies for decoding are basically the same (e.g., letter recognition, letter-sound correlation, blending in English or syllable recognition in Spanish, word recognition, spelling, and word application in own discourse). Knowing where MLLs fall within the dual language foundational reading subcomponents provides insights into reading difficulties or strengths in either language and where to focus instruction or extra assistance.

7. **Foundations of reading for older newcomers and long-term ELLs.** We must acknowledge in grades 4 to 12 that newcomers and even other more advanced MLLs still need foundational skills. Long-term ELLs probably missed quality basic reading instruction. Newcomers might have never developed reading skills in their native country. Without decoding skills, there can be no fluency and much less comprehension as they struggle through large dense pieces of reading in science, social studies, math, and language arts in middle and high school. Notwithstanding, the instructional approach to foundational skills (phonics) must be compatible with their age, educational background, and type of need (e.g., decoding, fluency, vocabulary).

8. **Interrelationship of both languages** occurs when the reading subcomponents are taught, compared, and contrasted in both languages. For example, even the smallest units of reading such as the /p/ in English and /p/ in Spanish can be recognized and practiced by contrasting the pronunciation of the phonemes in words such as "paper" and "*papel*." Students can hold a piece of paper up to their mouth and watch when the paper moves as they pronounce both words back and forth.

9. **To separate languages or not—or when and how?** There are several approaches to organizing the two languages of instruction:

   a. The 90/10 model concentrates more time on the home language and the gradual introduction of English. Yet there is typically no slide rule of percentages during the year.

   b. The 50/50 model proposes equal time on each language. Yet sometimes it becomes the co-teachers' choice. These approaches need better teacher and student monitoring in most programs. When team teachers are well prepared and have the materials to conduct a truly equitable schedule, this seems to be the most promising model for positive student outcomes. All the instructional strategies listed here excel 50/50 programs.

   The key is to monitor and document actual time on languages and adjust as necessary.

10. **Collaboration, communication, and critical thinking.** Multilingual learners enjoy listening to themselves and others read for pronunciation and fluency because reading with a buddy makes it a safe environment to take risks. They learn to delve deeper into their own thinking and comprehension by summarizing what they read while getting help from a peer. Working with same-language peers becomes an opportunity for translanguaging as they put together strings of discourse

(Continued)

(Continued)

> to build comprehension. Equally valuable, heterogeneous grouping is effective when the native Spanish speakers help the native English speakers during reading in Spanish, and the tables turn when it is time to read in English. Collaborating on summaries also gives second language learners opportunities to practice their new discourse skills and social-emotional competencies or collaborative skills. Albeit for collaboration to work well, establishing the importance of norms of interaction and cooperative skills become critically important. Whole-class interaction such as debriefing after reading a section provides additional opportunities to anchor both languages and prepare for elaborate writing.
>
> 11. **Equity.** Equity, in this context, involves giving all students access to excellent teaching and rigorous, rich, relevant learning opportunities in two languages. It means helping students learn as much as possible, and developing their talents and interests, as we meet and anticipate their needs along the way. It means helping them develop stronger relationships with their multicultural peers.

THE INTERSECTION OF ACADEMIC LANGUAGE AND READING COMPREHENSION IN BOTH LANGUAGES

The integration of language and literacy continuously adds depth to word knowledge, grammar, comprehension, and the "soft skills" that help students build confidence, appreciate their own talents and culture, and help them collaborate and communicate with peers. Figure 3.10 displays some of the subcomponents of literacy and biliteracy and how social and self-awareness skills and competencies can be developed. They are not in sequential order. It is more of a portrayal of vocabulary, grammar, reading comprehension, and social-emotional skills.

FIGURE 3.10 **Subcomponents of Reading to Address in Both Languages**

Word Knowledge	Grammar	Reading Comprehension	Undergirding Skills For Reading
Phonemic awareness	Parts of speech	Text elements (left to right) and sociocultural conventions	Self-awareness (e.g., mindset for reading, amnesia for past bad experiences with reading)
Pronunciation of words	Parts and/or types of sentences	Author's craft (e.g., irony, foreshadowing, dialog, simile, personification)	Self-management (e.g., resiliency, stamina, new mindset)

Word Knowledge	Grammar	Reading Comprehension	Undergirding Skills For Reading
Decoding	Capitalization	Academic vocabulary (Tiers 2 & 3) from the text	Collaborating effectively with peers in pairs or teams
Morphology	Punctuation	Comprehension strategies (e.g., ideas, inferences, summarizing, synthesizing, using references, evidence, refuting evidence)	Transfer of reading skills to other subject areas and life (e.g., ask questions, explore different perspectives)
Word meaning (Tiers 1, 2, 3)	Text features (e.g., indentation, title, bullets, bold letters, charts, graphs, maps)	Higher-order thinking or metacognitive strategies and cross-language connections	Transfer of reading skills and routines between languages
Word Fluency	Cross-language awareness (affixes, cognates)	Discourse (verbal and written)	Transfer of language and content to academic writing
Verbal discourse and fluency using those words	Written discourse using words from reading and explicit preteaching	Text structure (e.g., poetry, fiction, expository text, fictional biography, argumentative)	Bilingual, bicultural, and biliteracy awareness and goals
Continued word study	Complex text analysis	Close reading strategies	Research and sources

Source: Adapted from Calderón et al. (2023)

CAVEATS

Teachers reading to ELLs help model fluency and prosody and maybe introduce new words. However, it does not teach them to read. Second-language learners need to read, discuss, and summarize after each paragraph in the first and second language. For dual language students in the beginning stages, a text should be broken into small segments. This way, they read something different every day and are engaged in greater analysis and application as they learn and apply new vocabulary, grammar, and writing.

Repetitive reading of the same long passages does not help dual language learners. They will focus on "reading fast" and not on comprehension. Silent reading does not help either because the teacher cannot tell if students are comprehending. Students might begin to think that skimming and looking at pictures are considered "reading."

Close reading is not the same as repetitive reading. It entails going back into a paragraph to analyze, discuss, and construct meaning with a peer. After close reading, they can write questions to ask other students, use cognitive organizers to organize key concepts, and provide evidence for their assertions. They go into the text to delve deeper into meaning and content mastery.

FIGURE 3.11 Moving Away From Ineffective Reading Practices

Avoid	Why?
Jumping into reading without explicit instruction of vocabulary.	Students need to know 90 percent to 95 percent of the words in a text to comprehend what they read and excel in speaking and writing.
Sheltered instruction models that give a large menu of activities to choose from or have not proven to be effective.	Some instructional models let teachers choose at random strategies and/or activities from an array of popular "best practices" that don't have evidence and take up a lot of time, but delay language, literacy, and content learning. This is called the *activity trap*—great activity but no learning.
Using too much Shared Reading in K–3. Using long shadow reading times, the teacher reads aloud for students to mimic the teacher's reading.	A few minutes is fine for MLLs to hear new words and the prosody of reading by the teacher. Otherwise, students think that mimicking and memorizing what the teacher reads is reading. Teach them how to read; otherwise, they get used to the listen-remember-pretend-to-read sequence.
Teachers should not read whole novels, stories, large sections from history, or science texts to fourth- through twelfth-grade students.	MLLs in middle and high school are often read to because "they don't read well" and teachers want them to "learn the content." Unfortunately, it is difficult to remember something they only hear and do not read. Instead, teach them to read in that subject area. Even notetaking during teacher reading waters down the information learned, and students do not develop core content reading skills.
Teaching phonics alone.	Using only phonics programs without teaching comprehension or reading texts to apply phonics will leave gaps in skills for academic reading.
Round-robin reading or silent reading for ELLs.	There is no evidence these work. Instead, use evidence-based reading aloud with a partner alternating sentences. They learn more words, sentence structure, and punctuation. Partners clarify meaning for each other when they jointly summarize (verbally) after each paragraph. They stay engaged in reading. They use the new words and learn more words, discourse patterns, and collaborative and critical thinking skills.
Answer low-level simple questions after reading.	Instead, after reading, ask teams of four, ensuring a mix of English speakers and those with a home language other than English, to formulate questions. The teacher can then use these questions to test the other teams.
Guessing from context or pictures or using other cues.	Even older students might need explicit instruction and practice on how to decode (read) and encode (spell) words, including word-part analysis (e.g., syllables, morphemes). Assess or have a specialist assess all the foundational skills of a striving reader in both languages.
Emphasis is on speed reading so many words per minute.	Accuracy needs ample time to read slowly and deliberately because it develops accuracy, automaticity, fluency, and prosody in both languages.

Source: From Calderón (2009)

INTEGRATING ACADEMIC LANGUAGE, READING COMPREHENSION, AND WRITING COMPONENTS TO BECOME PROFICIENT IN WRITING

Multilingual learners must first go through a cycle of learning vocabulary, reading to learn content, and processing that content verbally before they are ready for writing. Without word and content knowledge, writing and composition skills will not develop.

Writing is the most challenging skill for all students. Colleges and business owners constantly lament that their students and employees lack adequate writing skills. Since teacher preparation rarely offers courses on academic content writing, all schools ought to revisit *writing* in embedded professional development.

FIGURE 3.12   **Writing**

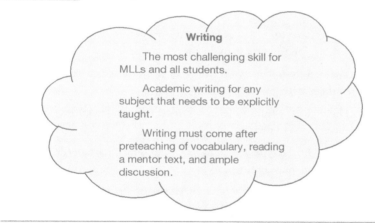

Writing

The most challenging skill for MLLs and all students.

Academic writing for any subject that needs to be explicitly taught.

Writing must come after preteaching of vocabulary, reading a mentor text, and ample discussion.

According to Graham and Perin (2007), Graham (2020), and Graham et al. (2020):

- About half of private employers and more than 60 percent of state government employers say that writing skills affect promotion decisions (Graham, 2020; National Commission on Writing, 2004, 2005).

- Since 2005, the National Commission on Writing has been finding that poorly written applications are likely to doom candidates' chances for employment and that writing remediation costs American businesses as much as $3.1 billion annually.

- The National Center for Evaluation Statistics reported that students' 2017 scores on writing were lower than those of 2011.

As most of us know

- Writing can be the most difficult domain for ELLs and their teachers.

- ELLs need to develop writing skills for each content area as they simultaneously learn, comprehend, and apply content-area concepts in their second language.

- ELLs are learning academic language as well as the mechanics of writing, genres, and editing procedures. Disjointing writing from reading and vocabulary won't work.

- Writing can be particularly painful for long-term ELLs if they have not been challenged or given the linguistic and literacy skills to do well in writing. For them, writing can be highly stressful, anxiety ridden, and terribly embarrassing. Their voices have been silent for many years. Yet it is essential that they become fluent and competent writers (Calderón et al., 2023).

How do we teach writing?

- Select a mentor text that helps students become aware of the type of writing you want them to do after they read it.

- Preteach five or six words from the mentor text that you want to see in their writing.

- Highlight the features (e.g., subtitles, bullets, dialog) that you want them to use in their writing.

- Highlight the type of writing (e.g., expository, narrative, argumentative) that you want them to use.

- Have students read the mentor text with a partner alternating sentences (to explore and feel punctuation) and stop after each paragraph to discuss the messages and the way the sentences and paragraphs unfold.

- Ask students to do a first draft with a partner or in triads using strategies such as Round Table.

- Ask students to edit and revise their draft by using strategies such as ratiocination (www.exc-ell.com).

- Finish with a powerful conclusion and an attention-grabbing title (Calderón, 2007; Calderón et al., 2023).

DEVELOPING BILITERACY: STRUCTURING WRITING IN TWO LANGUAGES SIMULTANEOUSLY

The process is the same in both languages. If a student is a better writer in one language, give the student opportunities to develop a voice and a writing process through that means. Writing in the language of their choice will develop skills and tools that will transfer into the other language. Equity begins with encouraging student background knowledge, interests, and culture.

Luckily, the writing process is the same across many languages. Editing entails finding one thing to look for to edit at a time. For example, students can look for too many repetitions of a word, missing punctuation, capitalization, and finding simple words that could be more sophisticated. Revising strategies include finding a place to add information, quotes, explanations, or details.

The strategies for editing and revising require quality time. Editing skills will not transfer across languages if they haven't been taught in one language first. Proficient writers will own a rich vocabulary bank, can read and comprehend a variety of texts, and have learned to draft, edit, revise, and write powerful conclusions and titles.

The key message from this chapter is that vocabulary, discourse, reading foundations, reading comprehension, critical thinking, and writing need to be integrated into each language and across both languages. We return to this figure as a closing visual to keep in mind how language, literacy, sociocultural awareness, and social-emotional competencies must be integrated into each subject area.

FIGURE 3.13 Integrated Language, Literacy, and Content, Each Containing Students' Voice, Cultural Application and Appreciation, Well-Being, and Self-Efficacy

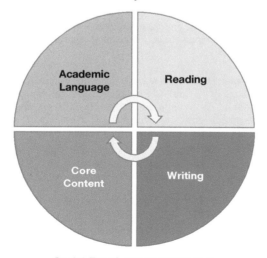

Academic Language

Reading

Core Content

Writing

Social-Emotional Attention and Discourse Undergird All

Conclusion: Key Take-Aways

For quality and sustainability of shifts in instructional practices and beliefs that benefit MLLs, enacting a comprehensive dual language professional learning program is fundamental. As noted in the publication *Guiding Principles for Dual Language Education* (Howard et al., 2018), the commitment to the goals of quality education for language minority students and emergent bilinguals must be a priority for all schools. With knowledge of evidence-based curriculum, instruction, and professional development as described in this book and in this chapter, all schools must now enact quality dual language programs.

Theory, research, and principles coincide on what that enactment means as aligned in figures 3.11 and 3.13. The extended principles and evidence-based studies have been collapsed into similar categories for the sake of space. Results from the four empirical studies and continuous implementation of those studies dovetail with Principle 2 Curriculum and key points, as well as Principle 3 Instruction and key points. Figure 3.14 summarizes the key points of what it takes to prepare educators to deliver those principles and strategies in a way that will have positive effects on all students in the school.

FIGURE 3.14 **Theory, Research, and Principle 2 of Dual Language Education Coincide**

Curriculum Principles and Key Points (Howard et al., 2018)	Empirical Research from 4 Dual Language and Multilingual Studies Cited (Two-Way Study, BCIRC, Transfer of Reading from Spanish to English, and ExC-ELL/ACE-LERA)
Quality Program The program has a process for developing and revising a high-quality curriculum.	The evidence-based plan described in this chapter developed and tested a process to integrate language, literacy, content, and social-emotional learning with core content in dual language curriculum.
Meets Needs of All MLLs Based on general education and bilingual education, adapts to ESL, SSL, special education, gifted education, and types of funding. The program is coordinated across grade levels.	The program was tested and continues to be implemented in general education and bilingual grades PK–5 and core content grades 6–12 classrooms, as well as ESL/ELD/SSL, sheltered classrooms, special education, and gifted education. The programs are coordinated across grade levels and across subject areas. These 5-year studies were funded by multiple sources and continue to be implemented through the typical federal and state funding sources.
Diversity Appreciation for multiculturalism and linguistic diversity. It is culturally responsive to all students' cultural and linguistic backgrounds.	The longitudinal studies took place in general and bilingual education settings. The studies were adaptable to different parts of the country (from Hawaii to New York City and in between). The programs were implemented in monolingual and bilingual and/or dual language settings for multicultural learners from diverse cultural and linguistic backgrounds.

Curriculum Principles and Key Points (Howard et al., 2018)	Empirical Research from 4 Dual Language and Multilingual Studies Cited (Two-Way Study, BCIRC, Transfer of Reading from Spanish to English, and ExC-ELL/ACE-LERA)
Standards-Based It is standards-based for language and literacy. Promotes and maintains equal status for both languages. Articulates measurable learning outcomes. Effectively integrates technology to enhance learning and meet standards.	All teachers in all programs are prepared to teach through this integrated language, literacy, and content curriculum model where it is implemented with high-quality MLLs. It aligns with state standards and district goals. Technology is used to measure learning outcomes and to support integrated learning.

FIGURE 3.15 Theory, Research, and Principle 3 of Dual Language Education Coincide

Instruction Principles and Key Points (Howard et al., 2018)	Empirical Research from 4 Dual Language and Multilingual Studies Cited (Two-Way Study, BCIRC, Transfer of Reading from Spanish to English, and ExC-ELL/ACE-LERA)
Methodology Instructional methods are derived from research-based principles of dual language education and ensure fidelity to the model.	**Methodology** Evidence-based strategies for teaching vocabulary, discourse, basic reading, reading comprehension, and writing appropriate for each subject area are part of the elementary and secondary components of instruction. An observation protocol accompanies each of those components to measure quality and fidelity. The protocol and training for coaching teachers also accompany the components.
Language Instruction The instruction incorporates appropriate separation of languages to promote high levels of language acquisition. Teachers integrate language and content instruction. Instruction in one language builds on concepts learned in the other language. Cross-linguistic (translanguaging) strategies are used to leverage students' bilingualism.	**Language Instruction** The Two-Way Bilingual study separated languages but kept the English-dominant and Spanish-dominant students together throughout the day. Teachers used techniques to facilitate understanding and practice of the new language with peers. Peers learned social-emotional competencies for working together effectively while developing metacognitive skills. The English and Spanish teachers taught to high levels of core content in a coordinated co-teaching approach to build on concepts and to meet grade-level standards. Translanguaging was used to process complex information, engage in language practice and reflection, and value home language and culture.
Literacy Instruction Teachers use sheltered instruction and other pedagogical strategies for bilingual learners to facilitate comprehension and promote language and literacy development.	**Literacy Instruction** Co-teachers use the same reading pedagogy (e.g., phonemic awareness, phonological awareness, decoding, fluency, word knowledge, reading comprehension, and metalinguistic awareness) to develop grade-level reading comprehension and content learning. Although languages are separated for instruction, differences and similarities between the languages are taught to facilitate transfer between both and to accelerate mastery of reading and writing.

(Continued)

(Continued)

Instruction Principles and Key Points (Howard et al., 2018)	Empirical Research from 4 Dual Language and Multilingual Studies Cited (Two-Way Study, BCIRC, Transfer of Reading from Spanish to English, and ExC-ELL/ACE-LERA)
Explicit language and literacy instruction is provided in both languages. Technology is used to display their language and further their skills.	Teachers went through extensive professional development on transfer between languages and building academic language in both. They learned to explicitly teach vocabulary before, during, and after reading expository and literary texts; students learned to discuss the content of the text, write summaries, anchor knowledge, and do content-based writing. Monthly performance assessments and grades demonstrated the progress of each student in the four domains and in the mastery of content. Those in need of extra assistance are identified. Co-teachers analyze their approaches based on those results.
Sociocultural Competence Student-centered instruction promotes sociocultural competence, language variation, independence, and ownership of the learning process.	**Sociocultural Competence** Sociocultural and social-emotional competencies are developed in the context of working with and getting to know the diverse students in the class as they work in a variety of interactive strategies. In student-centered interactive instruction, students learn to respect differences in language variation, talents, family background, and home situations. Social-emotional strategies are woven throughout the language, literacy, and content activities.
Appreciation for Student Diversity Teachers use strategies for meeting needs of diverse students: gifted, special education, newcomers, native speakers, and second language speakers.	**Appreciation for Student Diversity Ethos** Co-teachers using evidence-based studies use cooperative learning as a basis for all student interaction and learning. Students working in heterogenous teams or partners read and summarize, formulate questions in teams of three or four, and do drafting, revising, and editing with peers. Teams not only work to process and learn information but also to value the different cultures and student backgrounds. Students take turns becoming more capable peers and models for each other. Turn-taking and performance in each language are promoted to ensure equity.

THE UNDERGIRDING FACTOR FOR SUCCESSFUL CURRICULUM AND INSTRUCTION

A dual language–centered professional development design provides learning opportunities to expand educator expertise in evidence-based learning for MLLs. Educators have sustained opportunities to learn from each other as they share successes and common problems of implementation. Teachers are given time and spaces where they test and refine their practice and reflect with others. The time afforded to revise lessons to integrate new practices is not a luxury but a prerequisite to successful delivery. Leadership plays a major role in providing these collaborative structures and solicits feedback from teachers on how to improve their learning spaces. Continuous, focused, and authentic praise and encouragement are routine.

Professional development practices that changed teacher practice and enabled student learning gains were based in the curriculum content being taught; engaged teachers in active learning as teachers tried out the practices they would use; offered models of the practices with lessons, assignments, and coaching; extended over time (typically at least 50 hours of interaction over a number of months) with iterative opportunities to try things in the classroom and continue to refine. (Darling-Hammond, 2022)

The content and process for dual language–focused professional learning can be designed together. We can expect transfer from a training to go smoothly into a classroom when teachers experience iterations of theory and/or research, modeling or demonstrations of each strategy, and practice at each workshop with feedback and reflection with peers, followed by school-based coaching and teachers' learning communities (TLCs) (August et al., 2008; Calderón, 1999).

The content is also a reiteration of vocabulary, reading, and writing integrated with all content areas in two languages. Whereas monolingual program–focused professional development is mostly offered in English, the 50/50 proposition of time on both languages must also be considered in professional development for dual language programs.

> This made me think of the importance of ongoing job-embedded professional learning opportunities for teachers of ELLs/MLLs. One-shot professional development sessions must be replaced by collaborative approaches to shared inquiries, such as suggested here as TLCs.
>
> **Andrea**

FIGURE 3.16 Planning the Design of a Quality Implementation in K–12 Classrooms

Design Features	Implementation Features
1. Integrates language and literacy into all content in both languages.	The focus of disciplinary learning for MLLs is supported by explicit vocabulary, reading, and writing instruction integrated with math, science, social studies, and language arts in K–12 classrooms.
2. Professional development workshops incorporate theory, modeling, demonstrations, and practice of strategies in both languages.	Teachers, coaches, and leaders experience, analyze, and practice with peers the quality experiences they want for their students and the strategies they are to implement. They focus on successes and assets and how to be active advocates for MLLs.
3. Supports quality of implementation with continuous coaching in both languages.	Teachers and their coaches attend all professional learning together. They co-construct goals for observations, the type of data to collect, feedback format, and next steps. Teacher volunteers invite peers to observe or video their teaching for collaborative reflection in TLCs.
4. Provides relevant resources and time to develop lessons in both languages.	Student texts and ancillary materials for classroom and online learning are available to support the new instructional approach. Assessments are used to inform necessary adaptations.
5. Sustains the positive momentum.	School leadership actively and financially supports teacher efforts. Workshop refreshers are scheduled throughout the year, and teachers meet in teams to review curricula, lessons, and instructional processes, and to celebrate small and huge successes.

INNOVATIONS THAT BUILD EDUCATOR CAPACITY AND BETTER STUDENT OUTCOMES WILL TAKE TIME, EVIDENCE-BASED INSTRUCTION, AND WHOLE-SCHOOL COMMITMENT TO MLLS

Reflection Questions

1. Is our DLE program enacting the five design and implementation features?
2. Which might need more consideration?
3. Is our discourse and vocabulary instruction integrated into all subjects in both languages?
4. Are our students' reading skills at par in both languages?
5. Are our students mastering core content concepts in both languages?
6. What could be our next steps?

References

August, D., & Calderón, M. (2006). Teacher beliefs and professional development. In D. August & T. Shanahan (Eds.), *Developing literacy in second-language learners: Report of the National Literacy Panel on language-minority children and youth* (pp. 555–565). Lawrence Erlbaum.

August, D., & Shanahan, T. (Eds.). (2006). *Developing literacy in second-language learners: Report of the National Literacy Panel on language-minority children and youth*. Lawrence Erlbaum.

August, D., Beck, I. L., Calderón, M., Francis, D. J., Lesaux, N. K., & Shanahan, T. (2008). Instruction and professional development. In D. August & T. Shanahan (Eds.), *Developing reading and writing in second language learners. Lessons from the Report of the National Literacy Panel on language-minority children and youth* (pp. 131–250). Lawrence Erlbaum.

August, D., Calderón, M., & Carlo, M. (2001). *Transfer of reading skills from Spanish to English: A longitudinal study of young learners*. Report ED-98-CO-0071 to the Office of Bilingual Education and Minority Languages Affairs, U. S. Department of Education.

August, D., Carlo, M., Calderón, M., & Proctor, P. (2005, Spring). Development of literacy in Spanish-speaking English-language learners: Findings from a longitudinal study of elementary school children. *Perspectives on Language and Literacy, 31*(2), 17–19.

Berman, P., Minicucci, C., McLaughlin, B., Nelson, B., & Woodworth, K. (1995). Effective leadership. In K. Lindholm-Leary (Ed.), *Review of research and best practices on effective features of dual language education programs* (pp. 29–32).

Calderón, M. (1999). Teachers Learning Communities for cooperation in diverse settings. In M. Calderón & R. E. Slavin (Eds.), *Building community through cooperative learning.* Special issue of *Theory Into Practice Journal, 38*(2). Ohio State University.

Calderón, M. E. (2007). *Teaching reading to English language learners, Grades 6–12: A framework for improving achievement in the content areas.* Corwin.

Calderón, M. E. (2009). Professional development for teachers of English language learners and striving readers. In L. Mandel-Morrow, R. Rueda, & D. Lapp (Eds.), *Handbook of literacy and research on literacy instruction: Issues of diversity, policy and equity.* Guilford Press.

Calderón, M. E., & Minaya-Rowe, L. (2003). *Designing and implementing two-way bilingual programs: A step-by step guide for administrators, teachers, and parents.* Corwin.

Calderón, M. E., & Minaya-Rowe, L. (2011). *Preventing long-term English language learners: Transforming schools to meet core standards.* Corwin.

Calderón, M. E., Hertz-Lazarowitz, R., & Slavin, R. E. (1998, November). Effects of bilingual cooperative integrated reading and composition on students making the transition from Spanish to English reading. *Elementary School Journal, 99*(2). http://www.journals.uchicago.edu/doi/abs/10.1086/461920

Calderón, M. E., Tartaglia, L. M., & Montenegro, H. (2023). *Cultivating competence in English learners: Integrating social-emotional learning with language and literacy.* Solution Tree.

Calderón, M., & Carreón, A. (1994). Educators and students use cooperative learning to become biliterate and bilingual. *Cooperative Learning, 14*(3), 6–9.

Calderón, M., & Carreón, A. (2001). A two-way bilingual program: Promise, practice, and precautions. In R. E. Slavin & M. Calderón (Eds.), *Effective programs for Latino children* (pp. 101–142). Lawrence Erlbaum.

Calderón, M., & Espino, G. (2017), *Acelerando la comprensión en Español: Lectura, escritura y razonamiento académico* (ACE-LERA): *Manual para los maestros.* Margarita Calderón & Associates.

Calderón, M., August, D., Slavin, R., Cheung, A., Durán, D., & Madden, N. (2005). Bringing words to life in classrooms with English language learners. In A. Hiebert & M. Kamil (Eds.), *Teaching and learning vocabulary: Bringing research to practice* (pp. 99–123). Lawrence Erlbaum.

Christian, D., & Genesee, F. (2001). *Bilingual education.* TESOL.

Darling-Hammond, L. (2022, November 21). Linda Darling-Hammond wins International Prize for Educational Research. Interview by Rick Hess. *Education Week.* https://www.edweek.org/teaching-learning/opinion-linda-darling-hammond-wins-international-prize-for-education-research/2022/11

Escamilla, K., Olsen, L., & Slavik, J. (2022). *Towards comprehensive, effective literacy policy and instruction for English learner/emergent bilingual students.* National Committee for Effective Literacy.

Every Student Succeeds Act. Pub. L. No. 114-95, 114 Stat. 1177. (2015). https://www.congress.gov/114/statute/STATUTE-129/STATUTE-129-Pg1802.pdf

Genesee, F., Lindholm-Leary, K. J., Saunders, W., & Christian, D. (2006). *Educating English language learners.* Cambridge University Press.

Graham, S. (2020). The sciences of reading and writing must become more fully integrated. *Reading Research Quarterly, 55*(S1), S35–S44.

Graham, S., & Perin, D. (2007). *Writing next: Effective strategies to improve writing of adolescents in middle and high schools – A report to Carnegie Corporation of New York.* Alliance for Excellent Education.

Graham, S., Kiuhara, S. A., & MacKay, M. (2020). The effects of writing on learning in science, social studies, and mathematics: A meta-analysis. *Review of Educational Research, 90*(2), 179–226.

Hiebert, A., & Kamil, M. (Eds.). (2005). *Teaching and learning vocabulary: Bringing research to practice.* Lawrence Erlbaum.

Howard, E. R., Lindholm-Leary, K. J., Rogers, D., Olague, N., Medina, J., Kennedy, B., Sugarman, J., & Christian, D. (2018). *Guiding principles for dual language education* (3rd ed.). Center for Applied Linguistics.

Lindholm-Leary, K., & Genesee, F. (2010). Alternative educational programs for English language learners. In California Department of Education (Ed.), *Improving education for English learners: Research-based approaches* (pp. 323–382). CDE Press.

National Center for Evaluation Statistics. (2017). *NAEP 2017 writing assessments.* https://nces.ed.gov/nationsreportcard/writing/2017writing.aspx

The National Commission on Writing (2004). *Writing a ticket to work . . . or a ticket out. A survey for business leaders.* College Board.

National Reading Panel (U.S.) & National Institute of Child Health and Human Development (U.S.). (2000). *Report of the National Reading Panel: Teaching children to read: An evidence-based assessment of the scientific research literature on reading and its implications for reading instruction.* U.S. Department of Health and Human Services, Public Health Service, National Institutes of Health, National Institute of Child Health and Human Development.

The Reading League. (2022). *Science of reading: The defining guide.* https://www.thereadingleague.org/what-is-thescience-of-reading/

Slavin, R. E., & Calderón, M. (Eds.). (2001). *Effective programs for Latino students.* Lawrence Erlbaum.

Slavin, R. E., & Cheung, A. (2005). A synthesis of research on language of reading instruction for English language learners. *Review of Educational Research, 75*(2), 247–284. https://doi.org/10.3102/00346543075002247

Slavin, R. E., Madden, N. A., Calderón, M. E., Chamberlain, A., & Hennessy, M. (2011). Reading and language outcomes of a five-year randomized evaluation of transitional bilingual education. *Educational Evaluation and Policy Analysis, 33*(1), 47–58. http://www.edweek.org/media/bilingual_pdf.pdf

Snow, C. E., Burns, M. S., & Griffin, P. (Eds.). (1998). *Preventing reading difficulties in young children.* National Academy Press.

Takanishi, R., & Le Menestrel, S. (Eds.). (2017). *Promoting the educational success of children and youth learning English: Promising futures. Consensus Study Report.* National Academies Press

Thomas, W., & Collier, V. (1997). *School effectiveness for language minority students.* ERIC – ED436087. National Clearinghouse for Bilingual Education.

Vygotsky, L. S. (1978). *Mind in society: The development of higher psychological processes.* Harvard University Press.

chapter four

From Monolingual Assessment to Assessment in Multiple Languages

MARGO GOTTLIEB

PREMISE

As educators who strongly advocate for multilingual learners, it's time to revisit how we have been privileging English in assessment practices and take the multilingual turn (May, 2014). Increasing students' access to and use of multiple languages in assessment yields more equitable data that offer truer and richer portraits of multilingual learners' growth and accomplishments. Giving multilingual learners opportunities to provide multimodal evidence for learning in multiple languages shifts the locus of control to the student and allows student-driven assessment to prevail.

There is a growing awareness among teachers and other educational leaders of the importance of accentuating the strengths of multilingual learners by honoring and addressing their languages, cultures, experiences, and traditions. In asking educators at local and national conferences what the primary equity issue is in educating multilingual learners, inevitably, the number one response is "fair assessment." This chapter responds to the need for equitable assessment by offering ways to portray what multilingual learners can do across languages during instruction and classroom assessment.

Moving to assessment practices in multiple languages may sound challenging; however, the results are stunning. By shifting from a single monolingual mindset to one that is multilingual and contextualized, we can optimize linguistic and cultural sustainability in classroom assessment. Only then can we effectively portray multilingual learners' entire range of linguistic expertise and academic achievement. Using multiple languages for assessment purposes yields more robust and descriptive information to inform teaching and learning. When multilingual learners have language choice, there is the additional benefit of building their self-confidence, agency, and autonomy, traits that instill sociocultural competence and emotional stability.

We use the term *multilingual learners*, a subset of all learners, to acknowledge and honor these students' array of languages and cultures that contribute to their growing linguistic and cultural repertoires (Martínez, 2018; Ortega, 2014). *English learners*, the official legal term, applies to those multilingual learners who qualify for and receive language support according to individual state criteria. As seen in figure 4.1, students who participate in bilingual or dual language programs cross all three student population sectors.

FIGURE 4.1 The Range of Students in Bilingual or Dual Language Education Programs

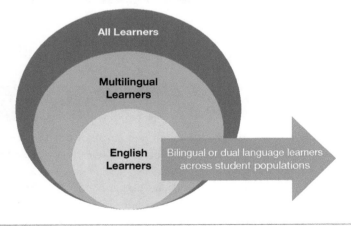

Source: Adapted from Gottlieb (2024)

Assessment is a multiphase process of planning, gathering, analyzing, interpreting, reporting, and using a variety of data sources over time (Gottlieb, 2016, 2021). We adhere to and advocate a strengths-based stance for assessment where we view languages and cultures as rights and resources (Ruíz,

1984). In contrast, we never portray multilingual learners as *disadvantaged, at-risk, struggling,* or with *barriers* or *academic gaps* that have been based on test scores or other factors. While assessment in multiple languages has broad applicability to all multilingual learners and their teachers, much of this chapter addresses students who participate in bilingual or dual language education programs.

VIGNETTE

In the last decade, Central Elementary School has undergone stark changes in its student population. Second generation Latinx families, now firmly established in the community, have opened their doors to immigrant families who have recently arrived from Mexico and Central America. The once passive *club de las mujeres,* an arm of the Parent Teacher Organization, has transformed into an advocacy group for bilingualism and biliteracy. These women no longer see developmental bilingual or dual language education as an enrichment program, but as a right and privilege for their children.

The principal of Central is sensitive to community issues and wants the entire school to embrace the languages and cultures of all the students. She is also keenly aware of how annual assessment data in English tend to dictate district policy and override the value of other languages as a learning metric. To showcase the necessity of multilingual data to meet the school's mission and vision, the principal recruits her coaches, teachers, and *el club de las mujeres* to wage a campaign for classroom assessment in multiple languages.

The leadership team shows the video *The Importance of ELL Strategies - Immersion (Moises in Math Class)* to launch a schoolwide professional learning series on multilingual data literacy. This poignant film illustrates how a newcomer who is well-versed in mathematical concepts is stymied by a math test in English. This most diligent student figures out the answer to a mathematical problem posed by the teacher but is laughed at by the class at his attempt to *explain* it orally in English. This vivid example is a call to action for educators to rethink how to create a welcoming classroom climate and for multilingual learners to have access to multiple languages for assessment to ascertain a more accurate account of their conceptual knowledge. Use the QR code adjacent here to view the video.

Video: The Importance of ELL Strategies - Immersion (Moises in Math Class)

THE URGENCY

Today, linguistic and culturally sustainable classrooms offer space for multilingual learners to engage in the languages of their community, home, and school. As shown in figure 4.2, the languages and cultures ever present in these three interdependent ecosystems help shape multilingual learners' identities (Zacarian et al., 2021). Multilingual learners navigate within and across all three ecosystems—the languages of interaction in the home, the languages students are exposed to in school, and the languages present in the community—yet the natural interweaving and flow of languages for students generally do not extend to assessment policy and practice at school. For instance, in the case of Moises, a newcomer to the United States, Spanish is the sole language of the home, English is the language of the school, and both exist in the community. The absence of linguistic crossover or consonance among these ecosystems has potentially harmful effects for multilingual learners.

When it comes to K–12 assessment in the United States, there is constant friction between the status quo, with its generally restrictive English-only policy for accountability, and the inauguration of policy that acknowledges and promotes multilingual learners' use of multiple languages for improving teaching and learning. While there has been a call to be inclusive of multilingual learners' languages and cultures within large-scale language assessment, there has been little to no movement in that direction (Chalhoub-Deville, 2019; Shohamy, 2011). Likewise, at the classroom level, monolingual data in English still abound as many bilingual programs seem to be in name only (Hinton, 2015). In addition to educators, families must become apprised (and at times, convinced) of the value and benefit of securing and sharing information in multiple languages.

Reform in assessment policies and practices for multilingual learners is urgently needed throughout the entire educational arena, with educators and families taking the lead in transforming the system. Integral to this movement are educators who support deep and engaging learning that celebrates multilingual learners' humanity and identities. Figure 4.3 invites teachers and administrators to take a needs assessment to ascertain the extent of assessment in multiple languages in their bilingual or dual language programs. It reveals the availability and use of languages for instructional and assessment purposes at the classroom, school, and district levels.

> This is such a powerful and crucial stance. And the harmful effects multilingual learners experience stay with them for a lifetime. A close friend of mine, now in his eighties, remembers being beaten in school (in a state on the west coast) for speaking Spanish—let alone ever being assessed in Spanish. He still hesitates to speak Spanish in public even though he worked hard on his own to stay bilingual and biliterate and everyone in his Fresno community speaks Spanish. Perhaps the visible beatings in schools have stopped; however, the internal shaming remains as long as we assess only in English.
>
> **Joan**

FIGURE 4.2 The Intersection of Linguistic Ecosystems for Multilingual Learners

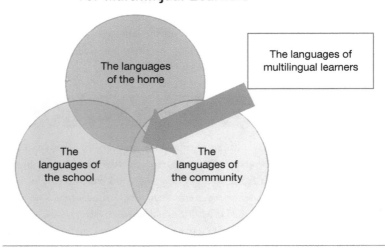

FIGURE 4.3 Assessment in Multiple Languages: Where Does it Occur in Your Setting?

Local educators hold the locus of control when it comes to assessment in multiple languages. After reviewing the assessment practices, identify the strengths you see in assessment for multilingual learners across classroom, school, and/or district settings.

Assessment Practice	Classroom	School	District
1. Instruction is in two languages, but assessment is in English.			
2. Instruction is in English; however, multilingual learners have access to their other languages for assessment purposes.			
3. Instruction is in two languages with corresponding assessment in both languages.			
4. Assessment in multiple languages matches the language allocation of the bilingual or dual language program.			
5. Assessment in multiple languages is a commitment of administrators and teachers.			
6. Assessment in two languages is systematically embedded in curricular units of learning.			
7. Assessment in two languages is infused in instruction.			
8. Multilingual learners have decision-making power in designing assessment and presenting evidence for learning.			
9. Multilingual families have decision-making power in designing local assessment.			
10. Teachers have decision-making power in designing and implementing assessment.			
11. Leadership teams of administrators, coaches, and teachers have input in formulating language and assessment policy for schools and/or districts.			

Follow-up Questions

- To what extent is there congruence in the languages of assessment for multilingual learners across the classroom, school, and district?

- How might figure 4.3 stimulate discussion among educators, multilingual learners, and families around equity in assessment practices?

- How might school leadership design or refresh your language policy to better represent the languages of multilingual learners in instruction and assessment?

The Force of Federal Mandates

The urgent need to accept multilingual assessment as a tenet of bilingual and dual language programs is not a recent phenomenon.

Born out of the civil rights movement, the modern-day wave of bilingual education in the United States can be traced to federal legislation of 1965, namely, the Elementary and Secondary Education Act (ESEA). In large part, what ensued was a series of compensatory programs that cast a negative light on multilingual learners (with labels such as *Limited English Speaking Ability* and *Limited English Proficient* students). On the positive side, the law brought about a national consciousness of this growing multilingual student demographic in our schools and communities.

Assessment for educational accountability is an outgrowth of this federal law. Initiated in 1994 with the Improving America's School Act (IASA), annual state assessments in reading/ language arts and mathematics for students in grades 3–12 have become instilled in state systems. Although initially exempt, the subsequent ushering of the No Child Left Behind Act (NCLB) in 2002 mandated the inclusion of multilingual learners. Here English language proficiency standards and an aligned assessment became state and/or consortium requirements, while the law simultaneously struck all references to bilingualism.

Fast forward to 2015. An opaque provision of the Every Student Succeeds Act (ESSA), as NCLB, states "to the extent practicable, assessments [shall be] in the language and form most likely to yield accurate data on what such students know and can do in academic content areas, until such students have achieved English language proficiency." In essence, the value-added nature of assessment in languages other than English for multilingual learners has been acceptable under federal law for over two decades, yet states have paid little heed to it (Solano-Flores & Hakuta, 2017).

To summarize, federal legislation has prompted tacit recognition of how assessment in multiple languages can yield rich data about our multilingual learners, yet most policymakers and educators have yet to tap its potential. As drivers of educational policy at the school and district levels, we must be sensitive to the force of federal mandates as we advocate and push for local control. Figure 4.4 illustrates the tension between assessment associated with state language policy stemming from federal legislation and litigation and competing language policy that represents the will of local communities, schools, and districts.

Secretary of Education Miguel Cardona makes a very relevant connection in his January 24, 2023, speech on the "Raise the Bar: Lead the World" iniative, whereby he calls for us [in education] to use assessments as flashlights to showcase what's needed rather than hammers to drive outcomes. He also asks the field to follow the research [like yours!] on second language development.

Joan

FIGURE 4.4 Policy-Driven Assessment in Multiple Languages: Macro (Top Down) and Micro (Bottom Up) Perspectives

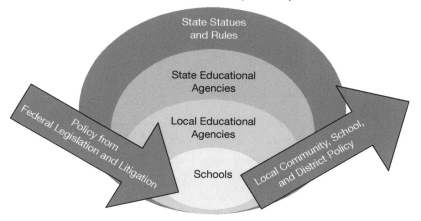

State and District Directives

Assessment policy for multilingual learners in bilingual and dual language education contexts tends to be a function of language policy. Given the boundaries of national language education policy under ESEA, states can shift their positioning regarding language education models and programs, understanding that their statutes and rules represent the floor or minimal requirements for compliance. Given the urgent need for multilingual assessment practices to represent what multilingual learners can do, we cannot be satisfied with just adhering to federal, state, or district policy without having the ability to infuse local provisions of schools and communities.

Given this legal precedent as de facto language policy, Gottlieb et.al. (2020) examined the websites of fifty states and the District of Columbia to ascertain additional guidance. The analysis yielded three distinct categories that mark the extent of reliance of states on the federal government as their source of language policy, from most (A) to least (C). The data reveal that

A. Three states (6%) have no statutes or rules regarding language education models or programming. They point directly to the Office of English Language Acquisition (OELA), the Title III arm of the United States Department of Education (ED), and information from its English Learners Tool Kit as its de facto language policy.

B. Fifteen states (~30%) rely on federal guidance under Title III for their language education policy. While there are no statutory mandates or administrative regulations, some have state-specific guidance.

C. Thirty-three states (64%) have substantive guidance that represents the interpretation of their individual state statutory mandates and regulations.

Follow-up Questions

- What is the language policy of your state, and where does it fall in this three-pronged categorical scheme?

- What is its primary source of guidance, and what other sources would you include?

- What else would you like your local language policy to address?

States have discretion in designing programs for multilingual learners, and school districts generally follow suit. In larger districts with greater heterogeneity in the multilingual student population, various program models often coexist. Figure 4.5 outlines a classification scheme of the most prevalent program models and their implications for assessment. The list goes from those programs that stipulate systemic use of multiple languages to those that are mainly English-centric.

FIGURE 4.5 Some Program Models for Multilingual Learners: Implications for Assessment in Multiple Languages

Program Model	Implications for Assessment in Multiple Languages
Dual language immersion	Use of languages other than English should mirror the program's language allocation plan (e.g., 90/10, 80/20, 50/50), if stipulated
Late exit or developmental bilingual	Use of languages other than English should be acceptable throughout the duration of the program
Transitional bilingual	Use of languages other than English should be contingent, to some extent, on the language(s) of instruction for specified content areas
English language development	Use of languages other than English (e.g., during student interaction or use of technology) should occur but not be considered compensatory *accommodations*
"Sheltered" content instruction	Use of languages other than English should reflect the classroom, grade-level and/or department, or school's language and assessment policy

Program Model	Implications for Assessment in Multiple Languages

Follow-up Questions

- How might you describe the program model(s) for multilingual learners in your district and school?
- How is language use treated for assessment? Does assessment match the languages of instruction?
- What kinds of decisions are made based on assessment in multiple languages?
- If you are familiar with translanguaging (if not, see the upcoming section), where might it come into play in assessment across program models?

The Counterforce of School- and Classroom-Level Data

Given federal and state mandates that generally set minimal criteria for language education policies, we desperately need additional data at the micro (school and classroom) level to convince nonbelievers of the power and positive impact of dual language and bilingual education for multilingual learners. In large part, data generated from assessment in these programs are tied to school and/or district accountability and used for program evaluation to determine the extent that programmatic goals have been met. We need to become more introspective and examine assessment that occurs day by day, week by week, and month by month within and across bilingual or dual language classrooms where instruction in multiple languages prevails.

In classrooms with multilingual learners, data from multiple languages are powerful providers of information from varying perspectives to help improve teaching and learning. One main source of these data is evidence generated from assessment where students have had input in formulating their own learning goals. Multilingual learners, their families, and teachers are all data informants in determining student growth toward goal attainment. Translanguaging, the natural and dynamic interweaving of languages among bi- and multilingual learners, can also serve as a data source.

> Program evaluation is such an important foundation for meaningful student assessment practices as described in this chapter. One question to consider might be "What type of instruction is taking place in the program model a school selects?"
>
> **Margarita**

The Role of Translanguaging in Instruction and Assessment

Translanguaging has been widely applied to language education as multiple language use has gained acceptance as part of schooling (García & Wei, 2013). As language policy and practice, translanguaging can be interwoven into all program models and therefore can (and should) be an expression of assessment. For example, in dual language classrooms with their strong presence of two languages, there is no reason why assessment can't include translanguaging to optimize what multilingual learners can do in different situations (Gottlieb, 2021). Here multilingual learners might interchange their languages as they seek to clarify concepts, dig deeper into content, or negotiate with peers of the same partner language in making decisions, all of which can be captured through observation.

The occurrence of translanguaging among multilinguals is flexible and dynamic, contingent on the purpose for language use, the context for the interaction, and the audience. If planned as part of a lesson on cross-linguistic transfer as a means of developing metalinguistic awareness, for example, the data from translanguaging during multilingual learners' interaction can be useful evidence for learning. For example, translanguaging can occur as multilingual learners dialog in designing projects whose end product is in a designated language. Figure 4.6 offers ideas for highlighting translanguaging during instruction and their integration into classroom assessment.

FIGURE 4.6 Ideas for Stimulating Translanguaging Practices in Classroom Instruction and Assessment

Teachers' Instructional Moves	Multilingual Learners' Opportunities to Translanguage During Assessment
Craft learning goals for units of learning or learning targets for lessons that are attainable through multiple languages	Co-plan with teachers ways to document evidence for learning in multiple languages
Invite multilingual learners to use online resources in multiple languages	Use multilingual websites and research tools (e.g., bilingual videos and podcasts) to explore content and show learning
Offer multimodalities (combining communication modes such as sight, sound, print, images, video, music, gestures with text) to show evidence for learning	Produce multimodal evidence, such as audio recordings, videos, or labeled graphics, to demonstrate learning
Promote interaction in multiple languages during discussions	Create models or other products according to bilingual criteria for success based on exchanges of information in multiple languages
Pair students or form groups to reflect on learning	Engage in peer assessment using languages of choice

Follow-up Questions

- Which translanguaging opportunities are available to your multilingual learners?
- How is translanguaging captured in assessment, or is it, in your language program?
- What do you see as the advantages of allowing multilingual learners to translanguage during instruction and classroom assessment?

In bilingual or dual language settings, no matter how strictly students and teachers adhere to a language allocation plan, translanguaging opportunities are going to pop up. There is no reason to suppress them because translanguaging ultimately enhances learning. Just look at the sentence at the top of the building in the next photo. The message, exemplifying translanguaging—*listen (you should) read more*—implies that the languages are of equal status and both contribute to maximizing meaning making (Hornberger & Link, 2012).

In Chapter 5, we also highlight the importance of translanguaging as an intentional pedagogical choice. Collaborating educators make decisions in preparation for their lessons and/ or during the delivery of instruction to tap into multilingual learners' full linguistic repertoires.

Andrea

Cautions and Caveats

The landscape of language education models and programs across the United States is wide and varied; it is also changing. As an educational community devoted to advancing multilingualism in instruction and assessment, we must be aware of and confront issues that are lodged against us. We must also understand that assessment in multiple languages cannot be uniformly applied to all programs with multilingual learners. Figure 4.7 addresses some issues of programmatic variability and their impact on assessment.

FIGURE 4.7 ## Dilemmas in Language Education and Their Implications for Assessment

Language Education Programs	Dilemma	Impact on Assessment
Variability in Theoretical Traditions	Dual language education builds on research and history of two related fields: foreign language and bilingual education, each with distinct foci, different student populations, and unique theoretical orientations. Programs tend to treat language learning either as a subject area, as in *world languages*, or a development process that integrates language and content.	Assessment should echo the program's research base and align with each program's philosophy and theoretical orientation. Assessment tools should reflect each program's overall goals and report results through the lens of its multilingual student population.

(Continued)

(Continued)

Language Education Programs	Dilemma	Impact on Assessment
Variability in Program Models and Goals	Bilingual program models have diverse language goals. Dual language education programs nurture two languages to move students toward and preserve their bilingualism and biliteracy. In contrast, transitional models capitalize on the students' other language as a springboard for their English language development.	Research shows that some dual language programs constrain equity by shielding multilingual learners from advanced electives, diminishing possibilities for rigorous assessment (Morita-Mullaney et al., 2020). In transitional programs, assessment in multiple languages is ephemeral, making it difficult to determine sustained language growth.
Variability in Language Use	Bilingual or dual language programs are built around different purposes, time allocations, and distribution of languages. Language policy, such as the treatment of translanguaging, should also be considered.	Local language policy (for classrooms, schools, or districts) should undergird instruction and assessment. Multilingual learners, families, and teachers should all have a voice in defining language-related assessment practices.
Variability in Terminology	There are varied meanings for individuals, communities, educational programs, and national groups; however, all terms must be strengths-based. Many students are bilingual (or multilingual) whether they participate in language programs or not.	Teachers should be sensitive to multilingual learners' language use during instruction, irrespective of their *label* or *category*, and allow opportunities to replicate it during assessment.

Follow-up Questions

- How do the different types of variability in bilingual and dual language education apply to your setting?
- What might you do to counteract their potential negative effects on assessment for multilingual learners?
- How can you remain sensitive to community circumstances and desires regarding language variability in instruction and assessment?

THE RESEARCH BASE

The research base for assessment in multiple languages is grounded in two different theoretical camps; one generally pertains to large-scale state assessment efforts (the structuralist or cognitivist side) and the other to instructional assessment activities (the socioculturalist or sociocognitivist side). Figure 4.8 outlines the characteristics of these two theoretical orientations showing the tensions that still exist. This contrast continues to appear in instruction and assessment.

FIGURE 4.8 Theoretical Foundations of Language Assessment and Their Implications

Theoretical Foundations	Structuralism	Socioculturalism
	• Assumes an order in language acquisition from sounds to words to sentences to discourse	• Assumes precedence of discourse with sentences and words being subsumed within it
	• Attends to mechanics, grammatical structures, and formal characteristics of language	• Asserts that learning revolves around social interaction
	• Is rule-bound, assuming *proper use* of language in oral and written expression	• Views meaning as negotiated among individuals in social and cultural contexts
	• Respects listening, speaking, reading, and writing as independent domains	• Accepts multiple modes (e.g., expressive, interpretive), including translanguaging (e.g., interactive)
	• Relies on error correction	• Reflects and values meaning over form
	• Emphasizes accuracy of communication	• Highlights effectiveness of communication
Implications for Instruction and Assessment	• Tends to rely on memorization of linguistic forms	• Relies on interaction among individuals across a variety of situations
	• Discourages creativity and experimentation	• Encourages creativity and deep thinking
	• Assumes one correct answer (e.g., multiple choice and cloze)	• Supports a variety of pathways and perspectives
	• Views language as hierarchical and sequential	• Considers students' cultural differences, identities, and interpersonal relations
	• Concentrates on students' accuracy of expression	• Emphasizes appropriateness of the communication

Rather than favor one theoretical orientation of learning over another, it might prove more effective for educators (and test developers) to blend aspects of each into multilingual assessment practices. The experiences and developmental paths of multilinguals are just too diverse to be shaped by a single theory. Bilingualism calls for unique contexts of sociocultural identity coupled with cognitive and neural functioning (Marian & Hayakawa, 2021). Given this reality, let's agree with Paradis (2004), who asserts that although structuralism serves a legitimate function, it does not suffice when viewing bilingualism. Bilingualism entails a reliance on neurolinguistic and sociocultural perspectives that include metalinguistic and/or metacultural knowledge and pragmatics.

Learning theories contribute to assessment practice. Often, they operate under the guise of monolingualism as the norm where multilingual learners are to be "accommodated" until they reach a level commensurate with their "monolingual English speaking peers." Although there has been gradual acceptance of the desirability of multiple languages for learning, we have yet to normalize bilingualism in school and systematize assessment in multiple languages.

The research of González et al. (2005) offers a shining light and promise for the education of multilingual learners. It reveals rich *funds of knowledge* that have been developed in community spaces for schools to tap as grounding for curriculum, instruction, and assessment. As an extension, in highlighting students' *funds of identity,* Esteban-Guitart and Moll (2014) find that multilingual learners grow more confident as learners, and as agents of their own learning, they gain more assurance.

TOWARD A UNIFYING THEORY OF MULTILINGUALISM AND ASSESSMENT

Although there is ample research and a growing interest in multilingual teaching and learning, the educational field remains quite devoid of assessment in multiple languages. Indeed, even acknowledgment of sociocultural theory as an accepted stance has not yet displaced the prevailing monolingual paradigm in assessment (Shohamy, 2011, 2022). Reports on large-scale assessment still tend to demoralize multilingual learners by emphasizing what these students lack, English language proficiency (Gándara, 2015). We must better attend to the linguistic and cultural diversity of our students; otherwise, we remain at risk of perpetuating a science that is rooted in deficit thinking and actions. There might be political and economic restrictions imposed on districts from state governments; however, that does not preclude *local* assessment policies and practices for individual schools and classrooms to draw from their own resources, stakeholders, and communities.

> These are very powerful questions that require all stakeholders' careful consideration, collaboration, and joint reflection.
>
> **Andrea**

Despite the body of research on effective teaching in bilingual contexts, classroom assessment has not strongly supported the credibility of these practices (Schissel et al., 2019). So why is the link between dual language teaching and assessment missing? How can programs and schools serving multilingual learners ever know the extent to which they are successful in realizing their educational goals if sound multilingual assessment is not in place?

To this day we have not reached a consensus on how to resolve the friction between contextualizing aspects of multilingual learners' multiple languages and cultures while simultaneously meeting the requirements of monolingual (English) assessment demands (May & Dam, 2014).

IMPLICATIONS FOR PRACTICE AND IMPLEMENTATION

There are a theoretical rationale and a strong research base that support the goals of dual language education—bilingual/biliteracy development, achievement, sociocultural competence, and critical consciousness. There is also the practical commonsense reason for reinforcing and building bilingualism of multilingual learners in school and beyond. When language and cultural practices of the community, school, and classroom are in concert with those of multilingual learners and their families, we build trust and come to share beliefs. Only then can we begin to overcome linguistic and cultural inequities that make tearing down monolingual walls necessary.

Yet when we examine school and classroom assessment practices, there is a paucity of data in multiple languages. Taking into consideration the assessment tenets and tips presented next, we invite you to pool your resources to create a compendium of data in multiple languages. With this solid evidence from local assessment, coupled with data from large-scale assessment, you will be equipped to leverage and defend assessment in multiple languages as a function of curriculum and instruction. You might also consider the evidence-based tenets as a precursor to crafting an assessment system inclusive of multiple languages or expanding your current assessment system.

Evidence-based Tenets for Assessment in Multiple Languages

The following tenets help shape a rationale for assessment in multiple languages for multilingual learners, especially for those students who participate in bilingual or dual language programs.

1. Multilingual learners, by definition, have been or are exposed to and interact in multiple languages and cultures; therefore, it is their right to use their assets to further their learning and show evidence for their learning in multiple languages. Assessment in bilingual and dual language programs should invite multilingual learners to build on their bilingualism and biliteracy within and across content areas.

2. Translanguaging is an evidence-based theory and practice that taps multilingual learners' linguistic and cultural resources to optimize their opportunities for success during instruction and assessment. Irrespective of language allocations of dual language education programs, translanguaging should be a viable and permissible policy and practice. In turn, assessment should be a tool for instantiating translanguaging within students' bilingual brains.

These four tenets are clear, concise, and pivotal. As we collectively share these via multiple venues and contexts, we have the pathway to change our field for the better. Additionally, these four tenets' rich layers of implication offer resonant invitations for further research. Finally, they solidify the ways in which we aim to prepare bilingual or dual language teachers via the National Standards.

Joan

3. Classroom assessment must be embedded in instruction; conversely, linguistic and culturally sustainable instruction must be infused into assessment. In bilingual and dual language education programs, the languages of assessment should not be a forced fit but a part of the natural flow of languages of everyday instruction. If multilingual learners' funds of identity anchor instruction, then as an extension, their languages and cultures should be embedded in classroom assessment.

4. Assessment *as*, *for*, and *of* learning features multilingual learners and their relationships with others; for example, students interact with peers, collaborate with teachers, and participate in their classroom's community of practice (Gottlieb, 2016). Together the three approaches offer a comprehensive system that humanizes assessment and exemplifies assessment equity. For bilingual and dual language programs, this principle translates into creating a balance among stakeholders' contributions (from families, teachers, and multilingual learners) and types of data (from large-scale state tests, district interim measures, school-based common assessment, and classroom assessment). Figure 4.9 illustrates this balanced assessment model that centers multilingual learners.

FIGURE 4.9 **Assessment *as*, *for*, and *of* Learning: A Model of Educational Equity**

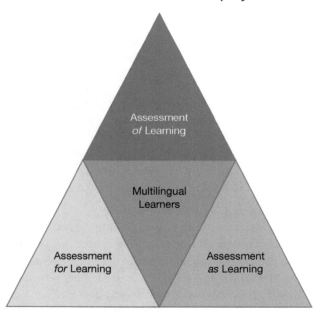

Source: Adapted from Gottlieb (2016)

Here are some thoughts about how to begin to enact these tenets to opti-mize the participation of multilingual learners and their teachers in equitable assessment practices.

From Tenets to Tips for Educators and Multilingual Learners: A Call to Action

In this section, we convert a solid research base on the efficacy of bilin-gualism and biliteracy to everyday practice. Figure 4.10 offers suggestions for district, school, and teacher leadership for incorporating assessment in multiple languages into practice.

FIGURE 4.10 **Actions by School and District Leaders and Corresponding Assessment**

Actions by School and District Leaders	Application for Assessment
Conduct an assessment audit to determine the weight of data from each language in decision making.	Collect and analyze data according to language use—English, another language, and/or both—to determine the extent of balance between or among languages.
Propose ongoing schoolwide or districtwide professional learning on assessment literacy for teachers, multilingual learners, and families.	Highlight the contributions of data in multiple languages across ecosystems—home, school, and community.
Establish grade-level, department, or schoolwide communities of learning to analyze and tackle inequities in assessment for multilingual learners	Generate a plan for how student data in multiple languages can help counteract a single monolingual perspective.
Initiate teacher-generated action research around data-related issues, such as examining grading practices for multilingual learners participating in bilingual or dual language education programs.	Present research findings from multiple assessment sources and languages to families, community organizations, and the local school board.
Craft a classroom and school language and assessment policy with input from multilingual learners and families around the advantageous role of bilingualism and multilingualism.	Address how language allocation, translanguaging, and language use can contribute to a vibrant multilingual assessment system.

We also need to look to more student-driven assessment where multi-lingual learners become agents and advocates for their own learning. One way in which students can play a more prominent role is by participating in assessment *as*, *for*, and *of* learning. Figure 4.11 illustrates how teachers and multilingual learners can be central figures in classroom assessment.

FIGURE 4.11 Ideas for Assessment *as*, *for*, and *of* Learning Based on Teacher and Multilingual Learner Actions

Actions by Teachers and Multilingual Learners	Application for Assessment *as*, *for*, and *of* Learning
Select and share mutually agreed-on student work that addresses bilingual or dual language education goals or student learning targets.	*Assessment as Learning* Promote student self-reflection of learning in two or more languages and cultures through personal journaling, annotated photo logs, or audio recordings.
Plan and practice student-led conferences for setting learning goals along with evidence of learning.	*Assessment for Learning* Verify that the evidence produced matches the agreed-on language(s) and personal learning goals by teachers and students.
Prompt data-initiated conversations revolving around feedback in their preferred language use in different contexts. Use the information to determine impact data.	*Assessment as Learning* Give concrete, timely feedback to peers in their preferred language according to predetermined descriptors and act on feedback received.
Invite students to engage in project-based learning, immerse themselves in the inquiry cycle, or conduct action research around a question of interest.	*Assessment of Learning* Co-construct criteria for success or rubrics for student projects or descriptors for action research.
Design assessment portfolios where students have language choice in selecting authentic samples as evidence for learning and meeting their individual learning goals.	*Assessment of Learning* Organize portfolio contents chronologically (digitally or manually) to document growth in language and content over time.

Teacher Tools in Multiple Languages Across the Assessment Cycle

Given the evolving roles of educators, students, and families in assessment, in this section we unveil an assessment cycle (see figure 4.12) for guiding the assessment process in bilingual and dual language education contexts. In it, educators make a commitment and concerted effort to offer multilingual learners the opportunity to access and use their multiple languages. For each of the five phases, we share a classroom tool for potential use in one or more languages.

Phases of the Assessment Cycle that Incorporate Multiple Languages

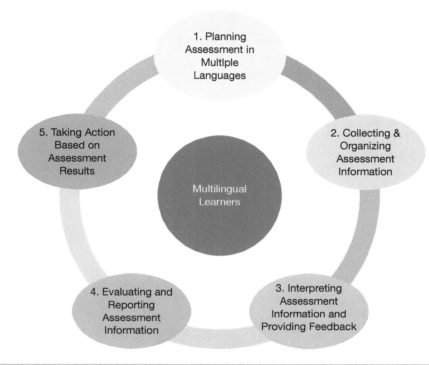

Source: Gottlieb, 2021, 2022

Phase 1: Co-plan Assessment According to Learning Goals

In dual language education programs, learning goals should correspond with the four established pillars—bilingualism/biliteracy, academic achievement, sociocultural competence, and critical consciousness—that are formally adopted as expected educational outcomes. The question then becomes, "How can we document multilingual learners' progress toward these goals?" That's where co-planning assessment among teachers comes into play.

When assessment is embedded in instruction, there is always consideration of the interplay between the two languages. Figure 4.13 lists some of the questions related to this initial phase of assessment.

It asks how you might, in collaboration with other teachers working with multilingual learners, respond.

Such a thorough checklist should be part of every school's agenda at the beginning of each year, then revisited frequently as a reminder of what has been accomplished. Many times schools focus on what is not in place instead of accomplishments or almost-there indicators.

Margarita

FIGURE 4.13	**Questions to Pursue in Co-planning Assessment in Dual Language Education Contexts**

Questions for Teacher Co-planning Assessment for Multilingual Learners	Your Response
What is the purpose of assessment, and which pillar(s) or goal(s) does it address?	
Which educators engage in co-planning, and what are their roles?	
What assets do multilingual learners and their families bring to this phase of assessment?	
When does co-planning occur, and is it on a regular basis?	
What role does technology play in assessment planning, including the archival and retrieval of student information?	
How does assessment in multiple languages seamlessly fit into instruction?	
Who is responsible for organizing and documenting content and language learning for multilingual learners?	
Who assigns the language(s) to different instructional and assessment activities, and when do multilingual learners have a voice?	
What is the language policy for language use throughout the day, including translanguaging, and how is assessment impacted?	
What are the criteria for success for different projects, and how are multiple languages treated?	
How do co-teachers plan activities and tasks in multiple languages that lead to assessment of end-of-unit projects?	
Who gives feedback, and how and when, during instruction and assessment?	

Phase 2: Collect Information From Students (and Families)

Gathering information to document multilingual learners' bilingual and biliteracy development that intertwines the students' sociocultural competence and critical consciousness, requires a nuanced instructional and assessment approach. Data collection can occur spontaneously, for example, when teachers observe multilingual learners interacting with each other, be built into student-led conferences, or be intentional, when students show evidence of meeting criteria for success for their project. During this phase of the assessment cycle, bilingual and dual language education teachers are to consider the

- oral language proficiencies in English and the other language of multilingual learners;

- biliteracy of multilingual learners;

- students' access to grade-level content;

- allocation of English and the other language for instruction and assessment, if applicable;

- language(s) of instruction for each content area;

- role and place of translanguaging as a classroom policy and practice;

- use of multiple modalities as a resource; and

- constraints imposed on schools and classrooms.

Multilingual learners should be given options in showing evidence for their content learning. In dual language settings, it is only logical that students express themselves in multimodal ways rather than be tied to one communication mode. For example, if a bilingual pair were to produce a video or an iMovie, it would be necessary for the students to minimally engage in oral interaction and gestures, in addition to visual and written artifacts (e.g., storyboards). Figure 4.14 is a chart for documenting multilingual learners' choices of communication modes, including language(s) for classroom assessment activities. In dual language programs, translanguaging should always be an option for multilingual learners.

FIGURE 4.14 **Gathering Multilingual Learners' Language Use and Modalities During Classroom Observation**

Example Instructional Assessment Activities Where Multilingual Learners . . .	Communication Mode(s)—Oral, Written, Visual, Graphic	Using English	Using Another Language	Using Both (i.e., Translanguaging)
Compare information in tables and graphs				
Defend perspectives with evidence				
Summarize and reflect on experiences				
Reenact historical or literary events				
Debate local issues at a school or community event				
Conduct interviews as part of research projects				

Phase 3: Analyze and Interpret Information from Multiple Sources

Once you have the data in hand, the next step is to make sense of it—that's where analysis and interpretation come into play. Figure 4.15 displays example instructional assessment activities for a range of purposes for three of the four pillars of dual language education. Critical consciousness, the fourth pillar, is a way of perceiving the world and a personal state of being that should not be directly measured.

FIGURE 4.15 Interpreting Results According to the Purpose for Assessment

Example Instructional Assessment Activities	Purpose for Assessment: to Ascertain a Dual Language Learner's (check all that apply)			
	Achievement in the Content Area of _____	Language Development for _____	Biliteracy Development	Sociocultural Competence and/or Social-Emotional Development
Compare information in various sources				
Defend perspectives with evidence				
Summarize and reflect on experiences				
Re-create historical or literary events from different viewpoints				
Conduct and analyze interviews and present findings				

Phase 4: Report Assessment Results and Give Feedback

In dual language education programs there are twice the number of sources of information as those in English-only programs. In reporting the results from the entire data pool, educators must be careful to balance the language(s), purpose, and data source. As shown in figure 4.16, the data sources should match with the types of assessment and their primary purpose of accountability.

FIGURE 4.16 Potential Sources of Assessment Data for Multilingual Learners According to Purpose

Types of Data Generated Throughout the Year	Primary Purpose(s) for Assessment	Range of Data Sources
Language proficiency data in English	Federal and local accountability Growth in English language development	• Initial state screening • State annual tests • District interim tests • Common standards-referenced assessment across classrooms • Classroom assessment *as*, *for*, and *of* learning
Language proficiency data in other languages	Accountability for dual language and other bilingual programs Growth in bilingualism and biliteracy	• District interim tests • End of unit performance assessment • Student portraits of language use across classroom contexts • Classroom assessment *as, for*, and *of* learning
Achievement data in English— English language arts and reading, mathematics, science	Federal and local accountability Growth in the content areas	• State annual content tests • District interim tests and common assessments • Classroom end-of-chapter tests • Classroom assessment *as, for*, and *of* learning
Achievement data in other languages	Accountability for dual language and other bilingual programs Growth in the content areas	• State annual content tests (if available) • District interim tests and common assessments • End-of-chapter tests • Classroom assessment *as, for*, and *of* learning

Reporting assessment results, giving feedback, and making assessment-related decisions should involve different pairs of stakeholders, such as partnerships between

- District and school leadership (e.g., for determining trend data)
- School leadership and teachers (e.g., for grouping students)
- Teacher teams (e.g., for updating criteria for success)
- Teachers and students (e.g., for determining next steps in learning)
- Students and classmates (e.g., for engaging in self- and peer assessment)
- Teachers, students, and families (e.g., for giving input on next steps for instruction and assessment)

Phase 5: Take Action Steps

Taking action based on assessment results in multiple languages requires overlaying and seamlessly infusing an assets-based lens into current routines while simultaneously eliminating bias and inequity. As bilingual and dual language educators and others shift their assessment practices to illuminate multilingual learners, there are six actions (repeated in figure 4.17) that summarize how assessment in multiple languages can be transformative (Gottlieb, 2022).

Action Step 5.1: Engage in reflective assessment practice and inquiry

Reflective assessment practice helps foster principal and teacher leadership (Day & Harris, 2002). School leaders need to take time to digest impact data from multilingual learners on their language proficiency and achievement in multiple languages before acting. In dual language programs, educators should also reflect on information gathered on students' social and emotional learning, sociocultural competence, and critical consciousness to deepen relationships with their students and support families.

Action Step 5.2: Decide priorities in assessing in multiple languages

The last years have been challenging for educators, families, and students; however, systematic assessment that encompasses multiple languages can readily fit into any school or district with multilingual learners. Being inclusive of multiple languages entails weighing possible constraints that can potentially impact making decisions. Determining priorities in assessment means considering

- the conditions of schooling or learning environments (i.e., face-to-face, hybrid, and/or remote) and types of educational programs;
- changes in the student population or community demographic;
- life events of students, families, and faculty;
- school or district schedules;
- faculty qualifications and positions;
- administration and/or leadership's dispositions toward bilingual and dual language education;
- school or district initiatives or mandates;
- a school's or district's mission, vision, and values; and
- a commitment to programs and policies for multilingual learners.

Action Step 5.3: Challenge the status quo in classroom and school assessment

Assessment in multiple languages needs a jolt. First, translanguaging should be treated as a linguistic and cultural asset of multilingual learners rather than be problematized (García-Mateus & Palmer, 2017). Second, assessment in two-way dual language programs should mirror the languages and cultures of multilingual learners, not privilege middle-class white English-speaking norms. Last, assessment in multiple languages should be normalized from the classroom to every district and state with bilingual and dual language education programs.

Action Step 5.4: Assess multilingual learners from a strengths-based perspective

Assets-based assessment goes beyond examining achievement and language proficiency data in multiple languages. Looking at data in a positive light extends across all multilingual learners, whether they participate in language education programs or not. Assessment needs to include descriptive information on multilingual learners'

- being inventive with translanguaging, giving multilingual learners latitude in using both their languages during instruction and classroom assessment;

- demonstrating creativity in one or more languages;

- critical thinking in one or more languages;

- expressing complex ideas through visual and performing arts;

- tackling challenges with enthusiasm;

- making deep connections between the known and unknown;

- possessing leadership qualities;

- engaging in self-initiated learning;

- representing ideas and concepts in multimodal ways;

- showing metalinguistic and metacultural insight; and

- developing social competence and being critically conscious.

Action Step 5.5: Enact effective assessment practices through access to multiple languages

In curriculum design, assessment *of* learning reflects students' interests that are represented in end-of-unit products, performances, or projects in one or more languages (Hilliard & Gottlieb, 2021). In lesson design, multilingual learners engage in assessment *as* and *for* learning in languages of their choice. Here multilingual learners collaborate with their peers and teachers to determine their learning targets and select a multimodal pathway to show evidence for success. Together, these three assessment approaches accentuate students as decision makers and agents of learning (Gottlieb, 2016).

Action Step 5.6: Use assessment data in multiple languages to leverage systemic change

Robust data produced by multilingual learners in multiple languages can stimulate change. To preserve classroom and school data from year to year, educators should devise a system to ensure their reliability and secure their archival. During joint planning time or professional learning, schools should adopt uniform criteria for success that are assets-driven and aligned from grade to grade. Anchoring the interpretation of student original work through a multilingual lens can produce strong defensible data.

Here is a recap of the six action steps with space to brainstorm how to bolster assessment in multiple languages.

FIGURE 4.17 **A Planning Sheet for Taking Action Based on Data From Multilingual Learners**

Action Step	What We Can Do to Promote Multiple Language Use
5.1 Engage in reflective assessment practice and inquiry	
5.2 Decide priorities in assessing in multiple languages	
5.3 Challenge the status quo in classroom and school assessment	
5.4 Assess multilingual learners from a strengths-based perspective	
5.5 Enact effective assessment practices for multilingual learners through access to multiple languages	
5.6 Use assessment data in multiple languages to leverage systemic change	

Conclusion: Key Take-Aways

The benefits of multilingualism are deep and are becoming increasingly visible across many facets of society here and around the world. If we accept these advantages as integral to the collective multilingual learner identity, then educational stakeholders must embrace moving from monolingual assessment to assessment in multiple languages. Taking this proposal further, the acceptance of multiple language use, including translanguaging, throughout schooling requires a change of mindset to one that embraces multilingualism and multiculturalism as integral to the school experience and a reflection of the community.

Accepting the changing landscape around assessment in multiple languages, especially in classrooms with multilingual learners, is nothing short of a paradigm shift. We must cast away equating assessment as a series of decontextualized scores or performance levels generated from tests given in one language or another at a single point in time. Instead, we must envision assessment as an ongoing process with numerous data sources that tell a comprehensive story of multilingual learners' growth over time. In doing so, we recognize the invaluable contributions of all stakeholders—multilingual learners, multilingual families, teachers, and other educational leaders—in leveraging the transition from assessment in one to that in many languages. Let's remember that

- all *multilingual learners*, by definition, are exposed to multiple languages and cultures; they should be entrusted to use their languages during instruction and assessment to focus on learning. Having an assessment policy at the school and classroom levels that promotes rather than inhibits multiple language use will contribute to a warm and inviting learning environment. Encouraging multiple language use will help shape multilingual learners' identities, boost their self-confidence, increase their motivation, and instill agency.

- all *family members* of multilingual learners should have a solid understanding of the linguistic, cognitive, economic, socioemotional, and educational merits of multilingualism (see the ED, OELA website) and their application to instruction and assessment. To become equal partners in discussing data, family members should have opportunities to develop assessment literacy. In that way, families can contribute to classroom assessment efforts to gain firsthand insight into the language, conceptual, and socio-emotional development of their children at home and school.

- all *teachers* of multilingual learners should become assessment literate as part of ongoing professional learning to enact the assessment cycle through a multilingual lens. Educators who understand the benefits of multiple language use in everyday life of multilingual learners, in classroom assessment, common/interim, and annual assessment are better equipped to draw data from multiple sources and in multiple languages to make sound, defensible decisions.

- all *educational leaders* (superintendents, principals, directors, coaches, and teachers) should realize how linguistic and culturally sustainable curriculum and assessment benefit all students. In addition, including accessibility to multiple languages for multilingual learners as a school or district policy is an equity move that helps level the playing field. Integrating multiple languages into a comprehensive assessment system has the potential of bolstering multilingual learners' language, literacy, social-emotional, and conceptual development.

In this chapter we offer tangible evidence and examples for how to enact linguistic and culturally sustainable assessment in multiple languages. We make a case for why multilingual learners should be entitled to access their entire linguistic, cultural, and experiential resources to show what they are learning and have learned to their peers, teachers, and family members. We also illustrate how educators can enact the assessment cycle through a multilingual lens.

In reaching consensus on the advantages of multilingualism, stakeholders can make greater strides to ensure that the multiple languages of our multilingual learners are integral to schooling and life. This shift in focus in research and practice will require nothing short of transformative systemic change in which assessment in multiple languages plays a central role. We attribute this multilingual movement to the perseverance of dedicated educators, multilingual learners, and families who are deeply aware that multilingual learners and other minoritized students are the faces of equity and the future of our nation.

Reflection Questions

1. How might you apply the tenets for assessment in multiple languages to your context whether you are multilingual or not?

2. How might you extend assessment in multiple languages to all teachers working with multilingual learners (e.g., through joint planning meetings, communities of practice) so that it becomes part of the school culture?

3. How might you and other educators design ongoing professional learning coupled with a coaching component around assessment literacy in multiple languages? Which topics might you wish to tackle?

4. What burning questions might you or a professional learning community wish to explore through action research?

5. Thinking of your multilingual learners, their families, and your context, how might you and your team strategically engage in the assessment cycle in multiple languages?

6. How might you counteract the argument that translanguaging, although an acceptable classroom practice, should not be part of assessment?

7. How might you energize and engage multilingual learners and their families in capitalizing on the strengths of assessment in multiple languages?

References

Chalhoub-Deville, M. B. (2019). Multilingual testing constructs: Theoretical considerations. *Language Assessment Quarterly, 16*(4–5), 472–480.

Day, C., & Harris, A. (2002). Teacher leadership, reflective practice, and school improvement. In L. Leithwood & P. Hallinger (Eds.), *Second international handbook of educational leadership and administration* (Vol. 8, pp. 957–977). Springer.

Esteban-Guitart, M., & Moll, L. C. (2014). Funds of identity: A new concept based on funds of knowledge. *Culture & Psychology, 20*(1).

Every Student Succeeds Act (ESSA). (2015). Pub. L. No. 114-95 §114 Stat. 1177 (2015–2016). https://www.congress.gov/bill/114th-congress/senate-bill/1177

Gándara, P. (2015, November 4). The implications of deeper learning for adolescent immigrants and English language learners. *Students at the Center.* https://www.jff.org/resources/implications-deeper-learning-adolescent-immigrants-and-english-language-learners

García, O., & Wei, L. (2013). *Translanguaging: Language, bilingualism and education.* Palgrave Macmillan.

García-Mateus, S., & Palmer, D. K. (2017). Translanguaging pedagogies for positive identities in two-way dual language bilingual education. *Journal of Language, Identity & Education, 16*(4), 245–255.

González, N., Moll, L., & Amanti, C. (2005). *Funds of knowledge: Theorizing practices in households, communities, and classrooms.* Lawrence Erlbaum Associates.

Gottlieb, M. (2016). *Assessment of multilingual learners: Bridges to equity* (2nd ed.). Corwin.

Gottlieb, M. (2021). *Classroom assessment in multiple languages: A handbook for teachers.* Corwin.

Gottlieb, M. (2022). *Assessment in multiple languages: A handbook for school and district leaders.* Corwin.

Gottlieb, M. (2024). *Assessment of multilingual learners: Bridges to empowerment* (3rd ed.). Corwin.

Gottlieb, M., Hilliard, J. F., Díaz-Pollack, B., Sánchez-López, C., & Salto, D. (2020). *Language education policy in the United States: A promising outlook.* Paridad Educational Consulting.

Hilliard, J. F., & Gottlieb, M. (2021, June). *Seeing multilingual learners' reflections en EL ESPEJO.* Bilingual Basics, TESOL International Association.

Hinton, K. A. (2015). "We only teach in English": An examination of bilingual-in-name-only classrooms. In D. E. Freeman & Y. S. Freeman (Eds.), *Research on preparing inservice teachers to work effectively with emergent bilinguals* (pp. 265–289). Emerald Group Publishing Limited.

Hornberger, N. H., & Link, H. (2012). Translanguaging and transnational literacies in multilingual classrooms: A biliteracy lens. *International Journal of Bilingual Education and Bilingualism, 15*(3), 261–278.

Improving America's Schools Act of 1994. (1993–1994). Pub. L. No. 103-382. Congressional Research Service, Library of Congress.

Marian, V., & Hayakawa, S. (2021). Measuring bilingualism: The quest for a 'bilingualism quotient.' *Applied Psycholinguistics, 42,* 527–548.

Martínez, R. A. (2018). Beyond the English learner label: Recognizing the richness of bi/multilingual students' linguistic repertoires. *Reading Teacher, 71*(5), 515–522.

May, S. (2014). Disciplinary divides, knowledge construction, and the multilingual turn. In S. May (Ed.), *The multilingual turn: Implications for SLA, TESOL and bilingual education* (pp. 7–31). Routledge.

May, S., & Dam, L. I. (2014). *Bilingual education and bilingualism.* Oxford bibliographies online datasets. https://oa.mg/work/10.1093/obo/9780199756810-0109

Morita-Mullaney, T., Renn, J., & Chiu, M. M. (2020). Obscuring equity in dual language bilingual education: A longitudinal study of emergent bilingual achievement, course placements, and grades. *TESOL Quarterly, 54*(3), 685–718.

No Child Left Behind Act of 2001. (2002). Pub. L. No. 107-110, § 115, Stat. 1425-2094.

Ortega, L. (2014). Ways forward for a bi/multilingual turn in SLA. In S. May (Ed.), *The multilingual turn: Implications for SLA, TESOL and bilingual education* (pp. 32–61). Routledge.

Paradis, M. (2004). *A neurolinguistic theory of bilingualism*. John Benjamins.

Ruíz, R. (1984). Orientations in language planning. *NABE Journal, 8*(2), 15–34.

Schissel, J. L., Leung, C., & Chalhoub-Deville, M. (2019). The construct of multilingualism in language assessment. *Language Assessment Quarterly, 16*(4-5), 373–378.

Shohamy, E. (2011). Assessing multilingual competencies: Adopting construct valid assessment policies. *Modern Language Journal, 95*(iii), 418–429.

Shohamy, E. (2022). Critical language testing: Multilingualism and social justice. *TESOL Quarterly, 56*(4), 1445–1457.

Solano-Flores, G., & Hakuta, K. (2017). *Assessing students in their home language*. Stanford University, Understanding Language. https://capri.utsa.edu/wp-content/uploads/2017/09/assessing-students-in-their-home-language-Hakuta.pdf

United States Department of Education, Office of English Language Acquisition. (2020). *Benefits of multilingualism*. https://ncela.ed.gov/sites/default/files/legacy/files/announcements/20200805-NCELAInfographic-508.pdf

Zacarian, D. E., Calderón, M. E., & Gottlieb, M. (2021). *Beyond crises: Overcoming linguistic and cultural inequities in communities, schools, and classrooms*. Corwin.

chapter five

From Educator Collaboration in a Monolingual Setting to Collaboration in a Dual Language Setting

ANDREA HONIGSFELD AND
JOAN LACHANCE

PREMISE

Teacher collaboration is an essential component of dual language (DL) education across all program models. By design, many DL programs are based on a partnership between and among two or more educators who come to the practice with language, [multi]literacy, content expertise, and cultural knowledge and skills in their respective languages and combine their fortes through regular collaboration and co-planning. At other times, DL teachers forge additional partnerships and collaborate or even co-teach with English

Language Development (ELD) teachers who may provide additional language instruction. There are also times when DL teachers, ELD teachers, and special educators collaborate. This is especially important given the longitudinal data that support special needs students' academic gains in DL education (Thomas & Collier, 2017). Some examples of special education (SPED) professionals collaborating with DL and/or ELD teachers include occupational and/or physical therapist providers, speech-language pathologists, LBS (Learning Behavior Specialist[s]), and other support personnel. In this way, culturally and linguistically responsive SPED services are provided in class to ensure that students' complex academic, linguistic, sociocultural, and social-emotional needs are met.

DL educators are in a critical position to support PK–12 dual language learners' (DLLs) multilingual development while simultaneously offering instruction that builds racial and ethnic identities, empowers home languages and cultural heritages, and debunks patterns of marginalization and minoritization. Given the many complexities of DL schools' programmatic formats and the communities where they are situated, DL educators (teachers, paraprofessionals, instructional assistants, coaches, and leaders) now more than ever are well-positioned to collaborate in strategic ways within the context of the classroom, school, district, and larger neighborhood community. We invite readers to take an unapologetic stance with us to tear down silos and dismantle segregated learning experiences for multilingual learners (MLLs). When educators forge partnerships and all members of the school community collaborate for the sake of their MLLs, everyone benefits. As you read this chapter, and this book, we invite you to consider the larger scope of district leadership responsibilities with DL programs. We note the need for shared leadership protocols to ensure ongoing and increased guidance for district leaders when creating policies, site-based protocols, and curricular and assessment decisions to then inform site-level administrators. For these reasons and more, this chapter defines the *who, what, where, when, how,* and *why* of collaboration in the DL context and offers actionable recommendations and tools to support collaborative planning, teaching, and assessment in PK–12 DL classrooms.

VIGNETTE

One Partnership's Assurance for Breaking Down the Monolingual Wall

The vignette presented is an exemplar of collaboration in one specific program. Readers are invited to draw connections to their own situations to see when and how there may be overlap with successes as well as look for ideas regarding ways to change mindsets and practices for growth.

My name is Olivia, and I'm a high school science teacher in a 50/50, two-way Spanish and English dual language (DL) program in Massachusetts. Some of our DL students are recent immigrant students while others are classified as long-term English learners (LTELs). Our math and science departments' professional learning communities (PLCs) within the DL program are grouped to facilitate cross-curricular collaboration. I teach my science classes in Spanish, and I'm paired with a partner teacher who also delivers his math instruction in Spanish for co-planning. Social studies and English language arts as well as the special subjects are taught in English. Our PLC teams make weekly, quarterly, and annual decisions together, discussing curriculum, classroom materials, and assessments that span grade levels across the math and science content areas. We discuss our unit plans, the students' biliteracy development, and content needs based on how they are progressing in all our classes. Then we really drill down to bridge curricular topics, supporting multimodal materials for biliteracy development, and the assessments to measure language and content across both Spanish and English. We co-create instructional strategies and parallel assessments that move our students forward to multilingual thinking about the knowledge and skills they learned in both program languages. We then share our results and creations with other teachers in other non-DL department PLCs, the instructional coaches, and our administrators. It is only in this way that we can ensure we are collaborating to complement each other's teaching rather than functioning in isolated classroom silos. Our successes are attributed to the fundamental ways in which our administrative leadership team created a changed mindset to promote multilingualism in our school. One crucial layer is that they protect time for us to collaborate. Another aspect is that they make DL program decisions with our [DL teachers'] input. We co-created collaborative protocols to keep detailed examples of student data across grade levels and content areas. These data facilitate our conversations to be structured, informed, and rich as we communicate to co-create shared goals with our students, parents, teachers and administrators, and community leaders, some of whom make open statements about English literacy needing to be the absolute priority. We've learned how to shift our conversations to promote DL, keeping multilingualism and linguistic equity as a part of the dialogue. We can respond to the challenging and confrontational questions from those who oppose multilingualism. We talk numbers, and we include people's voices. We have multidimensional assessment data readily accessible and are also intentional about sharing students' voices that more authentically represent their experiences. All of this makes the dialog impactful and transformational.

Figure 5.1 has a few examples of how we can work together to advocate and act by shifting our mindsets and dialogues, much like Olivia and her colleagues.

FIGURE 5.1   Transforming Dialogues: From Monolingual to Multilingual

Topic	What Leaders May Frequently Hear	Transformed Dialogues
(Bi/Multi) Literacy Development	It's taking too long for my child to learn two languages. The DL program is holding them back and they're behind in reading English.	It's very common for parents to be concerned about their child's progress, and we can probably all agree that we want our children to progress in their learning. When our students are becoming biliterate, the processes take additional time, which isn't a negative thing. DL students really show their academic and social gains in high school when the content area demands increase. Learning new content via two languages takes time, and we can show how students are successful with our multiple data sources.
Curriculum	We need a 90-minute block for English literacy development. Far too many students are not reading at grade level.	Research tells us that students enrolled in DL schools, especially when they are from diverse cultural, socioeconomic, racial, and linguistic backgrounds, tend to have increased biliteracy, which needs support through multilingual literacy development within the content areas.
Curricular Materials	While our school library has some selection of literature in both program languages, we don't have enough funding to purchase textbooks in English and Spanish.	It would be more cost-effective if we purchased materials in both program languages that complement each other rather than buying twice the number of books. In this way, we can also support bridging practices in our program. This is challenging to find, so we may need some strategic collaboration to do this for our school. We can also be innovative by facilitating opportunities for our bilingual paraprofessionals, community members, and immigrant families to create community-based, authentic materials for us to use in our schools. In this way, they are given options to showcase their multilingual writing skills, artistic talents, and success stories to embrace community assets. We also value the need to promote students' reading for pleasure in both program languages.
Assessments	Our state's high-stakes assessments are given in English. Therefore, we should focus only on English language and content development. Otherwise, the students will fail, and our district will have a poor reputation for academic success.	We know the consequences of high-stakes testing. We are committed to doing what we can at the school and classroom levels. We shifted our mindsets to work forward with data—to authentically reveal MLLs' rich and wide ranges of content and language capabilities. We use both program languages for assessment purposes so that we have deeper, descriptive, and more robust data to shape our teaching and learning. These practices, based on changed mindsets, allow us to also account for the additional benefits of multilingual assessments. Students demonstrate increased empathy, motivation to learn, self-confidence, innovative thinking, agency for problem solving, and learner autonomy. These are characteristics of more critically conscious, multilingual members of society, something our DLE program is committed to supporting.
Limited Space in Dual Language Programs	The spaces in DL programs should be held for the kids who are serious about school—for those who are already highfliers.	Research tells us that all kids benefit from DL education. Therefore, we really need to think about the students in our communities with the most needs. How can we focus on program expansion so we can offer DL to everyone?

Source: Adapted from Lachance and Honigsfeld (2023)

At this point in the chapter, we would like to have you make some preliminary reflections, which we expand on again at the end of chapter 5. For now, consider your thoughts regarding:

1. In what ways can you begin to shift your mindsets and dialogues via conversations with program stakeholders?

2. What do you believe is needed for school administrators to support teachers in collaboration?

THE URGENCY

We present the chapter by canvasing the current momentum in DL education, a movement we must collectively act upon with urgency for increased, informed advocacy. Families and communities who pursue students' participation in DL programs are quite certain about the countless sociocultural, cognitive, and academic benefits that consistently emerge in DL classrooms (Thomas & Collier, 2017). Those seeking access to DL schooling are all aiming to find themselves as a part of something greater, an interconnected, multilingual society where *all people* find a sense of belonging. People from all corners of the United States, representing over 30 partner languages, many of which are spoken by Indigenous peoples, participate in Dual Language Education (DLE). The urgency is similarly confirmed as our current Secretary of Education, Miguel Cardona, points directly to the importance of multilingual development and the need for reformed policy. He commented on January 24, 2023, as he spoke to the "Raise the Bar: Lead the World" initiative and said, ". . . learning another, or multiple languages should be expected of [all] our students and anchored as a skill that will enhance their global engagement and increase opportunities for success" (U.S. Department of Education, 2023). The U.S. Department of Education—also reported in *Dual Language Learning Programs and English Learners* (U.S. Department of Education, Office of English Language Acquisition, 2019)—indicates that nearly 75 percent of all U.S. states self-reported the existence of two- and one-way DL programs in their state, many of which serve English Learners (ELs).

From the state-level perspective, states like Massachusetts with the Language Opportunity for Our Kids (LOOK) Act (Massachusetts, 2017) and California with California Proposition 58 (2016) are passing more direct and strategic legislation to overturn monolingual mandates and steer state education agencies in the direction of providing resources and funding specifically for DL programs, with the inclusion of ELs and MLLs.[1] Nearly all fifty states and Washington, DC, have a state seal of biliteracy for high school graduation broadening the impactful scope of PreK–12 DL (Mudambi, 2022). The DL movement shows that programs continue to expand across many other states,

> We must keep up the momentum in growing DL programs where MLLs are advantaged in their bilingual and biliteracy development! We must insist on equity of opportunity and access for all MLLs and families. We must ensure that all school leaders and teachers of MLLs and other minoritized students collectively commit to breaking down those monolingual walls in their valuing and endorsing multilingual education. Finally, we must propose a robust research agenda so that, as an educational community, we have defensible data to propel DL education forward.
>
> **Margo**

---

[1] *We use the terms English Learners (ELs) and Multilingual Learners (MLLs) throughout the chapter with the strategic purposes of capturing and honoring the rich diversity of language learners in the United States in conjunction with the current federal terminology for policy.*

including Maine, New York, Virginia, Oregon, Idaho, and Illinois (CAL Center for Applied Linguistics, n.d.).

While the countless benefits of DLE are well documented in decades of research (ARC, 2021; Howard et. al., 2018; NCELA, 2022; Thomas & Collier, 2017), the monolingual wall remains. Woefully, the monolingual wall continues to be built on decades of strife from various political and social marginalizing agendas that attempt to further English-only movements, which are all directly contrary to the research on DLLs' academic, linguistic, sociocultural, and culturally conscious gains. Legislation and states' educational policies represent the historical and ongoing clashes that continue to divide language development stances, isolating resources for MLLs and increased access to DLE (see figure 5.2 and revisit chapter 1 for the federal policies and legislative impacts).

FIGURE 5.2 **A Snapshot of Select States' Legislation and Regulations**

Select Examples of State Legislation and Regulations		
Enactments	Summary	Impact on the Use of Languages Other Than English in U.S. Schools
Massachusetts LOOK Act (2017)	The Language Opportunity for Our Kids (LOOK) Act was unanimously passed by the Massachusetts Senate in 2017 with bipartisan support. This bill established a state Seal of Biliteracy and allowed school districts to offer bilingual programs without the requirement for waivers. It repealed the Sheltered English Immersion law (Massachusetts, 2002) that banned bilingual education, which stated that "all public school children must be taught English by being taught all subjects in English and being placed in English language classrooms."	The LOOK Act allows school districts more options to better meet students' needs with DL education as a promoted option to emphasize the value of bilingual students and communities. It also establishes a new Seal of Biliteracy to honor bilingual and biliterate high school graduates.
New Mexico as a bilingual state	New Mexico was the first state in the United States to have a bilingual and multicultural education law, passing the Bilingual Multicultural Education Act of 1973. There is no official language of the state, whereas many others note English as the official state language.	According to New Mexico's Language and Culture Bureau (2016), "Developing proficiency in two or more languages for New Mexico students has been the commitment of New Mexico educators, legislators, and other government leaders since the state constitution was approved in 1911."
Texas House Bill 3 (HB 3) (2019)	Texas Legislature passed HB 3, a widely publicized school finance bill. Under HB 3 programs with learners participating in a DL program receive additional Basic Education Allotment funds.	Overall, this means that schools enrolling students in DL programs may have additional state funding, which results in added resources to support their schools.

Select Examples of State Legislation and Regulations		
Enactments	**Summary**	**Impact on the Use of Languages Other Than English in U.S. Schools**
Washington State Transitional Bilingual Instruction Program	Starting in 1979 with the most recent update in 2020, this legislation mandates that school districts offer ELs transitional bilingual instruction, either through a bilingual program or an alternative program such as ESL.	In the Spring of 2021, the Washington State Board of Education adopted the National Dual Language Teacher Preparation Standards to oblige their use in all DL and bilingual teacher preparation programs (Guerrero & Lachance, 2018). We also recognize that Washington State is believed to be one of the first populated regions in the United States with Indigenous groups speaking more than fifty languages. The influence of language and culture remains today with the state's absence of an official language.
California Proposition 58 (2016)	Proposition 58 repealed the prior English-only policy of Proposition 227, which had been in effect for nearly two decades.	English learners are now freed up from the requirement to attend English-only classes under Proposition 58. Schools and districts may use a variety of language assistance programs, including bilingual programs taught by teachers who are fluent in both their native language and English, and programs are required to include community involvement.
Arizona's current English-only stance	In 2000, Arizona passed Proposition 203. The enactment mandated that all public school instruction take place in English. Children who do not speak English fluently are usually placed in a 1-year rigorous English immersion program to teach them the language as rapidly as possible while still learning academic subjects. For children who already know English, are 10 years old or older, or have unique needs that need a different educational method, parents may request a waiver of these requirements.	When Proposition 203 was passed in 2000, EL students could no longer receive instruction in their native language while learning English. This led to other regulations that hampered multilingual students, such as one that forced EL students to take English classes in 4-hour blocks every day. While the goal was to help ELs learn English, it has resulted in their missing out on other topics that are important for a well-rounded education, such as art, math, social studies, and science. It has also stopped EL students from naturally interacting with their native English-speaking peers. In 2019, the Arizona House of Representatives passed Senate Bill 1014, which gave districts and schools more flexibility in EL instruction. However, the bill stopped short of entirely repealing the state's ELD (English language development) requirements.

Source: Adapted from Lachance and Honigsfeld (2023)

The urgency to *advocate* policy that promotes effective multiliteracy via unique pedagogical and assessment practices at the local, state, and national levels is based on the need to interrupt the hegemonic systemic structures and power constructs in MLLs' education. Additionally, the advocacy obliges the inclusion of sufficient pathways to educate, accurately prepare, and hire more highly qualified DL teachers (Guerrero & Lachance, 2018; Lachance, 2017; NCEL, 2022). The urgency to *act collaboratively* in our classrooms, schools, and communities is based on remaining linguistic and cultural barriers. We take the stance that we must pivot away from monolingual pedagogical and assessment practices by demonstrating unwavering support for DL educators' collaboration to design, deliver, and assess multilingual, multidimensional instruction. When we view the societal and policy-level challenges side-by-side with the current momentous era of DLE, we assert that DL educators are now, more than ever, urgently situated to advocate and act in strategic ways with collaboration at the core.

RESEARCH BASE

The concepts of teacher collaboration, coteaching, and collaborative schools are not new. Over the years, several educational researchers and practitioners have offered their definitions and descriptions of collaboration. Many emphasize the importance of collaboration as an essential skill for bringing about much-needed educational and social change. Some seminal as well as current research also indicates that collaboration may hold the answer to improved teacher and student learning. As we highlight some key early findings in figure 5.3, we invite you to reflect on their relevance to today's educational context specifically connected to DL education:

FIGURE 5.3 Key Research Findings About Teacher Collaboration and Current Considerations and Connections

Research Findings	Current Considerations	Your Connections
Lieberman and Miller (1984) suggested that the norm in education is "self-imposed, professionally sanctioned teacher isolation" (p. 11).	*Do teachers continue to embrace a self-imposed, professionally sanctioned isolation?*	
Smith and Scott (1990) claimed that "collaboration depends inherently on the voluntary effort of professional educators to improve their schools and their own teaching through teamwork" (p. 2).	*Do teachers volunteer to collaborate in your context?*	

Research Findings	Current Considerations	Your Connections
Burns and Darling-Hammond (2014) reported that "more than any other policy area, actions that support collaborative learning among teachers appear to hold promise for improving the quality of teaching" (p. v).	*Is collaboration considered a dimension of teacher effectiveness in your context?*	
Jensen et al. (2016) noted that as adult learners, teachers learn "not simply from reading and observing others work, but from combining these passive activities with active collaboration and learning-by-doing" (p. 8).	*What opportunities do educators as adult learners have in your context to engage in active professional learning opportunities through collaboration and learning-by-doing something jointly?*	
In *What Works in Education*, Hattie (2015) synthesized some key understandings about collaboration: "Collaboration is based on cooperativeness, learning from errors, seeking feedback about progress and enjoying venturing into the 'pit of not knowing' together with expert help that provides safety nets and, ultimately, ways out of the pit. Creative collaboration involves bringing together two or more seemingly unrelated ideas, and this highlights again the importance of having safe and trusting places to explore ideas, to make and to learn from errors and to use expertise to maximize successful learning" (p. 27).	*Is teacher creativity (along with co-constructing new professional knowledge and skills) a part of your school's culture?*	

online resources

Based on our review of the literature, we found evidence-based and research-informed accounts of successful teacher collaboration with some recurring themes, including the following: an emphasis on building trust; sharing expertise; having a common goal (e.g., enhancing instruction for students, school improvement); participating in supportive, interdisciplinary endeavors; and finding multiple creative solutions while keeping it manageable. Although it has been recognized that "the long-standing culture of teacher isolation and individualism, together with teachers' preference to preserve their individual autonomy, may hinder deep-level collaboration to occur" (Vangrieken et al., 2015, p. 36), teacher collaboration has been an integral part of many schools and institutions of higher education (Kuusisaari, 2014; Multistate Association of Bilingual Education-Northeast, 2023).

Teacher collaboration and co-teaching have been extensively researched and practiced supporting English as a foreign language (EFL) as well as a second (or additional, or new) language (ESL, EAL, ENL) learners in a more integrated fashion for over 20 years (see for example, Dove & Honigsfeld 2020; Honigsfeld & Dove, 2012, 2022; Nagle, 2013; Yoon, 2022; and the Special Theme Issue of *TESOL Quarterly* [Farrell, 2012] dedicated to collaboration and co-teaching). A considerable volume of research has focused on collaboration among general- and SPED teachers, inclusion, and additional partnerships that all showcase an assets-based pedagogical approach to collaborative practices.

Inclusive pedagogy is based on the premise that teachers recognize and respond to all students' needs and extend what is available to some students and make it accessible to all:

> Human diversity is seen within the model of inclusive pedagogy as a strength, rather than a problem, as children work together, sharing ideas and learning from their interactions with each other. The inclusive pedagogical approach fosters an open-ended view of each child's potential to learn. (Spratt & Florian, 2013, p. 135)

While the notion of inclusive pedagogy is closely tied to instructional practices in the PK–12 SPED context, it provides a helpful framework for working with MLLs in collaborative, integrated programs, and DL education as well. At the core of successful inclusive pedagogy is teacher collaboration, often including or centering on collaborative instructional practices that allow two or more educators to plan, deliver, and assess instruction for unique groups of students while also setting challenging educational goals and delivering differentiated instruction for all students.

Research on co-teaching has also been expanding. It has been traditionally defined as the collaboration between general- and SPED teachers sharing all the teaching responsibilities for all the students assigned to a classroom (Gately & Gately, 2001). This definition has frequently been expanded to allow the collaborative partnership between a general-education teacher and a service provider or specialist other than a SPED teacher, such as a math intervention teacher, a reading specialist, a teacher of the gifted and talented, a speech-language pathologist, and, more recently, the ELD/EL specialist and bilingual or DL educators.

Villa et al. (2008) suggested that "co-teaching involves the distribution of responsibility among people for planning, instruction, and evaluation for a classroom of students" (p. 50). It is a unique professional relationship in which "partners must establish trust, develop and work on communication, share chores, celebrate, work together creatively to overcome the inevitable challenges and problems, and anticipate conflict and handle it in a constructive way" (p. 5). Often, educators working with MLLs look to borrow, adapt, and synthesize information and ideas from a related field. Thus, resources

> Teacher collaboration within DL settings can occur in many different configurations, which are all advantageous to MLLs. A language specialist can couple with a content specialist; a monolingual teacher with a bilingual teacher; a coach with a small group of DL teachers. What is important is that in their collaborative efforts, educators come to agree with their students on goals for learning, instructional strategies for reaching those goals, and types of evidence to show that the goals have been met.
>
> **Margo**

such as DuFour and colleagues' (2016) work on professional learning communities, Villa and colleagues' (2008, 2013) contributions, and Friend's (2008) and Friend and Barron's (2021) publications on co-teaching in the inclusive setting have been influential among specialists serving MLLs.

In the past 10 years, research more uniquely focused on collaboration and co-teaching for MLLs has expanded. Early research documented the challenges of developing effective collaborative relationships and co-teaching practices (Davison, 2006; DelliCarpini, 2008, 2009; Hurst & Davison, 2005). Documentary accounts of successful collaborative and co-teaching practices have also surfaced (Kaufman & Crandall, 2005). More recently, emerging research has documented that ELD/ELL specialists and their general-education co-teachers continue to struggle with establishing an equitable partnership (Daza, 2022; Fogel & Moser, 2017) or with defining their roles when it comes to content and language integration (Cordeiro, 2021; Martin-Beltran & Peercy, 2014; Norton, 2016).

Among others, Davison (2006) extensively researched collaboration among English as an Additional Language (EAL) and content-area teachers with a special emphasis on the nature and challenges of developing collaborative and co-teaching relationships. She was the first to use the term *partnership teaching* (also commonly used in research and publications originating in the UK) and emphasized, "It builds on the concept of co-operative teaching by linking the work of two teachers, or indeed a whole department/year team or other partners, with plans for curriculum development and staff development across the school" (pp. 454–455).

There is growing research-based evidence (Dove & Honigsfeld, 2014; Greenberg Motamedi et al., 2019; Honigsfeld & Dove, 2017, 2022; Peercy et al., 2017), practitioner-documentation (Foltos, 2018; Norton, 2016), and state and local policy initiatives (Massachusetts Department of Elementary and Secondary Education, 2019; New York State Education Department, 2018) to support teacher collaboration and integrated co-teaching services for ELs and MLLs. Similarly, collaboration within DL inclusion programs is gaining attention. For example, Baker et al. (2018) examined the common misconception that DL programs are not well-suited for students with disabilities, including those with autism. They emphasize that multilingual classrooms offer neurodivergent students integral and unique opportunities to practice linguistic repertoires while also building social relationships. With regard to inclusion practices in DL education, their research tells us "the philosophy of inclusive education holds that all children—regardless of disability category or learning needs should be fully accepted and should have the opportunity to participate in the entire range of public educational opportunities" (p. 175). Thomas and Collier (2017) also confirmed that "[i]f the dual language program is implemented effectively, English learners are no longer isolated from their classroom peers and pull-out instruction is not needed" (p. 24). The call for action is clearly emerging from the research: We must increase collaboration in DL education!

Building on literature reviews and our own examination of the research, several major themes have emerged that indicate the positive impact of teacher collaboration and co-teaching on the following:

1. Teacher learning and capacity building (Martin-Beltrán & Peercy, 2014)
2. Teacher relationship and trust building (Honigsfeld & Dove, 2017; Pawan & Ortloff, 2011)
3. Shifts in instructional practices and role definition due to collaborative and co-teaching approaches to serving ELLs/MLLs (Davison, 2006; Martin-Beltrán & Peercy, 2012; Peercy et al., 2017)
4. Equity in education and culturally responsive teaching (Compton, 2018; Scanlan et al., 2012; Theoharis & O'Toole, 2011)
5. Teachers' professional lives through reduced professional and social isolation (Safir, 2017)
6. Programmatic cost effectiveness (Thomas & Collier, 2017)
7. Combating teacher shortage (Guerrero & Lachance, 2018)
8. Collaboration increasing the effectiveness of DL education (Howard et al., 2018)

DLLs' development of countless sociocultural, linguistic, academic, and ideological competencies is noted as a direct result of bilingual and DL education (Cloud et al., 2000; Thomas & Collier, 2017). Numerous longitudinal analyses, balanced by extensive case studies, continue to emphasize that bilingual education is highly effective in increasing academic outcomes for **_all_** students, especially those who come from historically marginalized backgrounds and particularly emergent bilingual learners (de Jong & Bearse, 2014; Howard et al., 2018; Lindholm-Leary, 2012, 2016; Steele et al., 2017; Thomas & Collier, 2017).

Two key points from current research include the following (one invites explicit focus on planning for metalinguistic awareness, and the other one reminds us of the importance of collaborating to ensure that students engage in self- and peer-assessment and goal setting with clear expectations):

> *The explicit teaching of how language works can help multilingual learners expand what they can do with language, thereby growing their language toolbox. We want our students to become increasingly aware and strategic in their use of language to negotiate meaning and achieve their purposes in various contexts.* (WIDA, 2020, p. 20)

Gottlieb (2021) emphasized the importance of collaborating to engage multilingual learners: *"From the first day to the close of the school year, students should be participants in classroom instruction and assessment."* (p. 14)

Intentional planning and collaborative conversations about students' simultaneous development of academic, linguistic, cross-cultural, and critical consciousness are key to success in DL education. Many researchers and practitioners believe that learners' academic, linguistic, sociocultural, social-emotional, and critical cognitive development may be optimized when students' full linguistic repertoires are supported. In *Guiding Principles for Dual Language Education*, Howard and colleagues (2018) reminded us to consider "that if the two [program] languages are used concurrently, the use of both languages should be strategic" (p. 52).

When findings from research on DL programming and implementation are combined with evidence about the importance of teacher collaboration, we can more confidently approach DL education through collaborative practices.

Implications for Practice and Implementation

It is well-established in the professional literature and well-documented in evidence-based practitioner accounts that the intentional implementation of the collaborative instructional cycle consisting of collaborative planning, instruction, assessment, and reflection yields impactful teaching and learning experiences. While co-teaching is not always feasible, educators may be engaged in co-planning, co-assessing, and co-reflecting. But if they co-deliver instruction either via co-teaching or partnership teaching, co-planning, co-assessing, and co-reflecting are essential pre- and co-requisites (see figure 5.4 for a graphic representation).

FIGURE 5.4 The Collaborative Instructional Cycle

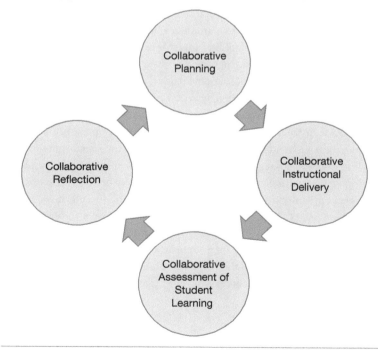

Applying the Collaborative Instructional Cycle to the Dual Language Classroom

For teaching pairs, trios, or quads who are either co-teaching or partnership teaching, and collaborative teams who devise and implement instruction for DLLs, we recommend that all members develop a clear understanding of the collaborative instructional cycle—co-planning, co-teaching or partnership teaching, co-assessment, and co-reflection.

Co-Planning

Co-planning is an essential activity; it provides teachers the opportunity to set general learning goals for students based on educational standards, to maintain continuity of instruction, to integrate curricula that include partner language and content objectives, to dialogue and discuss effective ways to leverage students' home language and cultural assets within instruction and assessment processes, and to co-create authentic multilingual, multidimensional materials that give all students access to content while developing both their basic and disciplinary multiliteracies. Without co-planning, there is no co-teaching or partnership teaching, the second element in the integrated instructional cycle. On the flip side, teachers do not have to co-deliver instruction and still can engage in co-planning.

Collaborative planning for strategic use of translanguaging in lessons ensures the creation of a classroom that is a safe and supportive space where students' multilingual talents are used authentically, regularly, and with purpose. For clarification, we describe translanguaging as the process and practice of providing space for students to use their full linguistic repertoire across all languages, instead of strictly holding students to speaking and writing in one language, depending on the language of instruction in a particular content area and/or portion of the instructional day. DL teachers collaborate to make careful decisions regarding when instruction in the two languages should remain separate and when it is beneficial to use both languages together (e.g., provide instruction in the partner language with primary sources in the original language or add in bilingual text, or model translanguaging for specific purposes and strategies). As noted in chapter 4 and figure 4.6, translanguaging opportunities naturally arise. Students benefit from DL teachers' collaborative planning to capture evidence of learning in and through both program languages. With these practices, we can also ensure equitable use of both program languages rather than giving greater emphasis to the majority language with English-dominant learners. Some educators might perceive translanguaging pedagogy as the sole responsibility of the bilingual educator, especially in classrooms that are serving emergent bilingual students with different abilities.

García and colleagues (2016) provided examples of how collaborative planning can leverage the development of bilingualism and biliteracy in the classroom. Recognizing it as a promising practice, you can work together to plan for a *corriente* (current) of translanguaging via heterogeneous grouping, the creation of activities that allow students to ask and answer culturally thought-provoking questions, and facilitation of frequent opportunities to solve real-world problems to promote critical consciousness. All of this can be done with the recognition that authentic, dynamic language use and metalinguistic discoveries are essential for MLLs. When teachers intentionally co-plan for their students' authentic use of language, they can communicate with each other in one language or the other, or even in a combination of program languages, when appropriate. Based on Solorza and colleagues' (2019) work, some intentionally planned activities may include

1. Conducting frequent and deliberate pre-assessments
2. Creating flexible language spaces for inquiry-based or play-based learning
3. Using instructional materials that invite flexible, dynamic language use and access to content in both languages
4. Building peer support that helps facilitate bridging between languages
5. Using translanguaging as an ongoing support

Built on the four pillars of DL education (1) bilingualism and biliteracy, (2) high academic achievement, (3) sociocultural competence, and (4) critical consciousness (also see chapter 1), we suggest a four-dimensional collaborative planning framework.

> What a wonderful idea to co-construct a four-dimensional collaborative planning framework to represent the four pillars of DL education! Collaboration strengthens, reinforces, and brings cohesion to DL education models.
>
> **Margo**

When all four dimensions are considered together, collaborative planning maximizes teacher effectiveness and meaningfully impacts students' language acquisition and literacy learning in both languages. In addition, students' grade-appropriate core content knowledge and skills develop along with sociocultural understanding and critical consciousness. Collaboration is vitally important whether the team includes DL partnering teachers or additional service providers such as special educators with or without the opportunity to co-deliver instruction. Collaborative planning upholds all other work, including assessments, that is done in DL classrooms. Figure 5.5 offers a four-dimensional example of thinking and discussion prompts for an integrated focus on collaborative planning in DL. We invite its use for co-creating planning notes across a wide range of DL program types such as two-way immersion with English and a partner language. We also give emphasis to DL programs in which the program languages may be a combination of languages other than English altogether. For example, an Indigenous language and Spanish. Or in the international context perhaps the two program languages are Dutch and French. In all cases, the criticality of four-dimensional planning remains.

FIGURE 5.5 Integrated Focus on Planning for Dual Language Teaching

Focus	Key Questions	Planning Notes
Language Expectations and Opportunities for Bilingualism and Biliteracy	What language learning standards do we target?	
	What academic language—general and subject-specific—is embedded in the target content in both languages?	
	What opportunities do our students have to practice the four key language uses (narrate, inform, argue, explain) across both of their languages?	
Academic Content Development	What content standards do we target and assess?	
	What scaffolds are needed to support comprehension of content and language through interpretive modes of communication (listening, reading, viewing)?	
	What scaffolds are needed to support the application of content and language through expressive modes of communication (speaking, writing, visually representing)?	
Cultural Competence	What materials can help students develop cross-cultural competence?	
	What learning tasks and activities can students engage in to demonstrate cross-cultural competence?	
Critical Consciousness	How have we ensured that both program languages are given equitable attention?	
	What aspect(s) of critical consciousness have we woven into the lesson content and/or materials?	
	What opportunities have we planned for our minoritized DLLs to serve in linguistic leadership roles?	

Source: Adapted from Lachance and Honigsfeld (2023)

An example from the Academic Content Development portion of the above template (figure 5.5) is presented here by one third-grade elementary school math and literacy partnership from Collinswood Language Academy. The partnership co-created a visual scaffold aligned with grade-level math standards to support students' interpretive language (reading) as they discussed math concepts to practice expressive language skills. Mrs. Alarcón, the third-grade math teacher, uses this anchor as a visual scaffold.

Mrs. Alarcón's third-grade math anchor chart

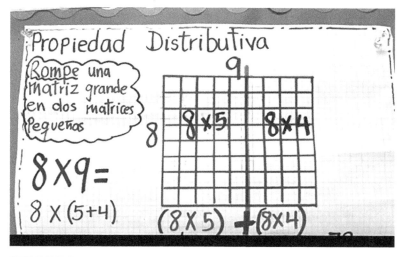

Source: Photo by Elia Alarcón. Used with permission.

Co-Delivering Instruction

Co-delivering instruction may take various forms and involve a range of educators in the DL context. Co-delivery requires coordinated purpose, equal teaching partnerships, and shared responsibilities for a class community of learners who are not separated for instruction by their labels. It involves the thoughtful grouping of students for learning, a clear understanding of one's roles and responsibilities during the co-taught lesson, and the coordination of teaching efforts. It challenges teachers to remain flexible, to be open to new ideas, and to trust one another.

Depending on the program model implemented in schools, we differentiate between two major approaches to collaborative instructional delivery in the DL context: partnership teaching and co-teaching. There are many unique similarities and differences between these two main approaches to co-instruction, but let's start with some straightforward, simple definitions:

1. **Partnership teaching** happens when two teachers systematically align their instruction, and work with the same group of students, but *do not (or rarely) co-deliver instruction in the same physical setting.*

2. **Co-teaching** takes place when two teachers physically *share the classroom space and the responsibility for all students through integrated instructional practices.*

Partnership teaching and co-teaching partnerships may also include ELD teachers, special educators, literacy or math intervention providers, and other educators, such as paraprofessionals or instructional aides (also referred to as paraprofessionals or teaching assistants).

Partnership Teaching in Two-Way Programs. Two-way programs are frequently designed to rely on two teachers collaborating and coordinating instruction for two groups of students. Do you recognize any of these basic configurations? How do they compare to your context?

Scenario 1:

Group 1/Class 1 begins the day with Teacher 1 in Language 1

Group 2/Class 2 begins the day with Teacher 2 in Language 2

Halfway through the day, the two groups are swapped:

Group 1/Class 1 finishes the day with Teacher 2 in Language 2

Group 2/Class 2 finishes the day with Teacher 1 in Language 1

Scenario 2:

Group 1/Class 1 spends an entire day with Teacher 1 in Language 1

Group 2/Class 2 spends an entire day with Teacher 2 in Language 2

The groups and teachers switch every day

Scenario 3:

Group 1/Class 1 spends an entire week with Teacher 1 in Language 1

Group 2/Class 2 spends an entire week with Teacher 2 in Language 2

The groups and teachers switch every week

If none of the above scenarios fit your context, consider the following possibilities:

- Through partnership teaching, some units of study are taught in Language 1 and others in Language 2. Alternatively, some larger, interdisciplinary units of study are started in Language 1 and then finished in Language 2, with strategic bridging of topics and materials.

- Each teacher of the DL partnership focuses on designated core classes (e.g., Teacher 1 teaches language arts and social studies in Language 1, and Teacher 2 teaches science and mathematics in Language 2 year-round).

- In some secondary programs the language partnerships may be more at the grade level rather than the classroom level. Each teacher delivers instruction in one of the two partner languages in one specific content area, and the school's schedule is created based on which teachers deliver which content subjects in the partner languages. For example, language arts, music, and social studies are delivered in program Language 1 while a second language arts class, math, science, and physical education are delivered in program Language 2.

A Closer Look at Co-Teaching. We start by taking a closer look at the seven co-teaching arrangements. You will notice that in the first three cases, the two teachers work with one large group of students, taking on different roles and responsibilities. In the next three models, there are two groups of students split between the two cooperating teachers. In the final model, multiple groups of students are engaged in a learning activity that is facilitated and monitored by both teachers. Based on Honigsfeld and Dove's (2019) work, we named the seven models using the group configurations and teacher roles:

1. One Group: One Leads, One "Teaches on Purpose"

2. One Group: Two Teach Same Content

3. One Group: One Teaches, One Assesses

4. Two Groups: Two Teach Same Content

5. Two Groups: One Preteaches, One Teaches Alternative Information

6. Two Groups: One Reteaches, One Teaches Alternative Information

7. Multiple Groups: Two Monitor or Teach

Each of these configurations may have a place in any co-taught classroom, regardless of the grade level, the content area, or the designated teacher assignment. We invite you to pilot various models in your classes to see which ones allow you to respond best to both the students' needs, the specific content being taught, the type of learning activities designed, and the participating teachers' teaching styles and own preferences.

Co-Assessment

Co-assessment provides teaching partners with opportunities to consider their students' individual strengths and needs by reviewing available student assessment data to establish shared instructional goals and objectives. Collaborative assessment practices allow teachers to decide the need for further building students' background knowledge or the requisite for re-teaching and review in both partner languages. Although the analysis of standardized assessment scores provides some information, for teaching teams to establish pertinent learning objectives, the examination of additional data such as local school assessments, unit tests, project-based outcomes, writing samples, learning summaries, journal writing, student observations, and other formal and informal evaluations may be best. Comprehensive data collection and analysis reveal a more holistic picture of students' progress, enabling assessors to then determine individual student needs. That picture may be used more effectively for DL bridging, planning follow-up, and continued instruction.

We can probably all agree that our students demonstrate extraordinary learning and language use in DL classrooms. We can probably also agree that there are countless, genuine, and multidimensional data that cannot be portrayed through test scores, reading levels, or other numeric forms of assessment. Rather, we must be attentive to capturing the rich, descriptive language our students use in our classrooms, the communities, and beyond. In figure 5.6 we offer an adapted version of Gottlieb's (2022) qualitative rubric designed to capture students' vivid and resonant use of multiple languages. As you reflect on the dimensions of language, we invite you to think about how they emerge in DL classrooms to then make direct connections to how you will change your collaborative practices (see chapter 4 for more on assessment practices in the DL context).

FIGURE 5.6 Multidimensional Assessment of Classroom Language Use in Dual Language Classrooms

Dimensions of Language	Evidence of Influence of Partner Language 1 on Partner Language 2	Evidence of Translanguaging	Evidence of Influence of Partner Language 2 on Partner Language 1	Evidence of Students' Metalinguistic Awareness
Discourse • directionality of writing • cohesion of thoughts • expressive language organization • cross-linguistic/ curricular representation of ideas • linear versus circular thinking and coherence of ideas • cultural patterns of dialog				
Sentence • syntactical order in both program languages				

Dimensions of Language	Evidence of Influence of Partner Language 1 on Partner Language 2	Evidence of Translanguaging	Evidence of Influence of Partner Language 2 on Partner Language 1	Evidence of Students' Metalinguistic Awareness
• complexity of structure in both program languages • connective language/ prepositional phrases in both program languages				
Phrase/Word • cognates and false cognates • multiple meanings • idiomatic expressions and when they are appropriate for use • collocations				

Source: Adapted from Gottlieb (2022, p. 136)

Co-reflecting

Co-reflecting on educational practices has many aspects, and it frequently sets the parameters for the next collaborative instructional cycle. Reflection provides insight into whether strategies and resources used during lessons are affecting student learning and can be particularly useful when teaching teams want to hone their collaborative skills. Successful teaching partners often reflect on both their challenges and successes to refine instruction. As we transform our collaborative practices in DL education to be truly multidimensional, we must also shift our actions to increase our collaborative reflections. Biliteracy development is based on the intertwining of both languages, a process we all agree to describe as deeply complex. Escamilla et al. (2014) remind us that collaborative approaches to classroom language and content development are highly beneficial and require teachers' ongoing reflection regarding students' momentums and movements within the trajectories toward biliteracy. In other words, collaborative reflections include discussions and data analysis to look for patterns in partner language literacy development alongside English language literacy development, capturing collective growth. In agreement, Brookfield (2017) advises the use of regular, disciplined, critical reflection. We invite you to try out the four-lens approach to reflection described below or devise different approaches to support your efforts with your collaborative team members and teaching partners to fully integrate reflective inquiry into your collaborative assessment practices. For reflection to be continual, its documentation needs to be easily and readily accomplished. As you begin to consider how your reflective practices will take shape, you may wonder what types of strategies are needed to make ongoing reflection a success. Brookfield (2017) suggests that we view what we do and how we form assumptions about the teaching-learning process that takes place in our classrooms through four different lenses. We've adapted them for the DL context:

1. The students' eyes:
   - What are the students seeing and experiencing as they assess their own and each other's multilingual/multiliteracies development?

2. Our colleagues' perceptions:
   - What are our colleagues seeing and experiencing within the collaborative assessment processes that are reflective of sociocultural competencies?

3. Our personal experiences:
   - What have we experienced in the past that is similar to or different from our MLLs' experience? What connections can I make my own sense of critical consciousness?

4. Relevant theory and research:
   - What does related educational theory and research have to say about these experiences as they align with all four pillars of DL education?

We recognize that many educators dedicate significant time and resources to the three aspects of the collaborative cycle, those of co-planning, co-teaching, and co-assessing. We take the stance that co-reflection is a critical aspect of the cycle whereby experiences provide empowering motivators to consistently renew the full instructional cycle. We offer some examples of tools and protocols educators may create and implement to support all four aspects, with students' ongoing language progression, content development, and sociocultural growth in mind (see figure 5.7).

As educators consistently create and implement key tools and protocols that support the collaborative instructional cycle in the DL context, we present a few examples of students' benefits from teacher collaboration in the DL context.

DL students will:

- Receive rich, multidimensional, culturally and linguistically responsive and sustaining curricula across the content areas in both partner languages

FIGURE 5.7   Key Tools and Protocols Supporting the Collaborative Instructional Cycle in the Dual Language Context

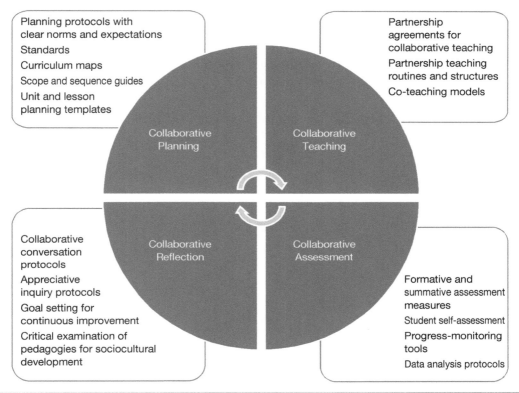

- Participate in instruction based on multilevel, differentiated unit, and lesson plans

- Engage in learning tasks that integrate content, language and biliteracy development, sociocultural competence, social-emotional growth, and critical consciousness

- Build cross-cultural understanding and positive identity development

- Develop critical understanding of and engagement with complex concepts, especially related to social justice and equity

A more specific example of students' benefits is shown here via a specific community-based biliteracy development initiative from the Eastern Band of the Cherokee Indians (EBCI). The following photos are from a multidimensional, multigenerational vocabulary/phrase-level development activity where three generations of Cherokee come together in an EBCI kindergarten classroom at the New Kituwah Academy. The Elder Cherokee Speakers, young-adult Speakers, and kindergarten learners play a collaborative language game they created, with the shared purposes of learning key words and phrases associated with daily routines and clothing combined with generational, multidimensional communication patterns in the Cherokee language. The significant critically conscious goal is to build students' linguistic and culturally relevant discourse with their EBCI community Elders as they regularly interact across generations, collectively contributing to the Cherokee language revitalization and reclamation. Tohisgi and Alsqwetawo, two young-adult Cherokee Speakers collaboratively interact with an Elder Speaker in the EBCI kindergarten classroom.

Conclusion: Key Take-Aways

We continue our efforts for breaking down the monolingual wall, and we urge DL educators to collaborate with national- and state-level policymakers, community and school leaders, immigrant families, and others seeking multilingual schooling for integrated collaborative instruction. DL programs and instructional practices must be based on the equity principle that MLLs should stay in their general-education classrooms, avoiding isolation from their English-speaking peers to develop proficiency in English. For students to have a welcome sense of belonging and to thrive academically, they need to be taught by subject-specific experts, that is, the content and grade-level teachers who are committed to promoting biliteracy development along with development of their English-language skills with instruction provided by a language-development expert so students can learn the core curriculum.

Collaboration in DL programs demands both. A conclusive representation of what we embrace and honor for success may be demonstrated through the words of Margarita Calderón and her colleagues as they claim, "the success of DL programs depends on collaboration between teachers, administrators, and students. In a DL school, teachers are well-prepared to co-teach and students to co-learn" (p. 163). Thus, collaboration is perceived to be the norm, simply stated, a solid necessity for breaking down the monolingual wall.

Reflection Questions

1. Hattie (2015) reminds us:

   Collaboration is based on cooperativeness, learning from errors, seeking feedback about progress and enjoying venturing into the "pit of not knowing" together with expert help that provides safety nets and, ultimately, ways out of the pit. Creative collaboration involves bringing together two or more seemingly unrelated ideas, and this highlights again the importance of having safe and trusting places to explore ideas, to make and to learn from errors and to use expertise to maximize successful learning. (p. 27)

   What does creative collaboration look like, feel like, and sound like in the DL classroom?

2. When researching collaborative leadership practices within New York City DL programs, Hunt (2011) found the following:

   Collaborative leadership is the reason many dual language programs last and continue to develop. Principals support teachers, teachers support their principals, and teachers support other teachers. [. . .] When a principal leaves the school, and leadership changes, it is the collaborative work of the teachers that maintains the program. Creating avenues for leadership to move beyond the principal is critical in promoting the enduring success of a dual language program. (p. 203)

   How are you, as a teacher leader, active in shared leadership with your administrative team?

3. What recommendations would you offer other educators regarding effective, collaborative ways to build equity within a DL program?

4. What essential tools do teachers and administrators need to transform professional discourse, supporting the increase in students' equitable access to high-quality DL programs?

5. How can DL program stakeholders increase strategic collaboration to gather, report, and authentically act on holistic program evaluation data?

References

ARC. (2021). *Canvass of dual language and immersion (DLI) programs in US public schools.* https://www.americancouncils.org/sites/default/files/documents/pages/2021-10/Canvass%20DLI%20-%20October%202021-2_ac.pdf

Arizona Proposition 203: English Language Education for Children in Public Schools Initiative. (2000). https://www.azed.gov/sites/default/files/2017/03/PROPOSITION203.pdf?id=58d003651130c012d8e906e5

Arizona SB 1014 English language learners; instruction; budgeting. (2019). https://www.azleg.gov/legtext/54leg/1R/bills/SB1014P.pdf

Baker, D., Roberson, A., & Kim, H. (2018). Autism and dual immersion: Sorting through the questions. *Advances in Autism, 4*(4), 174–183.

Brookfield, S. (2017). *Becoming a critically reflective teacher* (2nd ed.). Jossey-Bass.

Burns, D., & Darling-Hammond, L. (2014, December). *Teaching around the world: What can TALIS tell us.* https://edpolicy.stanford.edu/publication/pubs/1295

CAL Center for Applied Linguistics. (n.d.). *Dual language program directory.* http://webapp.cal.org/DualLanguage/DLListing.aspx

Calderón, M. E., Dove, M. G., Staehr Fenner, D., Gottlieb, M., Honigsfeld, A., Ward Singer, T., Slakk, S., Soto, I., & Zacarian, D. (2020). *Breaking down the wall: Essential shifts for English learners' success.* Corwin.

California Proposition 227: English Language in Public Schools Initiative. (1998). https://vigarchive.sos.ca.gov/1998/primary/propositions/227.htm

California Proposition 58: California Education for a Global Economy (CA Ed.G.E.) Initiative. (2016). https://vigarchive.sos.ca.gov/2016/general/en/propositions/58/

Cloud, N., Genesee, F., & Hamayan, E. (2000). *Dual language instruction: A handbook for enriched education.* Heinle & Heinle.

Compton, T. N. (2018, May). *Access to culturally responsive teaching for English language learners: Mainstream teacher perceptions and practice on inclusion* (Paper 2949) [Doctoral dissertation, University of Louisville]. ThinkIR: Electronic Theses and Dissertations. https://doi.org/10.18297/etd/2949

Cordeiro, K. E. (2021). *Positioning co-teachers in an integrated English as a new language class: Making sense of teaching roles* [Doctoral dissertation]. ProQuest Dissertations and Theses Global.

Davison, C. (2006). Collaboration between ESL and content teachers: How do we know when we are doing it right? *The International Journal of Bilingual Education and Bilingualism, 9*(4), 454–475.

Daza, E. (2022). *Openness to integrated English as a new language instruction and the co-teaching service delivery mode* [Unpublished doctoral dissertation].

de Jong, E. J., & Bearse, C. I. (2014). Dual language programs as a strand within a secondary school: Dilemmas of school organization and the TWI mission. *International Journal of Bilingual Education and Bilingualism, 17*(1), 15–31. doi: 10.1080/13670050.2012.725709

DelliCarpini, M. (2008). Teacher collaboration for ESL/EFL academic success. *Internet TESL Journal, 14*(8). http://iteslj.org/Techniques/DelliCarpini-Teacher Collaboration.html

DelliCarpini, M. (2009, May). Dialogues across disciplines: Preparing English-as-a-second-language teachers for interdisciplinary collaboration. *Current Issues in Education, 11*(2). http://cie.ed.asu.edu/volume11/number2/

Dove, M. G., & Honigsfeld, A. (2014). Analysis of the implementation of an ESL coteaching model in a suburban elementary school. *NYS TESOL Journal, 1*(1).

Dove, M. G., & Honigsfeld, A. (Eds.). (2020). *Co-teaching for English learners: Evidence-based practices and research-informed outcomes.* Information Age.

DuFour, R., DuFour, R., Eaker, R., & Many, T. W. (2016). *Learning by doing: A handbook for professional learning communities at work* (3rd ed.). Solution Tree.

Escamilla, K., Hopewell, S., Butvilofsky, S., Sparrow, W., Soltero-González, L., Ruiz-Figueroa, O., & Escamilla, M. (2014). *Biliteracy from the start: Literacy squared in action.* Caslon.

Farrell, T. S. C. (Ed.). (2012, September). Special Issue: Novice professionals in TESOL. *TESOL Quarterly, 46*(3), 435–604.

Fogel, L. W., & Moser, K. (2017). Language teacher identities in the Southern United States: Transforming rural schools. *Journal of Language, Identity and Education, 16*(2), 65–79. doi:10.1080/15348458.2016.1277147

Foltos, L. (2018, January 29). *Teachers learn better together* [Blog post]. Retrieved from http://www.edutopia.org/article/teachers-learn-better-together

Friend, M., & Barron, T.L. (2021). *Specially designed instruction for co-teaching.* Marilyn Friend.

Friend, M. (2019). *Co-teach: Building and sustaining effective classroom partnerships in inclusive schools* (3rd ed.). Marilyn Friend.

García, O., Johnson, S. I., & Seltzer, K. (2016). *The translanguaging classroom: Leveraging student bilingualism for learning.* Caslon.

Gately, S. E., & Gately, F. J., Jr. (2001, Mar–Apr). Understanding coteaching components. *TEACHING Exceptional Children, 33*(4), 40–47.

Gottlieb, M. (2021). *Classroom assessment in multiple languages: A handbook for teachers.* Corwin.

Gottlieb, M. (2022). *Assessment in multiple languages: A handbook for school and district leaders.* Corwin.

Greenberg Motamedi, J., Vazquez, M., Gandhi, E. V., & Holmgren, M. (2019). *Beaverton School District English language development minutes, models, and outcomes.* Education Northwest.

Guerrero, M. D., & Lachance, J. (2018). *The national dual language education teacher preparation standards.* Fuente Press.

Hattie, J. (2015). *What works best in education: The politics of collaborative expertise.* Pearson. https://www.pearson.com/content/dam/corporate/global/pearson-dot-com/files/hattie/150526_ExpertiseWEB_V1.pdf

Honigsfeld, A., & Dove, M. (2017). The coteaching flow inside the classroom. In M. Dantas-Whitney & S. Rilling (Eds.), *TESOL voices: Secondary education* (pp. 107–114). TESOL.

Honigsfeld, A., & Dove, M. G. (2012). *Co-teaching and other collaborative practices in the EFL/ESL classroom: Rationale, research, reflections, and recommendations.* Information Age.

Honigsfeld, A., & Dove, M. G. (2019). *Collaborating for English learners: A foundational guide to integrated practices.* Corwin.

Honigsfeld, A., & Dove, M. G. (2022). *Co-Planning: Five essential practices to integrate curriculum and instruction for English learners.* Corwin.

Honigsfeld, A., & Dove, M. G. (2022). *Portraits of collaboration: Educators working together to support multilingual learners.* Seidlitz Education.

Howard, E. R., Lindholm-Leary, K. J., Rogers, D., Olague, N., Medina, J., Kennedy, B., Sugarman, J., & Christian, D. (2018). *Guiding principles for dual language education* (3rd ed.). Center for Applied Linguistics.

Howard, E. R., Lindholm-Leary, K. J., Rogers, D., Olague, N., Medina, J., Kennedy, B., Sugarman, J., & Christian, D. (2018). *Guiding principles for dual language education* (3rd ed.). Center for Applied Linguistics.

Hunt, V. (2011). Learning from success stories: leadership structures that support dual language programs over time in New York City. *International Journal of Bilingual*

Education and Bilingualism, 14(2), 187–206. doi:10.1080/13670050.2010.53 9673

Hurst, D., & Davison, C. (2005). Collaboration on the curriculum: Focus on secondary ESL. In J. Crandall & D. Kaufman (Eds.), *Case studies in TESOL: Teacher education for language and content integration.* Teachers of English to Speakers of Other Languages.

Jensen, B. (2016). *Beyond PD: Teacher professional learning in high-performing systems.* Learning First.

Kaufman, D., & Crandall, J. A. (Eds.). (2005). *Content-based instruction in elementary and secondary school settings.* TESOL.

Kuusisaari, H. (2014). Teachers at the zone of proximal development – Collaboration promoting or hindering the development process. *Teaching and Teacher Education, 43*, 46–57. https://doi.org/10.1016/j.tate.2014.06.001

Lachance, J., & Honigsfeld, A. (2023). *Collaboration and co-teaching for dual language learners: Transforming programs for multilingualism and equity.* Corwin.

Lachance, J. (2017). A case study of dual language program administrators: The teachers we need. *International Journal of Educational Leadership, 12*(1), 1–18.

Lieberman, A., & Miller, L. G. (1984). *Teachers, their world, and their work: Implications for school improvement.* Association for Supervision and Curriculum Development.

Lindholm-Leary, K. (2012). Success and challenges in dual language education. *Theory Into Practice, 51*(4), 256–262.

Lindholm-Leary, K. (2016). Bilingualism and academic achievement in children in dual language programs. In E. Nicoladis & S. Montanari (Eds.), *Bilingualism across the lifespan: Factors moderating language proficiency* (pp. 203–223). American Psychological Association.

Martin-Beltran, M. A., & Peercy, M. M. (2012). How can ESOL and mainstream teachers make the best of a standards-based curriculum in order to collaborate? *TESOL Journal, 3*, 425–444. doi:10.1002/tesj.23

Martin-Beltrán, M., & Madigan Peercy, M. (2014). Collaboration to teach English language learners: Opportunities for shared teacher learning. *Teachers and Teaching, 20*, 721–737.

Massachusetts Department of Elementary and Secondary Education [DESE]. (2019). *Collaboration tool.* http://www.doe.mass.edu/ell/curriculum.html

Massachusetts. An Act Relative to Language Opportunity for Our Kids, Ma. General Laws § 138. (2017). https://malegislature.gov/Laws/SessionLaws/Acts/2017/Chapter138

Massachusetts. Question 2: English Language Education in Public Schools Initiative. (2002). *Official information for voters.* https://www.sec.state.ma.us/divisions/elections/download/information-for-voters/IFV_2002-English.pdf

Mudambi, A. (2022, June 29). *Honoring all dialects and regionalisms in languages.* https://duallanguageschools.org/columnists/honoring-all-dialects-and-regionalisms-in-languages/

Multistate Association of Bilingual Education-Northeast (MABE). (2023, June 14). *Department of elementary and secondary education (DESE): Guidance for dual language education programs.* https://www.doe.mass.edu/ele/programs/dle.html

Nagle, J. F. (Ed.). (2013). *English learner instruction through collaboration and inquiry in teacher education.* Information Age.

NCEL. (2022, February). *NCEL effective literacy white paper.* https://secureserver cdn.net/50.62.174.75/v5e.685.myftpupload.com/wp-content/uploads/2022/04/21018-NCEL-Effective-Literacy-White-Pa per-FINAL_v2.0.pdf

NCELA. (2022). *Benefits of multilingualism.* [Infographic]. https://ncela.ed.gov/sites/default/files/legacy/files/announcements/20200805-NCELAInfographic-508.pdf

New Mexico Public Education Department, Language and Culture Bureau. (2016). *Bilingual multicultural education programs (BMEPS).* https://webnew.ped.state.nm.us/bureaus/languageandculture/bilingual-multicultural-education-programs-bmeps/

New York State Education Department [NYSED]. (2018). *Program options for English language learners/Multilingual learners.* http://www.nysed.gov/bilingual-ed/program-options-english-language-learnersmultilingual-learners

Norton, J. (2016, October). Successful coteaching: ESL teachers in the mainstream classroom. *TESOL Connections.* http://newsmanager.commpartners.com/tesolc/issues/2016-10-01/3.html

Pawan, F., & Ortloff, J. (2011). Sustaining collaboration: ESL and content area teachers. *Teaching and Teacher Education, 27,* 463–471.

Peercy, M. M., Ditter, M., & Destefano, M. (2017). "We need more consistency": Negotiating the division of labor in ESOL—Mainstream teacher collaboration. *TESOL Journal, 8,* 215–239. doi:10.1002/tesj.269

Safir, S. (2017). *The listening leader: Creating the conditions for equitable school transformation.* Jossey-Bass.

Scanlan, M., Frattura, E., Schneider, K. A., & Capper, C. A. (2012). Bilingual students with integrated comprehensive service: Collaborative strategies. In A. Honigsfeld & M. G. Dove (Eds.), *Co-teaching and other collaborative practices in the EFL/ESL classroom: Rationale, research, reflections, and recommendations* (pp. 3–13). Information Age.

Smith, S. C., & Scott, J. J. (1990). *The collaborative school: A work environment for effective instruction.* National Association of Secondary School Principals.

Solorza, C. R., Aponte, G. Y., Leverenz, T., Becker, T., & Frias, B. (with García, O., & Sánchez, M. T.). (2019). *Translanguaging in dual language bilingual education: A blueprint for planning units of study.* CUNY-NYS Initiative on Emergent Bilinguals. https://www.cuny-nysieb.org/wp-content/uploads/2019/09/Translanguaging-in-Dual-Language-Bilingual-Education-A-Blueprint-for-Planning-Units-of-Study-RSVD.pdf

Spratt, J., & Lani, F. (2013). Applying the principles of inclusive pedagogy in initial teacher education: From university based course to classroom action. *Revista de Investigación En Educación, 11*(3), 133–140. http://thesendhub.co.uk/wp-content/uploads/2016/09/applying-principles-of-inclusive-pedagogy-in-itt.pdf

Steele, J. L., Slater, R. O., Zamarro, G., Miller, T., Li, J., Burkhauser, S., & Bacon, M. (2017). Effects of dual-language immersion programs on student achievement: Evidence from lottery data. *American Educational Research Journal, 54*(1_suppl), 282S–306S.

Texas Education Agency. House Bill 3. (2019). https://tea.texas.gov/about-tea/government-relations-and-legal/government-relations/house-bill-3

Theoharis, G., & O'Toole, J. (2011). Leading inclusive ELL social justice leadership for English language learners. *Educational Administration Quarterly, 47*(4), 646–688.

Thomas, W. P., & Collier, V. P. (2017). *Why dual language schooling.* Fuente Press.

U.S. Department of Education, Office of English Language Acquisition (OELA). (2019). *The top languages spoken by English learners (ELs) in the United States.* https:// ncela.ed.gov/files/fast_facts/olea-top-languages-fact-sheet-20191021-508.pdf

U.S. Department of Education. (2023, January 23). Remarks by U.S. Secretary of Education Miguel Cardona on Raise the Bar: Lead the World. https://www .ed.gov/news/speeches/remarks-us-secretary-education-miguel-cardona-raise- bar-lead-world

Vangriekena, K., Dochya, F., Raesa, E., & Kyndt, E. (2015). *Teacher collaboration: A systematic review.* University of Leuven, Centre for Research on Professional Learning & Development, Corporate Training and Lifelong Learning.

Villa, R. A., Thousand, J. S., & Nevin, A. I. (2013). *A guide to co-teaching: New lessons and strategies to facilitate student learning* (3rd ed.). Corwin.

Villa, R. A., Thousand, J. S., Nevin, A., & Council for Exceptional Children. (2008). *A guide to co-teaching: Practical tips for facilitating student learning.* Corwin.

WIDA. (2020). *WIDA English language development standards framework, 2020 edition: Kindergarten—grade 12.* https://wida.wisc.edu/sites/default/files/resource/ WIDA-ELD-Standards-Framework-2020.pdf

Yoon, B. (2022). *Effective teacher collaboration for English language learners: Cross- curricular insights from K–12 settings.* Routledge.

chapter six

From Leading in a Monolingual Program to Leading in a Dual Language Program

MARGA MARSHALL AND
DAVID NUNGARAY

PREMISE

Charlemagne once said, "To have another language is to possess a second soul." It's also often said, "*Quien habla dos idiomas vale por dos*, he who speaks two languages is worth two people." One of the many benefits of being bilingual is that it exposes an individual to diverse customs and ideas and increases awareness of other cultures. More than half the world speaks more than one language on a daily basis. and speaking two or more languages has many benefits such as bilingual and multilingual learners (MLLs) having greater problem-solving skills, a multicultural and awareness appreciation, higher academic achievement, and greater opportunities in college and career in the multilingual world of our times. Additionally, as the world and our own country become more multilingual, the need to provide successful dual language programs for students to become leaders in their communities and workplaces continues to grow. Fundamentally, we must also recognize the sense of belonging that occurs when our students see their languages and cultures reflected in our schools, honored and respected to the utmost degree. Multilingualism and multiculturalism simply speak to the dignity our human race must afford one another in a multicultural country made up of immigrants, refugees, asylum seekers, and descendants of immigrants.

The time has come for a fundamental and necessary shift to happen in the way our school systems serve our children, staff, families, and communities. If the pandemic has shown us anything related to education, it is that we can radically transform our systems overnight. It has also shown us exacerbation of inequalities and inequities inherent in how our current system was designed. We already know that the system is designed for the outcomes we see in our data, and quite frankly, in our students' lives and loss of opportunities. So much tinkering has happened around the edges of the system, and not enough resources, time, and energy are spent on what works to transform outcomes, especially for our most historically marginalized, yet fully capable, students. Having experienced monolingual programs and also having led dual language schools, we use this chapter to provide tactical ways to improve your current systems and to provide fundamental knowledge for program leaders.

UNESCO's research has shown that information and knowledge are key determinants of wealth creation, social transformation, and human development. Additionally, language enables the delivery of information and knowledge coded in different sociocultural, geopolitical, and economic contexts (Multilingualism and Linguistic Diversity, 2003). As leaders of schools, we should be able to provide linguistic diversity through communication with our families and communities since language is a direct connection with people's cultures. Posters and visuals are important, and we have to go deeper to the roots of what it takes to ensure academic and linguistic access for our students.

Schools need to be a place where students learn about today's global society and where they access high-quality instruction in bilingual or multilingual settings. Monolingualism has kept language learners separate from the core of instruction, unable to make meaning in each family's mother tongue, and all too often silenced into assimilation. America's history and legacy around engaging in forced assimilation practices in indigenous communities, and working to cut people's mother tongues through our practices in schools, are something we must reckon with. Ultimately, the development and high-quality implementation of excellent dual language programs is the hope on the other side of the wall that bilingual and multilingual leaders and families have been trying to take down for years. Together we must all take up the mantle and as system, school, and classroom leaders see to our collective responsibility to ensure that our students receive nothing but the best education possible.

We invite you to now read about each one of our own contextualized experiences, starting with Marga's time as a school leader at LOLA Language Academy (LOLA) followed by David's experience at Downtown Academy. Both schools are pseudonyms for their respective schools. Please know that what we have shared is just a fraction of the work it took to make things possible, and most important, that we did this work in partnership with our school staff, district support, families, students, and community partnerships. The myth of a superhero principal is not one we want to perpetuate. Our work was always done in community.

VIGNETTE: MARGA'S EXPERIENCE

LOLA was reopened in 2017 as a Spanish-English Two-Way Dual Immersion (TWDI) school. Its original iteration, LL Elementary, was unfortunately closed in 2011 due to low enrollment. When the district's leadership explored the reopening of the school, dual language programs were in demand, and families were requesting to have more programs to offer additive bilingual programs at the district. The TWDI program was created as an enrichment program designed for Spanish speaking students at all levels of English language proficiency, native English speakers, and students of other language backgrounds who are fluent in English.

When I was principal, I worked to make LOLA an example of an inclusive school that benefited MLLs as well as monolingual English students. Both groups had the opportunity to learn a second language, which allowed each group to be academically, linguistically, and socially successful. LOLA follows the 50/50 TWDI model (see more on the 50/50 model in chapter 3), where students received approximately 50 percent of their instruction in English and 50 percent in Spanish in each subject area (half day and half day, alternating languages at the beginning of the day daily), while core instruction was taught in both English and Spanish.

Another strategy we employed was *team teaching*, with a Spanish-proficient teacher and an English-proficient teacher at each grade level to serve as language models of the program. Since transferable skills and concepts are taught in either English or Spanish, this allowed for maintenance of 50/50 language allocation. The equal division of instructional time between each language allowed students' first and second languages to progress. As the founding principal selected to open LOLA, I co-created a shared vision with staff members, families, and the community; made a commitment to expose students to multiple languages; created a Continent Focus Learning model (see below); and aligned our Dual Language Program Goals to Positive Behavioral Interventions and Supports (PBIS) schoolwide.

One of our first initiatives was centered on Daily Morning Announcements, because they are such an important part of school life. We had a diverse population of students, and we wanted to celebrate each and every language spoken on campus. During the 2020–2021 school year, our diverse population consisted of African American 3.20 percent; American Indian 0.25 percent; Asian 2.50 percent; Filipino 1.70 percent; Hispanic 57.70 percent; Two or More Races 4.20 percent; Pacific Islander 1.20 percent; and white 21.60 percent. Therefore, we showcased each of the languages spoken by our diverse population during our Daily Morning Announcements.

All initiatives aligned with the school's TWDI Vision and Mission were as follows:

- **School vision:** Our vision is that all students reach high levels of achievement in a rigorous academic program while being provided the opportunity to learn in a bilingual, multicultural, and collaborative environment that develops character and the skills necessary for success in a diverse, global society.

- **School mission:** Our mission is to establish a school community dedicated to providing all students with a rigorous, standards-based education and the essential skills necessary to succeed as twenty-first century citizens. Through the emphasis on collaboration, critical and creative thinking, positive character development, and media literacy, our students take significant steps toward college and career readiness. We expect families, teachers, and staff to work together to foster a community environment with a focus on our children's success.

We implemented a *Language of the Week'* segment during our Daily Morning Announcements, where students would volunteer to teach theme words in their chosen language. This fun, student-produced, and collaborative effort fostered and promoted a sense of unity and belonging among our students. For example, Roberto (fourth grade), a student from LOLA since Transitional Kindergarten, shared with me that "[t]he 'Language of the Week' is very good for students learning new languages. I love how the language changes every week and students lead the announcements for the rest of school to learn new words."

Picture of Karen Hernandez's Dual Language Class Poster at LOLA Language Academy, Work inspired by "One Class Many Cultures" post at http://aplacetothrive.blogspot.com/

The Center for Applied Linguistics affirms that developing cultural competence is integral to language learning. In fact, language proficiency is enhanced when the culture it reflects is embedded in learning another language. Sociocultural competence, as a programmatic goal, is grounded in the idea that our emergent bilingual students would be willing and able to embrace ongoing and unending critical self-reflection. That is, they will be able to see the similarities and differences in each other but will embrace the differences as opportunities to connect rather than obstacles to overcome (Medina, 2018). One way we accomplished this was to connect our mascot, a jet, with the idea of traveling around the world and learning from different cultures and traditions. This is how we created the Continent Focus Learning Model. Each grade level would focus on an assigned continent and our students would have culture lessons in both Spanish and English focused on their continent during the school year. This special project was connected to the Center for Applied Linguistics Third Pillar of Dual Language Education, Cross-Cultural Competence (see chapter 1 for the breakdown of the four pillars). The lessons were engaging and taught students geography of the place they were learning at a deep level, including their culture, traditions, music, languages, and food. Throughout the years, we had multiple visits from other Dual Language Administrators/Teachers, district staff, and even neighborhood superintendents interested in sustaining or initiating dual language programs. We offered *consejitos*, or tips, they could benefit from as they planned and worked on their programs.

Consejito

Get to know your families and where they are from, their traditions and cultures, and invite them to make presentations about their experiences to the grade levels learning about the country or countries they have lived in. This is an amazing way for students to see what it looks like, what it feels like, and what it tastes like when parents bring traditional clothing, instruments, and/or food to classes.

VIGNETTE: DAVID'S EXPERIENCE

I first became aware of dual language programs when I was studying Spanish literature at my alma mater in California. One of my professors shared with our class that her daughter attended a school in Long Beach that taught her English side-by-side with Spanish, and that she had access to *folclórico* and other culturally relevant programming. I was in disbelief that such a school existed, especially as a native Spanish speaker and son of immigrants who attended schools in California during Proposition 227, which mandated English as the language of instruction, essentially eliminating or reducing access to bilingual programs. The proposition was passed in 1998 and was repealed in 2016, yet its legacy remains in how far too often English is considered the norm and the language of success in our country. It was not until I went to college that I was taught Mexican American history and the role the Chicano and civil rights movements had in my own education, including how *Westminster v. Mendez* paved the way for *Brown v. Board of Education* to desegregate schools. Most of my experiences in schools had been through what Dr. Angela Valenzuela (1999) describes as *subtractive schooling*, though my parents, thankfully, persisted in ensuring I maintained my language and a rich bicultural experience. In a sink-or-swim English-only model, I swam but not without experiencing the harmful effects of being submersed. At home it was *cumbias, novelas, y chilaquiles*, and at school it was English spelling tests, learning about Manifest Destiny without learning about the Treaty of Guadalupe Hidalgo and its true implications for how the border crossed our people, and Spanish but only when it was for my honors classes and college readiness. I am also thankful for the amazing teachers I had who saw me: Ms. Ivory who taught me English with care and compassion, Ms. Cao who helped me get identified for gifted and talented, and the many teachers I had along the way who worked to make sure I had the education and opportunities needed for me to be where I am today.

I was a first-generation college graduate. When the time came to decide what to do after my studies, teaching quickly rose to the top. I entered the workforce through Teach For America and was recruited after a recruiter reminded me that students like me did not make it to college without a strong K–12 education. A few months before the school year, I was selected to teach fourth grade at Downtown Academy, a dual language school in Texas. Being a dual language teacher and getting to see students from diverse racial, ethnic, cultural, and socioeconomic backgrounds was incredible. As a gay educator, I chose to eventually leave the classroom because the district I worked with at the time, like many districts across our country, did not have nondiscrimination protections for my identity. My service to this particular community would come full circle 6 years later when I returned to Downtown Academy as principal.

For context, at the time that I was a teacher, three schools had the additive model of dual language in a district of over 100 schools. The history of Downtown Academy was that it had once experienced declining enrollment, and in an effort to both increase enrollment and, more important, listen to the community's desire to add an enrichment model that would serve all students, including MLLs who had historically been marginalized, the school applied for and became an in-district charter. Through that charter, the school became a specialized model focused on multiple sections of TWDL classrooms per grade level. It also had one classroom per grade level focused on monolingual instruction, which meant that families had a choice. Additionally, the school had two more pillars of fine arts and sciences in its initial charter. The school grew in popularity as well as in enrollment, and academic outcomes for students consistently ranked high on Texas accountability systems.

At the time I was a teacher there, the school had been rated Exemplary, the highest designation a school could receive on the state accountability system. Enrollment increased as students from outside the neighborhood could apply to the lottery for dual language, and neighborhood students had priority for enrollment. The school also offered important programming such as *folclórico* and an after-school math club designed to engage students in math and improve their mathematics capacity through the use of the ancient Mayan abacus and digital, online mazes. The club also integrated Nahuatl and Mexican cultures through cultural games, dance, and language.

As a K–8 academy that served over 630 students comprising 90.7 percent Latinx students, 61 percent economically disadvantaged, and over 30 percent emergent bilingual students, the school itself also had almost 74 percent Latinx teachers, well above the state average of 29 percent. By their eighth-grade year, many students, including those who might not traditionally have had access (such as our MLLs), matriculated into high school English, Algebra 1, and environmental science (high school credit). Many challenged the AP Spanish Language test. Our AP Spanish teacher consistently had over 80 percent of her students who challenged the AP test receive a score of 3 or higher, meaning they'd receive college credit as part of our dual language program. This is and was a true testament to what is possible for students who have dual language access into secondary instruction, as well as to teachers who have high expectations and who practice rigorous instruction.

Situated in the urban core, the neighborhood surrounding the school began to experience gentrification, and yet despite a series of changes in district and school leadership, the school retained its status as an in-district school, and the dual language program and other pillars remained intact. When I returned as principal, it was clear that the instructional culture of the school was declining, according to a national normed teacher survey. Academic outcomes for most students had also been declining for almost 5 years, and it was considered an *improvement required* school. Enrollment was steady; however, there were opportunities to manage systems around recruitment of more Spanish-speaking families and to create access for enrollment by the monolingual families who were on waitlists for the dual language program. The makeup of classrooms made clear that ensuring that 50 percent of students were Spanish speakers and 50 percent were from monolingual English backgrounds had not been attended to. Additionally, MLLs were clearly experiencing opportunity gaps as evidenced by state and benchmark data. A program that was for MLLs was not by and large serving them well, and that data became more evident as the state upgraded its accountability system. At the same time, it was clear students were making progress on their English proficiency, and classroom observations revealed that there were strong teachers who were looking for direction on how to best ensure that their students were learning.

Previously, the school had only admitted students into the dual language program, but when I joined as principal, we worked with district staff to make changes in enrollment processes to allow more families to access the school's programming. The school had a robust waitlist, and families were clamoring for access. On the staffing end, I quickly prioritized hiring great talent and upgraded our hiring processes to ensure strong alignment with our mission and good teaching practices and coachability for the staff we did hire. Being intentional about hiring excellent teachers, especially those who understand equity, who build relationships with students and families, and who are collaborators, was key to our success. We incorporated a portfolio process, essays, a group interview process, a sample teach with our students, and most important, current staff voice and input into the process. Great teachers want to be hired early, and as we hired teachers who were first-year teachers, it was important their teams be invested in them as candidates and colleagues. We cannot overestimate the power of talented teachers in transformation work.

Downtown Academy teachers at our retreat to kick off the 2018–2019 school year, my first year as principal.

The experience of being principal of Downtown Academy taught me how important the interplay between research, policy, and practice, as Dr. Ofelia Garcia and others often speak about, must be attended to in this work.

It was clear from the professional development I had to engage with as a school leader that much of the field of dual language had taken multiple steps forward, and we needed to better align our practices within the school to support students' learning. Whether it was a focus on Dr. Kathy Escamilla's work on biliteracy or the need to understand translanguaging and metalinguistic connections, the professional development for teachers and staff was critical to the transformative work of the school (see more on effective Professional Development for Dual Language educators in chapter 7). We holistically improved and prioritized teacher planning, strong instructional materials, and building bridges between languages and content. Additionally, we needed to upgrade our language allocation plans, our focus on foundational skills in English and Spanish, and progress monitoring the growth of our students in both program languages. With support from the district, we also created a better process and tightened up our language of assessment plans for state testing. As principals, we cannot leave it to chance that our students are able to take their state tests in the language they will do best in. We cannot just move students into English testing without strong data to inform our decisions. We also have to understand that the state test is also not a true indication of our dual language program at work, meaning we cannot test students who are still developing their Spanish in third grade and test them in Spanish on the state assessment simply to see how their Spanish language development is coming along. We have to use other benchmarks for that because we know language development takes 4 to 7 years. That is why why we consistently saw much stronger data in our middle school: a true testament to the Thomas and Collier research, and why maintaining dual language programs into high school is necessary.

A key feature of this work was in the utilization of Diario Duo, which enabled us to see students' growth in writing through monthly writing samples that were displayed across the school. We chose this instructional priority because we know the cognitive demands that writing requires and the fact that it is a reciprocal process with reading. The school had stronger results in reading than in math, so focusing on writing allowed us to ensure that all arrows were pointed in the right direction and that all teachers at the school, including our specials teachers, received professional development and could engage in student work protocols during our professional learning communities and in ghost walk protocols for learning.

My experience in working with families and staff also saw new opportunities for advocacy and innovation in our programming. The school brought more culturally sustaining and responsive practices, such as the expansion of Mexican American Studies (MAS) (approved by the Texas State Board of Education) into middle school. One teacher had already begun teaching MAS in middle school. Elementary school teachers also introduced an MAS club so they could receive similar experiences. We also introduced the first school-based accordion-conjunto program in a public San Antonio school to expand our fine arts offerings and took a long-standing tradition of the community in its conjunto history to connect with students. The school already had a theater teacher and an art teacher, and we added one more and were able to expand from one music teacher to two, solidifying our guitar class in our master schedule as well.

Throughout this school transformation experience, the district where Downtown Academy is located was also expanding dual language programs, now spanning PK through twelfth grade at sixty-two out of the 100 schools, reaching more neighborhood schools, seven high schools, and the establishment of two wall-to-wall dual language schools. The school board also officially adopted TWDL as its preferred program, stating that it would be adopted to the maximum extent possible. Such a commitment to dual language also comes from listening to your community and engaging families in powerful ways.

THE URGENCY

As of October 5, 2021, the American Councils Research Center (ARC) announced the results of a systematic national canvass of Dual Language Immersion (DLI) programs in the United States. The results indicate that there are more than 3,600 DLI programs across the United States. Forty-four states report producing DLI programs, and California, New York, North Carolina, Texas, and Utah account for almost 60 percent of all programs. Spanish programs account for about 80 percent of all DLI programs, followed by Chinese (8.6 percent) and French (5.0 percent). These programs are a cost-effective approach to elevating equity and access with accountability in U.S. language education (American Councils of International Education, 2021).

Both California and Texas have strong declarations about the critical nature and importance of dual language programs and a focus on the improvement in outcomes for emergent bilingual and multilingual learners. Whether through adoption of legislative priorities or state board of education policies, these two states are examples of the urgency of ensuring that more students have access to a high-quality and linguistically responsive education. Across the country, more states, including Alabama, Louisiana, and Virginia, are focused on following the footsteps of states that are leading the way in bilingual education, but we still have such a long way to go nationally. We now do a dive into the guidelines in each of our respective states to better understand implications for our work and lessons learned.

In July 2017, the California State Board of Education (SBE) unanimously approved the English Learner (EL) Roadmap Policy, which lays a foundation for the education of language learners in TK through grade 12. The EL Roadmap Policy identifies high-quality multilingual programs as the most effective approach to educating MLLs (California Department of Education [CDE], 2017). The SBE policy ushers in a new era of MLL education that embraces linguistic diversity as an asset while providing the support necessary to allow learners meaningful access to an intellectually rich and engaging curriculum (CDE, 2017). This policy calls for the work on providing the support needed to ensure that MLLs have the same academic opportunities as English-only students. Getting familiar with this policy, going over this with your staff and families, and using it as a guide for your work as an administrator will shift the thinking about MLLs from a deficit- to an assets-oriented approach for your program. You can do this by unpacking each section, but especially Principle 1: Assets-Oriented and Needs Responsive Schools and Principle 2: Intellectual Quality of Instruction and Meaningful Access so that all teachers at your school site are on the same page about how to implement the two principles that apply to them most in their classrooms. Administrators, however, should also get to know Principle 3: System Conditions That Support Effectiveness and Principle 4: Alignment and Articulation Within and Across Systems. Specifically, administrators can work on how to implement all four principles with their principal colleagues by using the toolkits that have been developed for them. Use the adjacent QR Code to view the full road map policy.

English Learner (EL) Road Map Policy

In Texas, whether it's been through additional funding provided through House Bill 3 that increased and incentivized funding for dual language programs or the call for a strategic plan to improve outcomes for bilingual education as outlined in Senate Bill 560, steps are being taken to center the experience of multilingual and emergent bilingual students. The Texas Education Agency (TEA) also published the Texas Effective Dual Language Immersion Framework in 2021, focused on sharing key knowledge and actionable steps districts and schools can take to align their dual language work. The framework includes a rubric, checklists, and success criteria. TEA is the first state agency to design and release a framework for dual language. Districts across Texas are leveraging this framework to establish and refine programs with a focus on the key levers and essential actions. Building on the feedback from voters on Proposition 58 (2016), another California initiative emerged: *Global California 2030 Initiative: Speak. Learn. Lead* (CDE, 2018; for more on this, see chapter 1). In Texas, the state legislature passed Senate Bill 560: A Strategic Plan to Improve and Expand Bilingual Education. This bill requires TEA in collaboration with the Texas Higher Education Coordinating Board (THECB) and the Texas Workforce Commission (TWC) to set tangible goals and timelines that will focus on several aspects of bilingual education, including the expansion of one-way and two-way dual language programs.

A recent grant in California, the Dual Language Immersion Grant (DLIG), was established by Assembly Bill 130, chapter 44, Section 158 of the Statutes of 2021, to expand access to quality dual language learning and foster languages that MLLs bring to California's education system. It requires grantees to provide integrated language learning and academic instruction in elementary and secondary schools for native speakers of English and native speakers of another language, with the goals of high academic achievement, first and second language proficiency, and cross-cultural understanding (CDE, 2021). The DLIG has selected twenty-seven schools and districts, and each of them is receiving up to $400,000 to expand a current DLI program or establish a new one. With this new grant and more flexibility and resources to open dual language programs across California, school districts are developing, implementing, and expanding DLI programs.

In Texas, dual language schools that were brand-new leveraged funding from the state totaling $800,000 per school to be spent over 2 years for start-up costs. Through Senate Bill 1882, signed into effect by the Texas Legislature in 2017, incentives are provided for districts that partner with an open-enrollment charter school, institutions of higher education, nonprofits, or government entities. Both of these initiatives in California and Texas highlight the importance of state-driven policy and support to expand access to dual language programs. Many other states can learn from the lessons each state is experiencing as they implement this work, and champion dual language as the bar to ensure that our students receive the education they deserve.

Expanding the number of students who speak two or more languages will require more teachers and more programs to train those teachers. It will also require school leadership and superintendency preparation programs to ensure that there is systemic alignment and knowledge building around dual language. Unfortunately, we are far from solving this issue across the United States. More than half of states nationwide are experiencing bilingual teacher shortages, with shortages most acute in states that provide bilingual education to the greatest numbers of MLLs. These shortages were happening pre-pandemic and have only been exacerbated in the last few years. For more on teacher shortages, see chapter 7. For now, let's focus on possible solutions to adding more bilingual staff to your schools.

Partnerships between school districts and universities should be one of the key components to recruiting highly qualified bilingual and dual language teachers to create strong and successful programs that truly meet the academic, linguistic, and cultural needs of our students. When these partnerships are created, a shared vision will be supported with units and sessions that will align with school districts' visions and missions toward multilingualism. Additionally, the research is clear that when students have educators who share their racial, ethnic, and linguistic identities, student outcomes improve.

As part of David's work at Downtown Academy, the school worked to grow the partnership with the University of Texas at San Antonio, expanding how preservice teachers were embedded in their field placements. The school and university, along with the district, worked to align around the curriculum students were being taught, including the research based for dual language and biliteracy. Along with guidance from US PREP, they also increased the time of residency both regarding time during the day and in scope of activities preservices teachers had opportunities to shadow teachers doing, including professional development, grade-level meetings, faculty meetings, special education, dyslexia, and multilingual and dual language learning.

Another example is the Bilingual Authorization Program at California State University, Fullerton (CSUF). From 2014 to 2022, CSUF has multiplied by four the number of Bilingual Authorized Program completers. The work CSUF and other CSU campuses are doing has received substantial support with Assembly Bill 178 Budget Act 2022. Part of the $5,000,000 funds for this item is dedicated to increasing the number of credentialed teachers with Asian bilingual authorization. This initiative, among others, is a clear statement that the state of California is responding to the call for an increase in the number of teaching credential candidates who complete their programs with the Bilingual Authorization (Fernando Rodríguez-Valls, PhD Professor, California State University, Fullerton, personal communication).

> ## Consejito
>
> Check out universities around your community and neighboring cities, and see if they are offering the Bilingual Credential for new teachers. If so, invite them to learn about your program and create a system where any future bilingual teachers can join your school during their student teaching practice weeks. Consider "grow your own" programs as well to tap into the potential teacher pipeline you have within your own paraprofessional staff, which often reflects the community and among whom languages other than English might be a part of the skill set.

A national program that can help is the Exchange Visitor Program. The U.S. Department of State administers the Exchange Visitor Program under the provisions of the Mutual Educational and Cultural Exchange Act of 1961, as Amended. The Exchange Visitor Program for Teachers is a program with a long tradition in the United States (since 1986) whereby Spanish language teachers provide services as Spanish teachers in primary and secondary schools in the United States and Canada. The program promotes the interchange of knowledge and skills, mutual enrichment, and stronger links between research and educational institutions in the United States and foreign countries. The purpose of the Act is to increase mutual understanding between the people of the United States and the people of other countries by means of educational and cultural exchanges. All Exchange Visitors are registered in the Student and Exchange Visitor Information System.

The visiting teachers may remain in a school district or charter school for a maximum of 3 years and then are expected to return to their home country to share their experiences. School districts or charter schools may apply for an *extension beyond maximum duration* for an additional 1 or 2 years. The purpose of the Exchange Visitor Program is to promote the following:

- Cross-cultural exchanges
- Understanding and respect between U.S. teachers and non-U.S. teachers
- Professional growth opportunities for teachers and other countries
- Interest in international studies and cross-cultural awareness

Visit the link at bit.ly/43S6E0k for a brochure with more information about the Exchange Visitor Program.

As we continue to see an increase of dual language programs but a decrease of bilingual teachers, we need to be proactive and find the advantages of promoting the Seal of Biliteracy at schools so these students can turn into our future dual language educators. The Biliteracy Pathway Recognitions are established to recognize PK–eighth-grade students who have demonstrated progress toward proficiency in one or more languages in addition to English (Biliteracy Awards). Building pathways to biliteracy requires communities and school leaders to become familiar with the variety of language program options, the research behind them, and the conditions that support effective implementation. A collaborative process of dialogue about goals and purposes and planning for appropriate options for each community should engage all stakeholders. The California Department of Education has a Multilingual Support Division that supports local education agencies that may be looking into adding Biliteracy Awards and the Seal of Biliteracy for students. These resources can be used during workshops for parents where the information can be used to align with the benefits of being bilingual and the opportunities in education, and can start conversations at home about education and the opportunities for bilingual teachers.

RESEARCH BASE

A clearly delineated dual language program structure supports the three pillars of Dual Language Education (DLE): bilingualism and biliteracy, high academic achievement in both program languages, and sociocultural competence for all students. The latest research also proposes a fourth fundamental goal for TWDL education: critical consciousness for all (Palmer et al., 2019).

LOLA Language Academy Parent Night for incoming Transitional Kindergarten, and Kindergarten Students to the school. Educating parents on the three pillars of DLE and 4+1 language domains.

As equity continues to be a significant issue in DLE, policies need to ensure quality and rigorous instruction for all learners with a focus on MLLs who bring languages other than English to school. When school leaders and district administrators center their attention on strategic planning for the improvement of services and programs for students who are historically marginalized, and on the support for leaders to become effective and equity-focused with learners, what results is a powerful and effective education for all learners.

As a direct response to previous, deficit-based models that dominated education, there has been an increase in learning how to implement asset-based pedagogies in dual language schools. These asset-based pedagogies focus on the strengths that diverse students bring to the classroom, promoting equity for an increasingly diverse student population that still relies on educators viewing their differences as assets and not deficits. High-quality instruction and systems of support benefit students in a bilingual setting in strong dual language programs.

If critical consciousness for students, teachers, parents, and leaders is infused in the curriculum, pedagogy, policies, and leadership of TWDL programs, all involved will better maintain a focus on equity and fulfill their potential to support a more integrated and socially just society (Palmer et al., 2019).

As leaders, we must focus not only on bilingualism and biliteracy, academic achievement, and sociocultural competence, but also on calling out the inequities in the curricula and programs. Leaders must try to give voice to staff members and stakeholders to work together and make changes for an equitable and inclusive program for all. The more we educate ourselves as staff members and members of the community, the better we can serve our students. In your school, this might look like an intentional learning series focused on equity, engaging in shared readings to build knowledge and context, and attending to the gaps you might find in core curriculum due to a lack of a representation of your students' identities and languages.

> As a DL school leader, Marga explains how she intentionally grounds her day-to-day experiences in evidence-based research. For example, any new initiatives are always aligned with the Guiding Principles for DL Education, research in critical consciousness, and the school's mission and vision.
>
> **Lyn**

Consejito

Continue your fight for what is right for students during your monthly staff meetings with conversations about critical consciousness. Find articles calling for commitment to challenging social, cultural, and economic inequalities and be an advocate for culturally and linguistically representative curricular materials, ensuring authentic literature and stories that will showcase our communities as well. Ultimately, and as Dr. José Medina always mentions, DLE, and education in other settings, at the core, is about reparation for the oppression that we have inflicted on culturally and linguistically diverse student communities in U.S. schools.

The Guiding Principles for Dual Language Education is a resource for all practitioners that gives us a common framework and language that can guide our dual language work and instruction. Providing your staff with guiding principles should be the first action item for leaders implementing dual language programs, and they should be the foundation for all decision making. This is true at all levels. Superintendents, chief academic officers, assistant superintendents of school leadership, content executive directors, instructional coaches, front office staff, and anyone who works in a dual language district or school should be knowledgeable. For more on the Guiding Principles, see chapter 1.

Additionally, the C6 Biliteracy Instructional Framework from Dr. José Medina (2018) should also inform your school's thinking. The 6 Cs are create, connect, collaborate, communicate, consider, and commit. This framework is designed to create access to grade-level standards regardless of student language proficiency. It is also aligned to the *Guiding Principles for Dual Language Education, 3rd Edition*, and this framework targets the attainment of the three goals of dual language. Any school can use the C6 Framework since it may be used in dual, bilingual, and/or monolingual school settings because of the additive nature of the framework (Medina, 2018).

As former school leaders, we must note that the pressures of state accountability, educator beliefs, and even at times family requests can dilute the effectiveness of a dual language program when not followed with fidelity. State and district systems that fail to adequately support dual language programs and allow some practices on the superficial level run the risk of being dual language only in name, which is why it's important for us as a community to be rigorous and hold high expectations in the implementation of our students' bilingual programs. Moving away from a *pobrecito* (poor kid) mindset will enable us to fully see the assets and superpowers that our multilingual students bring.

We also want to impress the ownership school leaders need to take in being a part of and inspecting language of assessment decisions for state testing. At Downtown Academy, David worked closely with district staff and trained teachers on expectations related to the data that needed to be used to inform decisions for selecting the language of assessment (Spanish or English in Texas from grades 3 to 5). The district staff also audited decisions to make sure they were triangulating data on students who were on the cusp of proficiency between English and Spanish. District and school leaders need to ensure that these decisions are not made lightly and that they are informed by data, always.

> Building bilingual educators' capacity to understand the research that supports biliteracy instruction is crucial for the sustainability and expansion of dual language programs. To provide equitable education for all multilingual learners, professional learning must aim to prepare bilingual teachers to become instructional leaders and advocates in their field.
>
> **Rubí**

IMPLICATIONS FOR PRACTICE AND IMPLEMENTATION

In this next section, we go deeper into *Guiding Principles for Dual Language Education* with examples from our work. While all of the guiding principles are important, we've selected a few to highlight and dive into.

Because new hires might join your school throughout the year, the need for continuous program alignment can be met using the *Guiding Principles for Dual Language Education*. All new teachers should receive a copy at the beginning of the school year, even if some of them are already familiar with this resource. The Practice and Implementation of the seven strands in the *Guiding Principles for Dual Language Education* is a particularly powerful and effective instructional approach you can employ as a cohesive team.

Within the Guiding Principles, there is also Appendix A: Templates for Self-Evaluation. The tools found here are great to utilize with your team whether you have a newly opened program or a well-developed one. These templates can be used to document evidence of the program's level implementation for each principle and key point, to compare the perspectives of stakeholders on the current level of implementation, and to identify current strengths of your program and areas in need of improvement. The progress indicators are intended to provide a path that programs can follow toward mastery of the principle and beyond, as well as a metric on which current practice can be appraised (Howard et al., 2018).

FIGURE 6.1 Appendix A: Templates for Self-Evaluation / Strand 3: Instruction

STRAND 3: INSTRUCTION

Principle 1
Instructional methods are derived from research-based principles of dual language education and ensure fidelity to the model.

Key Points	Comments	M	P	F	E
Key Point A The program model and corresponding curriculum are implemented with fidelity.					
Key Point B Instruction incorporates appropriate separation of languages to promote high levels of language acquisition.					
Key Point C Standards-based academic content instruction is provided in both program languages in a coordinated way.					
Key Point D Explicit language arts instruction is provided in both program languages, is based on language-specific standards, and is coordinated across languages to ensure biliteracy development.					
Key Point E Instruction that promotes sociocultural competence is provided in both program languages in a coordinated way.					
Key Point F Teachers who provide support services (e.g., special education, gifted education, ESL) and specials (e.g., art, music) align their instruction with the dual language model.					
Key Point G When delivering instruction, teachers take into consideration the varying needs of students with different language learner profiles (e.g., native speakers, second language learners, new arrivals, students who are already bilingual in English and the partner language).					

Principle 2
Instructional strategies support the attainment of the three core goals of dual language education.

Key Points	Comments	M	P	F	E
Key Point A Teachers integrate language and content instruction.					
Key Point B Teachers use sheltered instruction and other pedagogical strategies for bilingual learners to facilitate comprehension and promote language and literacy development.					
Key Point C Instruction in one language builds on concepts learned in the other language.					
Key Point D Instruction promotes metalinguistic awareness and metacognitive skills.					
Key Point E Instruction leverages students' bilingualism by strategically incorporating cross-linguistic strategies.					
Key Point F Instruction promotes an awareness of language variation.					
Key Point G Teachers use a variety of strategies to ensure equitable participation among all students.					
Key Point H Teachers use a variety of strategies to promote the sociocultural competence of all students.					

Principle 3
Instruction is student-centered.

Key Points	Comments	M	P	F	E
Key Point A Teachers use active learning strategies in order to meet the needs of diverse learners.					
Key Point B Teachers create meaningful opportunities for sustained language use.					
Key Point C Student grouping maximizes opportunities for students to benefit from peer models.					
Key Point D Instructional strategies build independence and ownership of the learning process.					

Principle 4
Instructional staff effectively integrate technology to deepen and enhance the learning process.

Key Points	Comments	M	P	F	E
Key Point A Instructional staff use technology tools to engage all learners.					
Key Point B Students use technology to display their understanding of content and to further develop their language and literacy skills in both program languages.					

M: Minimal alignment **P**: Partial alignment **F**: Full alignment **E**: Exemplary practice

Figure 6.1 shows an example of a Template for Self-Evaluation from Strand 3, Instruction. During LOLA's monthly scheduled TWDI meetings, participants would choose a strand to work on for the school year and would prepare self-evaluations as teachers, grade level, and school. After the strand was chosen, and self-evaluations compared, they would look for strategies, professional development, and learning rounds throughout the school year to move themselves from the alignment that resulted from the templates to the next one—and always shooting for exemplary practice. They used the information from the templates to schedule learning walks where teachers would observe each other and would look for student-centered instruction focusing on the four key points noted under Principle 3 (more on that next). After learning walks and observations from teachers to teachers, the next step was meeting to collaborate with notes and see if they were able to move from the progress indicators they initially found to the next one.

Consejito

This is a tool that should be used every year to identify your program's areas of strength and areas for growth. Once you have identified your program's areas of strength and areas for growth, we encourage you to select only one or two areas for growth that the team can focus on for the remainder of the year to move it to an area of strength.

Now, let's cover some key strands and principles. We also show examples of how we incorporated this work during our time as school leaders. We encourage readers to be inspired by these ideas and incorporate them in your dual language program, if they seem appropriate.

Strand 1: Program Structure

This strand and its principles are what really drive the program and are aligned to the Three Pillars of Bilingual Education. Within this strand exist four principles:

- **Principle 1.1:** All aspects of the program work together to achieve the three core goals of DLE: grade-level academic achievement, bilingualism and biliteracy, and sociocultural competence.

- **Principle 1.2:** The program ensures equity for all groups.

- **Principle 1.3:** The program has strong, effective, and knowledgeable leadership.

- **Principle 1.4:** An effective process is in place for continual program planning, implementation, and evaluation.

You can use this strand and its principles as an entry point for the rest of your program's features.

Principle 1.1

The focus here is on achieving the goals of the three pillars: bilingualism and biliteracy, academic achievement, and cross-cultural understanding for all students. The program in a dual language school needs to be well defined and articulated across grades because educators need continuity and alignment schoolwide. Your language allocation plan is key to this process, as is your stakeholders' (students, families, and staff) knowledge of the *why* behind dual language.

Principle 1.2

Equity can be achieved by getting to know all the students and families in our schools, as well as their backgrounds and traditions traditions. This means intentionally building community within your staff and with families through practices like "I Am" poems and language and culture stories, for example. The more you know about your students, families, and staff, the more you can ensure an equitable program based on their needs. Additionally, progress monitoring data of students' biliteracy trajectories through linguistically appropriate assessments is key. Academic outcomes must be at the center of how we ensure equity, and addressing discrepancies between groups of students is key.

Additionally, the high-quality instruction needs to be aligned; all grade levels in a school need to provide the same instruction with fidelity to the program model. Leaders should ensure that the instruction and program model are consistent across the grade levels.

Finally, we can ensure we are intentional in our work by having books in our school libraries that include bilingual books for all reading levels, as well as books that reflect students' cultures and identities. Leaders should also encourage and welcome families to visit their libraries and to read to students from books written in their languages. Families should be able to check out books if they do not have these resources at home. Given the recent increasingly polarized controversy around books and book bans, leaders have the responsibility to insist on diverse and robust selections of books for their students.

Picture of diverse books purchased for the LOLA school library

Principle 1.3

This principle is mainly aimed at the responsibility district offices and their Human Resources Departments have to ensure that principals and assistant principals hired to lead dual language programs must believe in the program they will be leading. Not only do they have to believe in it, but they also have to live it, make it their own, and participate in the decision making around it.

We strongly believe that if you are a principal who has been placed in a bilingual or dual language school and you do not believe in the program, then the program will not succeed. If you don't speak the languages of the programs, then you are not modeling the program. This does not mean you have to be fluent, yet engaging in the languages of your school matters. We have seen strong monolingual English principals and assistant principals who alongside their bilingual and biliterate colleagues help move the mission of the school forward.

Overall, it's important to ensure you have strong talent at all schools, and the skill sets and mindsets needed to lead a dual language school are something that should be vetted for intentionally in hiring practices. There is far too often a legacy of district and school leaders who do not understand the program, say it isn't working, and want to toss it out without understanding the needs of the community, without having an asset-based belief system about the power of bilingualism and biliteracy. Families should also be empowered to demand that their children receive strong school leadership that will support teachers and students to do their very best in pursuit of academic excellence. Including input from student, staff, and family voices in hiring processes is critical.

Principle 1.4

This principle is truly about ensuring that any changes made are informed by data as well as current research and are implemented in the interest of improvement. Leaders should prioritize ensuring that all students have a bilingual and dual language pathway through twelfth grade, and this can happen only with a commitment from the district to increase language acquisition, biliteracy, and college, career, and life preparedness.

Strand 2: Curriculum

The core curriculum for students in bilingual or dual language programs must be based on national and state achievement standards specific to bilingual or dual language programs for students learning English as a new language and growing in their native language. An effective curriculum includes literacy goals and objectives in the first language and for English as a new language development as well as content standards that are developmentally appropriate and properly scoped, sequenced, and articulated within and across grade levels. In addition, the curriculum must be structured so that students meet the ultimate goal of language instruction programs: becoming competent in listening, speaking, reading, and writing in their first language and English (Project Estrella, n.d.). Teachers and even district-created materials, while well-meaning, can often dilute the rigor and grade-level appropriateness needed for students. Within this strand exist three principles:

- **Principle 2.1:** The program has a process for developing and revising a high-quality curriculum.

- **Principle 2.2:** The curriculum is standards-based and promotes attainment of the three core goals of DLE.

- **Principle 2.3:** The curriculum effectively integrates technology to deepen and enhance learning.

Leaders must insist on curriculum that is linguistically and culturally appropriate and that meets the language allocation plans put in place for dual language or any other bilingual model.

Principle 2.1

This principle calls for training and equipping the faculty with the same information, protocols, systems, and processes. Program norms and protocols that are created at the beginning of the school year need to be reviewed and updated in subsequent years, and new protocols should be added when needed. English Language Development (ELD) and Spanish Language Development (SLD) must be included in the curricula to serve students who are learning those languages as a second language. This could look like sending your teachers to any district training aligned with your mission and vision so that all have the same knowledge, foundations, learned research, and strategies to better deliver the curriculum when teaching.

Leaders should also prioritize grade-level team meetings and professional learning communities to ensure that teachers collaborate with a goal of delivering instruction that meets the needs of all students; at the same time, we recommend coordinating vertical team meetings to have various grade levels working together to help students acquire the academic skills necessary for success.

Principle 2.2

Curriculum must be planned based on rigorous standards, and you should always include the two languages of the program. The work aligned to this principle can be done in many forms of appreciation of multiculturalism, for example, students in assemblies presenting to the rest of the school about their traditions, students sharing newly learned content about a new country with their classes, or learning with 123 Andrés—the Latin Grammy-winning children's music duo.

For example, Marga was often invited to classes to present her country of birth to students when they were learning about Europe during Continent Focus Learning time. This was a fun time because she would demonstrate how to play the castanets and have students taste some of her favorite snacks from Spain. At Downtown Academy, students had access to Mexican American Studies courses based on the state-approved ethnic studies programs. While not all students were Mexican American, considering San Antonio's history, students learned a lot about the community they lived in. This also built cultural awareness and appreciation for other cultures. Pre-pandemic, David, along with incredible educators, built the Mexican American Studies Leadership Institute that served over 100 students from twenty different schools in the district. Ensuring that students have access to culturally sustaining and responsive content is important in building self-knowledge and knowledge of other cultures.

Principle 2.3

Students can greatly benefit from an effective digital integration of technology in both languages. Not only are they able to access resources in two languages, but they also benefit from exposure to the technology itself. However, we offer a cautionary note: Books or online resources that are a strict translation from English to Spanish (or other target languages) or vice versa deny students the opportunity to appreciate the richness and authenticity of the language, so be sure to vet your resources. What leaders should aim for are authentic translations.

During the COVID-19 pandemic, laptops and often Wi-Fi were quickly introduced into children's homes and became more accessible in schools, but that did not close the digital gap overnight. It is important to note, however, that leveraging technology to support the 4+1 language domains and how to plan for that skillfully is an area we need to continue to grow in and receive professional development and coaching around.

While some think of technology as programs, technology can be as expansive as we choose to make it. For example, at Downtown Academy, we began to leverage FlipGrid so that students could practice their speaking and presentation skills during intentional portions of the lesson cycle and/or as assessment pieces. In Texas, we have the Texas English Language Proficiency Assessment System (TELPAS) that has moved to a digital platform, including for the speaking portion, so authentic practice through FlipGrid in the classroom can enhance students' learning and help make them familiar with how they will be assessed on TELPAS. Additionally, artificial intelligence use is rising across schools, so it's important that educators and students know how to navigate these new resources to support dual language learning.

Strand 3: Instruction

Dual language programs offer students the benefit of exposure to all content areas in both languages. "Effective instruction is associated with higher student outcomes, regardless of the educational model used (Hightower et al., 2011; Marzano, 2003; O'Day, 2009), and the effects of quality teaching are cumulative and long-lasting (Hightower et al., 2011)" (as cited in Howard et al., 2018). Within this strand exist two principles:

- **Principle 3.1:** Instructional methods are derived from research-based principles of DLE and ensure fidelity to the model.

- **Principle 3.2:** Instructional strategies support the attainment of the three core goals of DLE.

Principle 3.1

This principle is especially important for making hiring decisions. Dual language staff must have an understanding of the program requirements and methodologies, including what the classroom looks like, the use of color coding in classrooms (e.g., green for Spanish, blue for English, red for bridging), a knowledge of when and how to deliver lessons related to culture, and the ability to explain the program to families, community partners, or visitors to the school. Ideally, specialized support teachers (music teacher, PE teacher, art teacher, enrichment teacher, etc.) should also be bilingual to ensure that students receive dual language support over the course of the instructional minutes of the day. At Downtown Academy, writing was seen across the curriculum and across all the specials classrooms using "Talk, Read, Talk, Write" by Nancy Motely. Additionally, the school focused on *7 Steps to a Language Rich-Interactive Classroom* by John Seiltz and Billy Perryman, and *¡Toma la palabra!* by Monica Lara. All teachers saw themselves as language teachers. It is imperative to also hire special education and dyslexia teachers who speak the program's target language and English.

Creating class rosters in dual language schools requires special consideration of the students' home languages. For example, when a class incorporates one third of English-only speaking students, one third of Spanish-only speaking students, and one third of bilingual English-Spanish students, all students will be able to be the models of instruction in the target language. When a classroom is balanced with that equation, it provides all students with the instruction necessary to allow them to be exposed to the language target, and they learn from peers who also participate in the classroom using the language we want the students to learn. In a one-way model, that balance will generally happen more naturally; however, as we've seen the gentrification of programs, it's important to hold true to ensuring that the program stays focused on meeting the needs of your students who are most historically marginalized.

Principle 3.2

Here, it is important to focus on the 4+1 language domains: listening, reading, speaking, and writing, plus metalinguistic awareness. Bridging is another word for the plus one in the 4+1 domains. This metalinguistic awareness is the natural state for our bilingual students when they are making those connections. As Dr. José Medina says, "[M]etalanguaging is the command of the language that allows students to make natural connections between the languages that are part of their linguistic repertoire." This can be achieved by providing students with the 4+1 language domains icon system, created by the Language Learners/Dual Language Department for all dual language schools in the district. Teachers can refer to these icons and use them in their daily lessons. Students can also own the language domains when engaged in active student participation strategies. At LOLA, these 4+1 language domains were sent home at the beginning of the school year so that students continued their learning by referring to them when doing homework or working on projects. If there is a language domains icon system and the students know how to use the icons, the students can own this process.

Strand 4: Assessment and Accountability

This strand and its five principles are key to the Dual Language work. The five principles are as follows:

- **Principle 4.1:** The program creates and maintains an infrastructure that supports an assessment and accountability process.

- **Principle 4.2:** Student assessment is aligned with program goals and with state content and language standards, and the results are used to guide and inform instruction.

- **Principle 4.3:** Using multiple measures in both languages of instruction, the program collects and analyzes a variety of data that are used for program accountability, program evaluation, and program improvement.

- **Principle 4.4:** Student progress toward program goals and state achievement objectives is systematically measured and reported.

- **Principle 4.5:** The program communicates with appropriate stakeholders about program outcomes.

While we do not go into depth on this strand, we wanted to highlight that one of the greatest challenges in a DLI program is identifying where the program is regarding the trajectory of high academic achievement seen in the research literature. Developing and implementing an assessment and evaluation plan is only the beginning of the work. There is a need for a well-planned assessment and data conversation schedule, and during every trimester and/or quarterly evaluation, there must be data analyzing what is working and what is not working. Leaders should constantly ask themselves, "What should we teach again, and what can we skip since the students are mastering those standards?" It is our responsibility as school leaders to work with the information we receive about the results and make plans of action.

One way leaders can gather such data is by providing intentional team planning and/or collaboration days during the school year. These planning days become powerful opportunities for teachers to engage in rich conversations around what is going well, areas for improvement, and specific actions they need to take to adjust instruction. For a deeper dive on assessment, please see chapter 4.

Strand 5: Staff Quality and Professional Development

This strand covers a critically important component of successful dual education schools and programs. Principals play an important role in both hiring decisions and creating opportunities for high-quality professional learning. School leaders need to attend to the varied learning needs of their staff and work to build up teaching excellence and cohesive systems for learning. The principles in this strand are the following:

- **Principle 5.1:** The program recruits and retains high-quality dual language staff.

- **Principle 5.2:** The program provides high-quality professional development that is tailored to the needs of dual language educators and support staff.

- **Principle 5.3:** The program collaborates with other groups and institutions to ensure staff quality.

Principle 5.1

Effective staff have a great impact on turning schools into successful dual language programs. We both consider ourselves social butterflies, and we are always meeting new people all the time, especially when attending conferences. These conferences are the best place to meet bilingual educators from all over the country. They are also prime locations for recruiting bilingual educators. Leaders should prioritize attending not only state-based conferences, but also national ones as well. We highly recommend La Cosecha, one of, perhaps the largest convening of dual language researchers and practitioners in the country. The most important part in this principle is ensuring that your staff is committed to the program. Recruiting highly qualified staff means that all staff members in your school need to be committed to bilingual education.

Office staff should also be bilingual and able to communicate with students, families, and the community. Having hiring components, such as role-plays, that ensure individuals can perform tasks associated with their job is important. Leaders should ask candidates about their knowledge of dual language programs. If they are comfortable doing a scenario in the target language, make it a part of your hiring process. Most important, get to the root of the beliefs about meeting the needs of your diverse student population and families.

As mentioned earlier in the chapter, another possibility is hiring teachers using an exchange program and forming strong partnerships with state universities. For example, during her time as principal at LOLA Language Academy, Marga hired teachers from the visiting teacher program and had the honor of working with bilingual professionals from Spain and Mexico. Another organization that might be of interest when you are hiring qualified bilingual teachers is the Amity Institute. We offer the following timeline and tips for leaders who would like to enhance their staff with these hires (see figure 6.2).

> In many communities, myths and misconceptions about biliteracy and multilingual instruction continue to overshadow the benefits of DLE. Leaders must have a plan to build capacity across all stakeholder groups on the foundations of DLE. All district staff must have common language and research data to share when addressing questions and concerns from families and the community.
>
> **Rubí**

New Teachers from Spain and Mexico for the 2021–2022 school year with Marga Marshall (third from left)

FIGURE 6.2 Tips for Dual Language Program Administrators Interested in Participating in the Visiting Teachers Program

Timeline	Tips for Dual Language Programs Administrators
November–December	Plan out the need for bilingual teachers for the next school year.
January	Attend the CDE/Office of Education Presentation about the Visiting Teachers Program.
February	Administrators submit their requests for teachers.
March	Send "Agreement of Collaboration" to CDE/Spain Office of Education.
April–May	Virtual interviews will be conducted tentatively between April and mid-May (dates vary every year). After the interview, if interested in a candidate, send a Letter of Offer of Employment.
May–June	Contact candidates for their tentative assignments for the next school year.
June–July	Continue contact with new visiting teachers and support with links about the district, school assignment, and platforms to get familiar with. When visiting teachers arrive, support with getting familiar with the town, district, and school; help in assisting in getting their Social Security cards, support with housing—best areas, safe areas to stay—schedule contract signing with HR (if more than one teacher coming to the same district, schedule all together for an easier meeting).

Timeline	Tips for Dual Language Programs Administrators
August	Welcome visiting teacher(s) to school, assigned classroom, school calendar, and schedules. Meet and go over Dual Program Norms and Protocols, give a copy of *Guiding Principles for Dual Language Education*, and contact a TISP coach if applicable to help get teachers familiar with the educational system.
September–June	Continue to support teacher(s) throughout the school year in chunks. Meet before Back to School Night, Parent-Teacher conferences, Field Trips, Assemblies, and so on so they know the expectations and guidelines of these key components of the school for a successful school year.

One standout teacher was Beatríz Rodríguez de Cepeda, one of the teachers who joined LOLA through the Spain Visiting Teachers Program during the opening 2017 school year. Of the experience, she shares the following:

My experience in the Visiting Teachers Program was without a doubt a turning point in my professional career. If there is an intention to work from an intercultural approach, a stay outside the educational system in which we have been trained as students, and of which we want to be part of as teachers, this should be mandatory, with the goal of not repeating patterns that don't work and creating change in the classroom.

Given the large number of dual language programs that have been implemented, it is necessary to observe, reflect, and share globally to grow as teachers and then be able to select the most convenient programs, strategies, and methodologies in our school context.

Beatríz explains that during her time at LOLA

deconstructing and rethinking ourselves as teachers was a hard process, but when you have a great team and leadership that supports you, the teaching process gets easier. In my case, being from Spain and coming as an exchange visiting teacher, this school was my family. It was my first experience in a dual immersion school. Principal Marshall increased my strengths and supported me in my professional development, sending me to conferences, training and coaching me in strategies to be used in our bilingual school, and providing meaningful Two-Way Dual Immersion meetings based on the *Guiding Principles for Dual Language Education*, a training process based on practice and reflection that provided me with the tools needed to be able to implement strategies at the moment in my classroom and that allowed us to observe that everything made sense, that it worked. I will always remember how I even had the opportunity to have the visit of Dr. José Medina in my classroom and my class full of materials that my principal had provided me with such as color charts to facilitate the transfer and bridging process and pictures of the Three Pillars of Dual

Education. . . . During my time at this school under Marga's leadership, I felt supported and strong on the education I was providing to my students.

To further our mission of increasing to promote the rise of dual language programs after Proposition 58, Marga teamed up with Dr. Rodríguez-Valls, COE, Bilingual Authorization Program Coordinator from the California State University, Fullerton, to present to his classes about the *Guiding Principles for Dual Language Education*. The future bilingual educators would collaborate on an engaging presentation where they were able to make connections with the work done in class and what it would look like when they worked in a bilingual class. This was a very positive partnership because the presentation was based on feedback new bilingual teachers usually shared on the lack of preparation to be successful in bilingual schools. Dr. Rodríguez-Valls is always up-to-date in teaching policies and frameworks to his college students and how to implement best practices as his students get ready for the bilingual education field.

When Marga hired Ariana Cárdenas as the Bilingual School Secretary, she immediately learned the program vision, mission, and program structure to be prepared for her position. School secretaries are the face of the school, so when Ariana would answer the phone or assist families visiting the school office, she drew on her training to explain the program, the teacher partnering work, and the 50/50 program model. When asking her about joining the team, Ariana shares,

> When Principal Marshall approached me with the chance to utilize my biliteracy on a daily basis, I jumped at the chance. The opportunity for me to explain the program to new families searching for schools for their new students was very rewarding. Not only was I able to explain the program in English, but I was able to inform our Spanish-speaking parents as well of this wonderful opportunity. Many of them were delighted to learn that their student would have two teachers for instruction 50/50 percent of the time. They were extremely thankful that this program was being offered at a public school, not having to pay the high tuition in which these programs are usually offered. I would explain to them that current students who had English as their first language would come into the office and I would ask questions in Spanish, in which they would respond perfectly in Spanish, it was so #LOLAwesome!

Ariana also shares that informing families about how the program worked—as well as telling the families that everything from school signs, announcements, award certificates, and much more was done in both languages—made the parents' commitment to having their students at LOLA even easier. She believed that having the correct bilingual program information at hand was key in helping our new parents make the decision to enroll their student at LOLA. "Families hung up the phone reassured that they were making the best decision for their student by enrolling in a program that is now becoming more popular in California and beyond."

Similarly, leaders must be every bit as discerning when hiring stewards for dual language schools, as well as carefully train future dual immersion principals to be prepared to lead this program. All who are to be involved in the program must be fully educated on what they need to make the program successful. If this program is going to be implemented at your district, the board, the superintendent, and the core district need to be fully aware of the curriculum and of the rigorous endeavor that it takes to run the program and make it successful. Start by learning about the program from your district's Multilingual Learner Master Plan. What kind of program is at your school? How does it work? Are there other schools you could partner with? What is the district's plan for middle school, high school?

Consejito

Attend state and national conferences with specific training for Dual Language Administrators. Every spring the California Association for Bilingual Education (CABE) offers a fantastic conference with sessions for new and experienced dual language leaders. In the past, CABE has also offered the Administrative Leadership Success Series for dual language administrators to develop expertise around effective program, structure, staff quality, support and resources, and professional development for dual language programs.

Principle 5.2

This principle is another that is vital to the success of any dual language program.

The research literature is replete with studies demonstrating the importance of training to promote more successful administrators, teachers, and staff (Ballantyne et al., 2008; Epstein et al., 2016; Mater et al., 2016; Valdés, Menken, & Castro, 2015) as well as higher student achievement (Master et al., 2016; Valdés et al., 2015). (as cited in Howard et al., 2018)

At Downtown Academy, David established a professional learning committee of staff who would give input and help design and implement the professional development of the entire staff. It was important that teachers in both the monolingual classes and dual language classes had the opportunity to plan together, and this was prioritized during additional professional development days that were added to the instructional calendar. Downtown Academy also partnered with district content leads and bilingual specialists to support staff learning throughout the school year. Professional development days at

Downtown Academy also focused on educator well-being and giving staff choice and voice in how they approached their own learning as adults. There were unified learning experiences on priority areas as well as grade-level and content-specific training. By providing the priorities, the professional learning committee could ensure that staff were getting relevant and timely learning experiences. Professional development schedules were shared in advance, and community building was an important part of that continued work for staff culture. An integrated approach to professional development is key.

Strand 6: Family and Community

"Family engagement is ongoing, meaningful interaction between schools and families that is characterized by two-way communication. Its focus is on supporting student learning (Garcia et al., 2016)" (original emphasis removed, as cited in Snyder & Fenner, 2021). Studies show that family involvement in the school environment leads to student success.

> A significant feature of effective programs is the incorporation of family and community engagement and collaboration with the school (National Academies, 2017). Research shows that most families of ethnically and linguistically diverse students have high aspirations for their children and want to be involved in promoting their academic success (Glick & White, 2004; Ji & Koblinsky, 2009; Lindholm-Leary, 2001; Sibley & Dearing, 2014). (as cited in Howard et al., 2018)

The principles in this strand are the following:

- **Principle 6.1:** The program has a responsive infrastructure for positive, active, and ongoing relations with students' families and the community.
- **Principle 6.2:** The program promotes family and community engagement and advocacy through outreach activities and support services that are aligned with the three core goals of DLE.
- **Principle 6.3:** The program views and involves families and community members as strategic partners.

Principle 6.1

Families are key in growing and sustaining a dual language program. Being able to continue engaging them and developing a partnership in support of the program as it grows is extremely critical. As school leaders in dual language programs, we need to provide opportunities for families to be active participants in the school and classroom. All family and community members need to be welcomed because their voices are important to improving our programs.

Both Marga and David prioritized authentic family engagement and empowerment from the start. David would invite families in as partners in their child's education; the growth of their involvement was tangible.

By going beyond the traditional ways of engaging families, Downtown Academy increased its family engagement through ensuring language access and multiple methods of communication. From weekly messages shared via text, email, and Facebook lives, David focused on ensuring that families were informed. An important and intentional decision David made was to always send messages (including via social media) in the target language of Spanish first. This choice was grounded in elevating the target language and ensuring that families saw the representation of both program languages. Meetings were translated simultaneously and often started in Spanish; then English was interwoven. Families were also looped into how the school was measuring growth, its academic focus areas, including writing and math, as well as activity in small-group efforts. Many families volunteered to support small-group instruction, especially Spanish-speaking families who were welcomed as volunteers, several of whom also eventually were hired on as subs. Their perspectives as family members and staff were vital to helping the school build bridges of understanding. It is important to note that all the family engagement and empowerment work at Downtown Academy was the history of the community in many ways; however, when David started it was made clear to him that some Spanish-speaking families had not felt as empowered. The same was true for families at the nearby Section 8, low-income apartments, where many heritage language speakers and students in the monolingual program families lived. David and the staff set out to ensure inclusion by establishing a family engagement committee with staff. Events were even held at a site close to the apartments, and the school worked with the apartments to ensure signs for main school events were put up in the apartments.

Last, it was important to ensure that the staff at Downtown Academy had training to support all students. This included training with the Parent and Friends of Lesbian and Gay (PFLAG) organization and the Transgender Education Network of Texas, recognizing the intersectionality of our students as well as the need to support our educators in creating welcoming environments. Being more systematic and prioritizing this development around identity and how to create supportive classrooms is vital.

Marga knew how important it is to focus on the fourth fundamental goal—critical consciousness—and provided tools and resources to support culturally and linguistically diverse students and their families. At LOLA, these resources were found in the lessons provided to students or in articles on weekly newsletters for families and workshops offered to families and community members. Those culturally and linguistically diverse lessons were intentionally planned by our teachers using their knowledge about our students' cultures and backgrounds as they designed and delivered effective instruction. Meanwhile, parents learned what was happening in the class from teachers sharing with families in their weekly and monthly newsletters.

All communications to families were always bilingual, and they always included the mission or vision of the school. In her weekly *Mensaje de la*

Directora, Marga included what to expect next week or month and what had happened during the week, and resources were sent to families to help support their students at home. Resources included articles about the benefits of being bilingual, and many more related to DLE. That way, families were always informed of the latest best practices as part of the positive, active, and ongoing relationships with students' families and the community.

Principle 6.2

Leaders can use many strategies in this principle to build strong partnerships with our families and community. For example, at LOLA Language Academy, there was a weekly letter to families (*Mensaje de la Directora*). The call messages always went out in both Spanish and English, all school signs through the school were bilingual, and the social media platforms (Twitter, Instagram, and Facebook) always posted in both languages. Marga would also collaborate very closely with the school's Parent Faculty Club Committee, and during the school year they would plan and organize Cultural Reading Nights, campus beautification days, Science Fairs, Unity Day, Great Kindness Challenge Week, Multicultural Night, and many other cultural events that were always well attended by LOLA's families and the community.

We understood that family involvement was more than a plus, and we planned Family Workshops during the school year. A Google Form was sent to families for feedback on what they were interested in learning about, and our teaching team worked together to plan and organize evening sessions for our families. Our Family Workshops always included a principal presentation about our TWDL program. We shared data about the school program, and we went over the importance of the 4+1 language domains. After the main presentation, different sessions were offered to parents, like literacy, reading strategies, Spanish support, and so on. This was always a well-received event with high interest and attendance.

Another family and community engagement activity was #FollowMeFriday. Typically, it involved a 12-minute walk around the playground before the bell rang on Fridays to start the last day of the week exercising, being active, meeting other families, and *por supuesto, bailando*. A message would go out to families the evening before, reminding families to join Marga, LOLA's staff members, and students in walking together and chatting with one another. During this short amount of time, but a weekly event, we would see grandparents, families with strollers, siblings, and many family and community members join in on Fridays right before school. On cold days, families would even serve hot cocoa for all joining the walk.

At Downtown Academy, the kindergarten team organized Kinder Camp, which focused on onboarding our newest families. Part of the camp included activities for welcoming the students; however, the important element of the event was explaining the dual language program goals and ensuring that families felt comfortable and connected to one another through their journey. This intentional meeting of families across languages, cultures, and socio-economic backgrounds was important to modeling what their own students would experience. The school also started a food pantry, which would come in handy during the pandemic, and the school would regularly connect with local churches, nonprofits, and community organizations to ensure that families had what they needed, including drives during the holidays.

Principle 6.3

Involving families and the community as strategic partners is key to increasing buy-in from parents and students alike. Since LOLA had many languages represented in their school, another way to engage with families was through the Morning Announcements. Families were also invited to do the Language of the Week during the assigned week and would teach everyone new words. There were many ways and opportunities for instructional leaders to engage with our families.

At Downtown Academy, families were a part of the selection of the principal. Families were surveyed prior to David's selection and became part of a panel to select the principal; the process stayed in place after David transitioned from the school. There is power in student and family voices in selecting their principal, along with the staff. One of the most important decisions in ensuring a strong dual language school is selecting a principal who believes in the work, understands the research, and will uphold high expectations for the program.

David also implemented *Friday Fenomenal* programming, where the school would incorporate student voice and choice into specially crafted experiences that allowed teachers to innovate and be creative in service of their students. The students went to photography classes at a nearby lake and park, while others went to tech offices to learn about how startups work, and other students enjoyed a Harry Potter experience with a high school librarian down the street. Each *Fenomenal* experience was teacher and student driven in partnership with the community. Downtown Academy even provided *Fenomenal* programming through the pandemic, including important topics like "Knowing Your Rights" in partnership with ImmSchools, which supports families who are undocumented. They also did *Fenomenal* programming during Black History Month, where we explored issues of intersectionality, including being Black and having disabilities, as well as the anti-Black phenomenon in our Latinx community. Dual language programming was also provided with Story Time in Spanish and English, featuring a local drag group. There were also a number of annual festivals, such as Las Posadas, and eventually a Pachanga organized by a committee of family members and staff, which was 100 percent free to families.

The annual Las Posadas tradition at Downtown Academy, a schoolwide celebration of culture and community

As we close out these examples from the Guiding Principles for Dual Language, it's important to acknowledge our collective responsibility to make sure we are reaching out to families and providing them with the support they need so they can feel like a member of the school community. At a time when school choice and enrollment are critical, making our schools the center of our community matters. Leaders need to ensure that communications and systems are clearly understood and accessible to all families. And most important, we need to harness the power of our community for the betterment of our children's education and future. We owe it to them.

Conclusion: Key Take-Aways

Anyone who is currently a principal or has been one since 2020 knows just how rewarding and challenging the role can be. People often talk about how lonely the principalship can be. That outdated mindset and belief must be washed away, especially in the context of being dual language leaders. We cannot go it alone. Whether with a cadre of fellow dual language principals, or through connections and mentors from other districts or Even Start programs, find and leverage community to make yourself a better leader. Even on the hardest days, remind yourself how vital relationships are, especially to achieving any of the work we've described. Listen to your people, ask for and act on their feedback regularly, and ensure that you get them the resources and support they need so they can best serve your students. It's often said, "Feed the teachers so they don't eat the children." Staff members and educators are human beings, too. They too need positive reminders of just how meaningful their work is. To be a dual language teacher is one of the hardest jobs in schools, and as principals of dual language programs, leaders must move barriers out of their way so that educators can do their job justice.

Relationships are also critical with the students at your school. Remember their names, ask them about their weekends, sit down and have lunch with them. Take a moment to stop and visit classrooms not just to hit a walk-through quota but to enjoy the learning process alongside students. Be visible; stand out in front of the school and welcome the staff, families, and students. Relationships are a vital part of the work of building your school into a real community.

We also hope you have taken away the importance of your role in actively interrogating, dismantling, and moving the needle to battle inequities. Fight for what is right. The culture wars are not going away, and yet you must stand firmly by the tenets of sociocultural competence and critical consciousness to stand by those who are often most marginalized in our communities. Guard against the gentrification of your programs. Educate families on the role of privilege, engage in the hard conversations with staff who are not upholding a high belief in your children, and lean on your team to tackle the hard issues that will inevitably come up.

Be strategic in the work you do. Calendar your year and identify when you'll do quarterly step-backs with your administrative and teacher leadership teams to revisit your priorities, to measure your progress toward your goals, and to take the time to simply reflect. Schools can often be go, go, go, and you have to remember that, if you want to succeed, sometimes you have to go slow to go fast. It is important to draw on the wisdom of the African proverb: "If you want to go fast, go alone. If you want to go far, go together."

Most important, be gentle on yourself. If you are reading this book, and specifically this chapter, it is likely because you want to learn and improve yourself. Being a reflective leader who learns what is important, yet the most important lessons you are going to need to engage with, are in getting to know yourself first. Harness the power of your own story, be clear, and consistently revisit your values and beliefs. Start with one thing to focus on as you finish out this chapter. You won't be able to improve or implement everything all at once; you don't need to. Simply take a deep breath and remind yourself of your *why*. Remind yourself of who you were as a teacher and why you decided to step into the role you are in today. Your dual language leadership is needed now more than ever. Hold the bar high for your families, students, staff, and community, and give them all the love and support they deserve. And at the same time, take care of yourself and lean into the journey you have chosen to embark on as a dual language leader. Your community will be better for it, and so will you.

Reflection Questions

1. What connections are you creating with other dual language leaders in your school and/or district to create a collaboration that will make you and them better leaders?

2. What are your systems at your dual language school that support positive relationships with your staff members, students, families, and community?

3. How are you using your voice as an agent of change for your dual language program? When are you having those courageous conversations about inequities in your program?

4. What is your story in the world of DLE? How are you, as a dual language leader, taking the steps necessary to reflect and make a positive change in the future of your multilingual students?

References

American Councils for International Education. (2021). *ARC completes national canvass of dual language immersion programs in U.S. public schools.* https://www.americancouncils.org/news/announcements-featured-content/arc-completes-national-canvass-dual-language-immersion-programs

California Department of Education. (2017). *EL roadmap at a glance: Information sheet.* https://www.cde.ca.gov/sp/el/rm/roadmapinfosheet.asp

California Department of Education. (2018). *Global California 2030: Speak. Learn. Lead.* https://www.cde.ca.gov/eo/in/documents/globalca2030report.pdf

California Department of Education. (2021). *Dual Language Immersion Grant* (DLIG). https://www.cde.ca.gov/sp/el/er/dliginfo.asp

California Department of Education. (2023, February 27). State Seal of Biliteracy: Resources. Education Code sections 61460–51464. https://www.cde.ca.gov/sp/el/er/sealofbiliteracy.asp

Medina, J. (2018). C6 Biliteracy Instructional Framework. Educational Solutions Dual Language Immersion Grant (DLIG). Assembly Bill 130, Chapter 44, Section 158 of the Statutes of 2021.

Gibney, T. D., Kelly, H., Rutherford-Quach, S., Ballen Riccards, J., & Parker, C. (2021). *Addressing the bilingual teacher shortage.* CCNetwork. https://www.compcenternetwork.org/sites/default/files/2.%20Addressing%20the%20bilingual%20teacher%20shortage_Acc.pdf

Howard, E. R., Lindholm-Leary, K. J., Rogers, D., Olague, N., Medina, J., Kennedy, B., Sugarman, J., & Christian, D. (2018). *Guiding principles for dual language education* (3rd ed.). Center for Applied Linguistics.

Multilingualism and Linguistic Diversity. (2003). *UNESCO.* Retrieved March 10, 2023, from https://www.unesco.org/en/multilingualism-linguistic-diversity

Palmer, D. K., Cervantes-Soon, C., Dorner, L., & Heiman, D. (2019). Bilingualism, biliteracy, biculturalism, and critical consciousness for all: Proposing a fourth fundamental goal for two-way dual language education. *Theory Into Practice, 58*(2), 121–133. https://doi.org/10.1080/00405841.2019.1569376

Project Estrella. (n.d.). *Curriculum considerations for students in bilingual or dual language programs*. http://estrella.obaverse.net/learning-modules/bilingual/instruction/curriculum-considerations#:~:text=Curriculum%20is%20designed%20to%20allow,and%20productive%20proficiencies%20in%20English

Proposition 58. (2016). *Official Voter Information Guide*. California Secretary of State: California Proposition 58: California Education for a Global Economy (CA Ed.G.E.) Initiative. https://vigarchive.sos.ca.gov/2016/general/en/propositions/58/

Snyder, S., & Fenner, D. S. (2021). *Culturally responsive teaching for multilingual learners: tools for equity*. Corwin.

Valenzuela, A. (1999). *Subtractive schooling: U.S.–Mexican youth and the politics of caring*. SUNY Press.

From "One-Size-Fits-All" Workshops to Job-Embedded Professional Learning for Dual Language Teachers

RUBÍ FLORES

PREMISE

Dual language (DL) and biliteracy teachers strive to design intellectually challenging instruction as well as culturally and linguistically responsive learning experiences to meet the needs of their diverse learners. To succeed in their efforts, they require a unique set of pedagogical knowledge and instructional strategies that must align with the research on multilingual teaching and learning. Regrettably, most professional learning available to DL educators tends to focus on instructional practices designed for monolingual learners. Rarely are biliteracy teachers provided with professional learning that addresses the context and instructional needs of a DL setting, and even more rare is the access to professional learning delivered in the partner language that they teach (Howard et al., 2018).

As our field becomes increasingly aware of this issue, it is critical to explore the connections between the DL teacher shortage that has been highlighted due to the rapid expansion of DL programs in the last few years and the need to provide culturally and linguistically responsive professional learning support for new and experienced bilingual educators. Due to the increased awareness of the multiple benefits of bilingualism, more and more multilingual and monolingual families have engaged in advocacy efforts for access to DL instruction (Howard et al., 2018). Both state and district school leaders across the country have responded to these efforts by promoting the implementation of new DL programs or by expanding the programs they currently offer. Although this is most definitely a cause for celebration, especially for non-English dominant multilingual families, this has also augmented the staffing challenges that already existed in DL programs.

Due to the increased demand for highly qualified bilingual teachers needed to serve in these new or expanding programs, districts often struggle to find qualified staff who already possess the pedagogical knowledge and language skills needed for biliteracy instruction. As a result, they often find themselves hiring teachers who may be bilingual and may even have previously taught in traditional bilingual settings, but may not have trained in a bilingual teacher preparation program or may not have recently participated in professional learning specific to DL and biliteracy settings. In some states, a bilingual credential or preparation program is not even an option. As also discussed in chapter 1, a brief published in 2021 by the Comprehensive Center Network (Rutherford-Quach et al.) states that after reviewing policies on bilingual teacher credentialing across all fifty states and Washington, DC, at least fifteen states require teachers to hold a bilingual endorsement. The decision to hire some of these teachers with limited preparation may provide a short-term solution to DL staff and biliteracy programs; however, it does not solve the teacher shortage dilemma, given that without the appropriate professional learning and coaching support, many of these educators may eventually become overwhelmed and leave the DL program or the teaching field entirely (Mitchell, 2020; Stavely & Rosales, 2021).

VIGNETTE

It was Mrs. Torres's first day of new employee orientation. She had learned that a neighboring district was implementing the region's first DL program and decided to apply for one of the teaching positions. Although she had taught in transitional bilingual programs in the past, she knew that her passion and ideologies were better aligned with the goals of additive multilingual programs (programs that develop biliteracy) like the one she had applied to. Mrs. Torres was born and raised in the United States, and although she had spoken Spanish since birth, her level of academic language proficiency was stronger in English than in Spanish.

After attending all the required sessions for new hires, she learned that she was also required to attend a 2-day training while the rest of her monolingual peers would be given those days to plan and work in their classrooms. During an intensive 2-day training, she couldn't help but feel overwhelmed after learning about the additional requirements of the program while also realizing that she now had less time than the rest of her peers to prepare for the first days of school. She also found out that many of the materials needed to teach in Spanish were not yet available given that district leaders themselves were still learning the program requirements. As the only DL teacher in her grade level, she could not rely on her monolingual peers to support her with finding, translating, and creating the additional instructional resources she needed. She was told that there would be a district DL instructional coach to support her through the process; however, this coach would be at her site only one day a week because she was also responsible for coordinating the recruitment and testing of new DL students. Nevertheless, Mrs. Torres knew that this was the right program for her and spent many evenings and weekends trying to plan and prepare to implement everything she had learned in those 2 days.

That first year was extremely challenging and overwhelming, but Mrs. Torres remained hopeful that once the program got off the ground, more support would be available to help her become a more effective DL teacher. Unfortunately, that was not the case. By her third year, Mrs. Torres had become more and more disillusioned given that apart from the initial 2-day training, the district never provided any additional professional learning to address the needs of her multilingual context. She was required to attend professional learning that would provide examples only of instructional practices for monolingual classrooms and would be questioned and even disciplined when she would push back on mandates to implement practices that would not be appropriate for her biliteracy classroom. At the district level, the support she was promised never came to fruition.

Aside from the curriculum adoptions, very few resources were provided in the partner language, and the district instructional coaches eventually became interventionists with no time to support teachers with planning or ongoing professional learning. Inevitably, Mrs. Torres's level of confidence in her teaching abilities began to decrease because she felt that no matter how hard she worked, she couldn't keep up with the demands of the program, the needs of her students, and the mandates from the district. And so, although her passion kept her coming back every year, by her fifth year of teaching, she knew that she needed more than passion to continue.

THE URGENCY

There is overwhelming research that shows that effective DL and additive biliteracy instruction can close the opportunity gap for students whose home language is a language other than English (Thomas & Collier, 2012). The research also suggests that all students regardless of home language, socio-economic status, and cultural background can benefit from bilingualism and biliteracy instruction (Thomas & Collier, 2012). DL and biliteracy instruction can level the playing field for linguistically diverse students. Therefore, we must be advocates for expansion and effective implementation of these programs (Cloud et al., 2000).

Due to the high stakes of DL and biliteracy instruction, the lack of high-quality and linguistically and culturally sustaining professional learning for DL and biliteracy educators is a social justice issue. As suggested in the vignette, it is unfair to expect DL teachers to replicate the results of the research on effective DL and biliteracy programs without equitable access to resources or professional learning opportunities that align with that research. Successful DL and biliteracy programs require a collective mindset shift, meaning that professional learning on effective biliteracy practices must be made available to all educational partners and must address the specific role they play in the program and their level of experience with biliteracy instruction.

Unfortunately, new and experienced DL and biliteracy teachers must often overcome additional obstacles to feel confident in their teaching skills. Like our students, DL and biliteracy teachers come with a diverse range of academic, linguistic, and sociocultural experiences that will influence the type of professional learning support they will need. Effective DL professional learning must be differentiated and strategically planned to fully address the teaching and learning needs of all educational partners in the program (Howard et al., 2018).

As also suggested in the vignette, when not provided with the fundamental pedagogical and linguistic resources needed for successful implementation of biliteracy instruction, DL teachers must often spend much more time and personal resources than their monolingual peers preparing high-quality learning experiences. Unfortunately, as also mentioned in chapter 6, many teachers facing these challenges tend to become discouraged, and, unable to keep up with the demands of the job, some may eventually decide to return to English-only settings where the workload feels more manageable. Like Mrs. Torres, some of them may leave the teaching profession entirely. DL and biliteracy teachers deserve to feel valued, supported, and capable of meeting the needs of their students, or we risk the chance of losing them to the over-whelming demands of the job (Mitchell, 2020; Stavely & Rosales, 2021).

The National Teacher Shortage Issue

The road to validating the benefits of bilingualism and biliteracy instruc-tion has been a very strenuous and lengthy one. In California as well as in many other parts of the country, it has taken over two decades of battling against English-only sentiment and policies by multilingual communities and advocacy organizations, but in the last few years, activists have finally started harvesting the fruits of their arduous labor. One example is the passing of Proposition 58 in California, which overturned the deficit-based, English-only legislation Proposition 227 with an overwhelming 73.5 percent voter support, opening the door for parents to request biliteracy instruction for all children (detailed information on Proposition 58 is provided in chapter 1). With this change in policy, and renewed community interest in multilingual education, districts across California are now faced with the challenge of finding the resources needed to respond to the requests for more multilingual programs.

Since the passing of Proposition 58 in 2016, the California Department of Education has launched a variety of initiatives and programs to support and fund the expansion of biliteracy programs across the state. Nevertheless, although we welcome and encourage this critical rectification of our educational system, we must also keep in mind that these victories come with certain staffing and teacher retention challenges that can affect the sustainability and success of DL and biliteracy programs. More information on the California initiatives can be found in chapters 1 and 8.

Unfortunately, the bilingual teacher shortage is not exclusive to the California context. According to a 2021 brief published by the Comprehensive Center Network (Rutherford-Quach et al.), the bilingual teacher shortage continues to be a national issue. The brief further states that at least half of the fifty states are facing critical bilingual teacher shortages, and it goes so far as to present three major factors that contribute to this issue (Gibney et al., 2021):

1. Teacher recruitment, preparation, and certification challenges, as well as an inadequate teacher pipeline

2. Lack of competitive compensation and incentives

3. Inadequate working circumstances

Another report published by the University of Houston (Horn et al., 2021) concluded that Texas continues to face the bilingual teacher shortage across the PK–12 grades that it has been battling since the 1990s. Given that Texas is one of a few states that mandate bilingual education when twenty or more speakers of one language enroll in a district, finding and retaining highly qualified bilingual teachers to meet this demand is critical. One suggested cause for the limited availability of bilingual teachers in Texas is the certification process that requires bilingual teacher candidates to take five rigorous assessments to receive their bilingual certification as opposed to the three assessments that their general education counterparts are required to pass. This imposes an additional financial burden on bilingual teacher candidates because they are financially responsible for every assessment they have to take or retake when necessary (Piñón, 2022). Nevertheless, Texas has taken steps in the last few years to address this issue by providing funding for Grow Your Own programs to recruit bilingual educators (Garcia, 2020), among other recruiting and retention strategies.

Meanwhile, New Jersey is currently facing a similar scenario because it is also one of a few states that mandate bilingual education when the district has twenty students enrolled who speak the same partner language. As of 2014, about 30 percent of New Jersey's residents older than 4 years old spoke a language other than English, and as its population becomes more diverse, the need for more bilingual teachers has become a critical issue (León, 2017). New Jersey has also been facing a teacher shortage since 2004 that has only increased throughout the years, especially on account of the pandemic (León, 2017). These circumstances have driven some districts to recruit teachers from Spanish-speaking countries as well as to rehire retired teachers who can now work full time while still receiving their pensions (Rodas, 2022).

Last, Illinois is another example of a state that continues to face critical teacher shortages. This is partly due to the increase in numbers of non-English fluent multilingual learners entering schools and to the pool of educators who hold a nonrenewable transitional bilingual educator license due to changes in their teacher certification process in previous years. It was reported that about ninety-eight open vacancies for bilingual teachers were unfilled in 2021 across the state (Smylie, 2022). To address these shortages, the Illinois State Board of Education has made available a four-million-dollar grant to increase the bilingual certified teacher pipeline. The goal is to provide support for teachers with a nonrenewable license to obtain their professional renewable license and to also encourage certified nonbilingual endorsed teachers to pursue their bilingual certification (Smylie, 2022). This means that a large number of educators will need to complete the appropriate professional learning requirements to meet the requirements for certification.

Although the contributing factors fueling the teacher shortages may differ from state to state, it is clear that if states do not address the professional learning needs of bilingual teachers serving in DL and biliteracy programs, teacher recruitment and retention will continue to be a major obstacle for the expansion of DL and biliteracy programs across the country.

As illustrated in some of these scenarios, districts across the country are developing programs to recruit bilingual educators with a wide range of experience and preparation levels. However, leaders must keep in mind that although it is in fact a great idea to recruit teachers armed with a variety of pedagogical knowledge and experience, it is critical to understand that a large majority of these educators may not be up to date with new methodology or language development strategies specific to DL settings. In many cases, educators may also need to reclaim or even relearn the academic language needed for partner language instruction in DL or biliteracy programs. Instruction in DL and biliteracy programs is not equivalent to instruction in transitional bilingual programs or in world language programs (Thomas & Collier, 2012). Experienced, novice, and international bilingual teachers must be provided with professional learning that clearly delineates the expectations of additive language programs such as Dual Language Education (DLE). By the same token, this professional learning must address the need for all teachers to continue to refine their academic language abilities in the partner language they teach. In addition, because our field is still recovering from the barriers created by English-only policies, teacher ideologies about the role of students' non-English home languages in the classroom must be addressed through meaningful and coordinated support. For more information on the effects of English-only policies, see chapters 1 and 8.

Long-term Impact of COVID-19 Pandemic on DL and Biliteracy Teacher Retention

District leaders must also consider the impact of the COVID-19 pandemic as it relates to DL and biliteracy teacher burnout and attrition. We found that teaching content and language through virtual instruction proved to be extremely challenging for teachers of multilingual learners. They experienced more pressure than ever to address the individual needs of their students with even more limited resources and support than they had before the pandemic (Villegas & Garcia, 2022). The reopening of schools brought a heightened pressure to get students back on track and, for DL and biliteracy teachers, this pressure doubled as they work tirelessly to accelerate learning in more than one language. Unfortunately, this pressure has prompted a resurgence of literacy teaching practices that focus on a much more narrow view of literacy instruction and do not take into consideration the unique needs of multilingual learners in biliteracy settings (Escamilla et al., 2022).

If not addressed through a multilingual lens, these circumstances have a serious potential to break our DL and biliteracy teachers and, consequently, drive many of them to consider leaving the profession altogether. A survey conducted by the National Education Association found that "a disproportionate percentage of Black (62 percent) and Hispanic/Latino (59 percent) educators, already underrepresented in the teaching profession, were looking toward the exits" (Walker, 2022). As most of our DL teachers are teachers of color, it is clear that we are in danger of losing more DL teachers due to the added pressures and limited support available to meet the demands of their multilingual context. This information is critical as district leaders plan for ways to prevent and address teacher attrition and shortages (Walker, 2022).

A Call for Strategic Professional Learning Practices in Multilingual Settings

As addressed earlier in this chapter, DL and biliteracy educator professional growth is a matter of urgency for the sustainability of DL and biliteracy programs. However, we exhort district leaders not to respond to this call for urgency with quick-fix approaches and rushed initiatives, but to thoroughly consider the recommendations of the research on effective professional learning practices (Learning Forward, 2022). For DL and biliteracy teachers to effectively address the academic, linguistic, sociocultural, and critical consciousness needs of multilingual learners, there must be intentional and systematic planning of professional learning supports. These supports must reflect a commitment to investing in the short- and long-term professional growth of DL and biliteracy educators. In other words, professional learning in biliteracy settings must encompass a set of differentiated and strategically coordinated approaches aimed at addressing the unique learning needs of multilingual students (Howard et al., 2018). These approaches must be designed to go beyond building capacity to improve teaching practices; they must also empower bilingual teachers to become transformative intellectuals and experts in the field who will disrupt and redesign the inequitable structures in our current educational system (Giroux, 1988).

RESEARCH BASE

Defining Professional Learning

The Every Student Succeeds Act (ESSA; 2015) defines professional development as:

> activities that—"(A) are an integral part of school and local educational agency strategies for providing educators (including teachers, principals, other school leaders, specialized instructional support personnel, paraprofessionals, and, as applicable, early childhood educators) with the knowledge and skills necessary to enable students to succeed in a well-rounded education and to meet the challenging State academic standards; and "(B) are sustained (not stand-alone, 1-day, or short term workshops), intensive, collaborative, job-embedded, data-driven, and classroom-focused . . .

This much more expanded definition has prompted a conversation in the field of education regarding the general perception of the commonly used term *professional development*. As stated in a 2019 position statement by the National Council of Teachers of English, many educators relate professional development with one-time training or dreaded short-term workshops that are usually disconnected from their current teaching context and rarely include teacher input or interest. To change perception and align practices toward a more responsive and effective view of teacher training and development, the field has been increasingly using the term *professional learning* when referring to more comprehensive capacity-building supports designed to positively impact teaching and learning outcomes over time. Through this chapter, we use the term *professional learning* when referring to the practices that align with the definition included in the ESSA (2015).

Characteristics of Effective Professional Learning in DL and Biliteracy Contexts

To provide DL and biliteracy teachers with effective professional learning that will address the teaching and learning needs of the program, district leaders must ensure that they have a strategically crafted professional learning plan that

1. aligns to the research on effective professional learning practices; and

2. is also informed by research on effective biliteracy teaching and learning practices.

To address the two components, we first present the research on effective professional learning practices as it applies to general learning contexts. We then expand on those recommendations by connecting them to the research on effective biliteracy teaching and learning practices. In other words, we explore the research on effective professional learning practices through a multilingual lens.

In a 2017 study conducted by the Learning Policy Institute on effective professional learning practices, the authors defined effective professional learning "as structured professional learning that results in changes in teacher practices and improvements in student learning outcomes." Therefore, district and site leaders must ensure that their professional learning initiatives can show a direct connection to student learning outcomes as well as to evidence of teacher professional growth. For DL and biliteracy programs, this means that district and site leaders must be able to show a direct connection to student academic and linguistic outcomes in both languages of the program as well as to evidence of teacher professional growth in biliteracy instructional practices. More information about the role of leaders as DL advocates can be found in chapter 6.

This study also found seven common characteristics among effective professional learning programs and initiatives. Their conclusions about effective professional learning are shown in figure 7.1.

> Teacher quality is a key component in student achievement and biliteracy development. Effective professional learning that supports teacher growth needs to align to the specific goals, mission, and vision of the school's DL program. It is a must that professional learning include reflective practice and critical thinking while it maintains its focus on content, active learning, and collaboration.
>
> **Marga**

FIGURE 7.1 **7 Characteristics of Effective Professional Learning**

1. **Focuses on content:** Teachers benefit from professional learning that improves both their content knowledge and their understanding of best practices that align with their instructional goals. Professional learning must build understanding of the concepts specific to the content area they teach (science, math, etc.) while also building their capacity to make pedagogical decisions when applying and reflecting on content-driven instructional practices.

2. **Integrates active learning approaches:** Effective professional learning integrates and models the same or similar active learning strategies that educators are expected to use in their classrooms. These may include collaborative strategies, inquiry approaches, and student-centered practices. It also provides opportunities for educators to try out the strategies while learning to create similar experiences for their students.

3. **Fosters collaboration:** High-quality professional learning creates dedicated spaces to foster collegial collaboration between all educators. This cultivates a positive learning and teaching culture and also builds instructional alignment across the teaching and learning community.

(Continued)

(Continued)

4. **Includes modeling:** It's essential to provide educators with concrete examples of the instructional practices and pedagogical expectations as they learn to refine their craft. These models may include model lessons that may be available, videos of instructional strategies, and so on.

5. **Includes coaching provided by highly qualified experts:** Coaching and mentoring support provide an opportunity to address the individual professional learning needs of each educator.

6. **Utilizes feedback and reflective practices:** In effective professional learning, reflective cycles are embraced as a core practice. Teachers are provided with opportunities and strategies for engaging in self and collective reflection as well as opportunities to provide and request feedback from their peers to refine their practice.

7. **It is provided over a sustained period of time:** High-quality professional learning is strategically planned and delivered over a sustained period of time to ensure that teachers acquire not only the conceptual knowledge of the content but also the job-embedded support enabling them to practice, implement, and refine their understanding of the content and the strategies they are learning.

Source: Adapted from Darling-Hammond et al. (2017)

The findings above accentuate the expectations for effective professional learning as defined in the previously cited ESSA definition (Learning Forward, 2015). This is helpful to district leaders because it provides a framework to follow as they reflect and work toward refining their planning and implementation of professional learning supports. This information is especially critical when they address the professional learning needs of DL and biliteracy educators, as DL professional learning often tends to be viewed and provided as an "add-on" or "on top of" other districtwide professional learning priorities. This common practice contradicts the research on effective professional learning, because this uncoordinated approach will not support or contribute to multilingual students' academic and linguistic success (Howard et al., 2018).

To avoid this common pitfall, we can draw both on the existing body of research on effective professional learning practices and on the research on effective multilingual teaching and learning to reimagine professional learning through a multilingual perspective. Figure 7.2 presents the expanded characteristics of effective DL and biliteracy professional learning that is viewed through a multilingual lens.

FIGURE 7.2 **General and Expanded Views of Professional Learning**

General View of Professional Learning (Adapted from Darling-Hammond et al., 2017)	Expanded View of Professional Learning Through a Multilingual Lens
Focuses on content	Is content, language, culturally sustaining, and critical conscious-focused. As well as being content based, it addresses the linguistic needs of the classroom and embeds culturally sustaining pedagogies that take into consideration the sociocultural needs of the student population (Howard et al., 2018).

General View of Professional Learning (Adapted from Darling-Hammond et al., 2017)	Expanded View of Professional Learning Through a Multilingual Lens
Integrates active learning approaches	Incorporates active learning in English and the partner language utilizing adult learning theory and focuses on developing critically conscious educators. As well as preparing teachers through active learning, it also prepares them to become critical intellectuals who will work toward ensuring equitable and socially just teaching practices (Giroux, 1988; Palmer et al., 2019).
Fosters collaboration	Supports collaboration among DL teachers within and across grade levels, typically in job-embedded contexts. District leaders prioritize opportunities for DL teachers to observe, collaborate, plan, and co-teach with other DL teachers consistently and as part of a larger plan to align instructional practices across the grade levels (Howard et al., 2018).
Includes modeling	Uses models and modeling of high-quality biliteracy instructional and linguistic practices that are based on research on multilingual instruction. Also, model lessons, videos, and so on are available in both languages of the program (Escamilla et al., 2022).
Includes coaching provided by highly qualified experts	Provides coaching and expert support by bilingual and biliterate instructional leaders who are well versed in research on effective multilingual instruction in both English and the partner language and on effective coaching practices in multilingual settings (Howard et al., 2018).
Utilizes feedback and reflective practices	Offers opportunities for feedback and reflection of instructional, linguistic, sociocultural, and critical conscious capacity and opportunities for growth (Howard et al., 2018; Palmer et al., 2019).
Provided over a sustained period of time	Provided over a sustained period of time and includes structures to develop instructional biliteracy leaders and experts: aims to prepare future coaches, administrators, advocacy leaders, and professors (Palmer, 2018).

Overcoming the Common Barriers of Implementation

The Learning Policy Institute's comprehensive study also identified the common barriers district leaders must address to successfully implement an effective professional learning plan. It is useless to create a very well-crafted plan if the barriers preventing effective implementation and fidelity to the plan are not systematically addressed. Some of the common implementation issues identified in the study include (Darling-Hammond et al., 2017)

- lack of shared vision about what high-quality instruction entails;
- lack of time for planning and implementing new instructional approaches;
- conflicting requirements, such as scripted curriculum or pacing guides; and
- lack of adequate foundational knowledge on the part of teachers.

It is commonly known that these barriers are also present, and in most cases are even more pronounced in DL and biliteracy programs. It is important to address the additional barriers that DL and biliteracy programs must overcome to create the conditions that will yield successful professional learning outcomes.

FIGURE 7.3 **Common Implementation Barriers and Additional Considerations**

Common Monolingual Professional Learning Implementation Barriers (Darling-Hammond et al., 2017)	Additional Considerations for DLE and Biliteracy Classrooms
Inadequate resources, including needed curriculum materials	Inequitable access to high-quality resources including linguistically responsive, needed curriculum and assessment in both languages of the program
Lack of shared vision about what high-quality instruction entails	Lack of shared vision or limited knowledge by district leaders and professional learning providers about what high-quality instruction entails in multilingual settings
Lack of time for planning and implementing new instructional approaches	Lack of time for planning and collaborating to implement new biliteracy approaches such as co-teaching, as these are viewed as additional to other district/site priorities
Conflicting requirements, such as scripted curriculum or pacing guides	Conflicting requirements such as scripted curriculum written through a monolingual lens that doesn't provide differentiation for multilingual settings Pacing guides that are created based on monolingual delivery of instruction and do not take into account the need to include cross-linguistic transfer opportunities
Lack of adequate foundational knowledge on the part of teachers	Lack of adequate foundational knowledge of DL and biliteracy instruction and second language acquisition theory and practices

Ultimately, professional learning practices must positively impact student learning and build teacher capacity. In DL and biliteracy settings, district leaders must ask themselves if they are effectively creating the conditions and building the systems that will lead both teachers and students to meet the goals of DL and biliteracy programs.

Further Research Informing Effective Professional Learning Practices for DL and Biliteracy Teachers

Collective DL and Biliteracy Teacher Efficacy

One unique feature of DL programs is the natural built-in shared responsibility element that occurs as students progress through the grade levels. In programs with low DL teacher turnover, district leaders can predict the level of instructional quality students will receive because it is more likely that each cohort of students will have the same teachers throughout their duration in the program. This element presents a valuable opportunity to strengthen the quality of instruction through the lens of collective teacher efficacy, which according to Hattie (2019) is the number one factor related to student achievement. Stemming from Bandura's (1993) self-efficacy theory, collective teacher efficacy is defined as "a group's shared belief in the conjoint capabilities to organize and execute the courses of action required to produce given levels of attainment." Many former DL teachers can attest to the loneliness and disconnect that can be felt when there are no systems in place to support cross-grade-level collaboration. It's easy to doubt one's abilities and wonder about the abilities of your peers when there are few or no opportunities to discuss, share, and learn from each other. We often see pockets of greatness being highlighted and celebrated in DL programs. These are often the educators who have the reputation of being the strength of the program and are celebrated and recognized for their exceptional instructional skills. Although it is necessary to celebrate and recognize those educators who exemplify instructional greatness, we must also create opportunities to leverage the abilities of these exceptional educators to replicate these conditions in all DL classrooms. Through the lens of collective teacher efficacy, as shared in chapter 6, district leaders would plan for professional learning that would instill a culture of trust and collegial collaboration to ensure that all DL teachers become confident in their abilities to provide high-quality instruction to all multilingual learners (Hattie, 2018).

Pedagogical and Ideological Clarity in DL and Biliteracy Programs

Johnson (2021) states that DL and biliteracy educators must have pedagogical clarity when it comes to the unique pedagogical, linguistic, and philosophical foundations of effective multilingual instruction. Without this clarity, it is more likely that teachers of multilingual learners may miss valuable teaching and learning opportunities when they present themselves. Teachers must learn to be conscious of their own capacity as biliteracy practitioners and also of their understanding of partner language structures to make pedagogical decisions that will yield positive student outcomes (Johnson, 2021). Lack of clarity could endanger the sustainability of the DL and biliteracy program because its effectiveness may be questioned if students fail to meet the expected outcomes in both languages. Therefore, specialized training to develop teachers' biliteracy pedagogical clarity is required so that teachers can meet instructional, linguistic, and sociocultural demands of the DL or biliteracy program (Johnson, 2021).

Also, because social justice is an integral part of DL education, teacher professional learning must be based on the foundations of transformative pedagogical practices. In a program that was designed to serve the linguistic, academic, and sociocultural needs of historically underserved populations, equity and social justice must be at the center of teaching and learning (Alfaro & Hernandez, 2016). In addition to the three pillars of DL found in *Guiding Principles for Dual Language Education* (Howard et al., 2018), Palmer et al. (2019) propose the inclusion of the development of critical consciousness as the fourth goal for teaching and learning in a DL program. This foundational goal would position teachers as transformative intellectuals who, according to Giroux (2002), understand that "the teacher task is not to mold students, but to encourage human agency, to provide the conditions for students to be self-determining, and to struggle for a society that is both autonomous and democratic." Professional learning in DL programs must also aim to strengthen DL teachers' ideological clarity to prepare them to address issues of inequity, discrimination, and oppressive language politics, which can have negative effects on the lives of all multilingual educational partners (Bartolomé, 2000).

IMPLICATIONS FOR PRACTICE AND IMPLEMENTATION

A Systematic Approach to Addressing the Professional Learning Needs of DL and Biliteracy Programs

Through this chapter, much has been shared about the *why* and the *what* of professional learning in DL and biliteracy settings. However, as it is important for district leaders to understand the urgency and to be knowledgeable about the topic, it's the *how* or the actions they must take that lead to teacher and student success. The following exemplary practice example is presented to illustrate some of the actions leaders can take to build or refine their DL and biliteracy instruction professional learning plans.

Exemplary Practice Example

A new multilingual director had recently learned that two of the six DL teachers at the district's only DL school had requested to transfer out of the program. Aware of the DL teacher shortage, she knew that replacing the teachers would be a significant issue. After meeting with them, she learned that they had been meeting at least two Saturdays a month and, because of staff and grade-level meetings, they didn't have time to plan for their Spanish lessons. Since both were in their second year of teaching, they were finding it difficult to keep up with the demands of the program. They had approached the principal with their concerns, but he felt it was important to build rapport with their monolingual grade-level teammates and preferred that they all plan together as a team.

The program was only in its third year of implementation, and only one of the six teachers was an experienced DL teacher, so she was afraid to lose more teachers. The director scheduled a meeting with the teachers, and through collaborative strategies, she asked them to share some successes and some challenges they faced as DL teachers. She also asked each one of them to fill out a survey to collect data on their individual needs. A few days later, she scheduled a meeting and invited the principal, superintendent, director of teaching and learning, the HR director, two volunteer DL teachers, and one monolingual member of the site's leadership team who teaches in a general education classroom. She prepared a presentation to share the goals of the program, research on multilingual learners, benefits of bilingualism, and most important, the importance of retaining DL teachers. She proceeded to share the data she collected during her meeting with the DL teachers. After analyzing the data, the team of leaders agreed that it was critical to address the teachers' concerns, and they planned to meet once a month to create a support and retention plan. During those meetings, the multilingual director facilitated article discussions on effective multilingual instruction, coordinated visits to other effective DL programs, and contracted a DL consultant to provide recommendations and facilitate the development of a DL teacher support plan.

By the end of the year, the team had developed a plan that included hiring a DL instructional coach, allocating funds for teachers and leaders to attend one self-selected DL conference or training of their choosing, providing two full days per trimester for planning for DL teachers, contracting a consultant to coach the DL instructional coach and the experienced DL teacher, and allocating funding to hire two bilingual, full-time, job-embedded substitutes to support implementation of a professional learning and support plan. By the end of the first year of implementation, although at first hesitant about the investment they were making, they saw not only positive results in the attitudes and practices of teachers but also a noticeable improvement in multilingual student achievement. The team continued to meet twice every year to review new teacher and student data and to refine the plan as needed. Eventually, after 5 years of implementing the support plan, the campus had 90 percent of DL teacher retention, and their multilingual student testing scores had increased by 20 percent. After evaluating its success, the DL support plan was replicated across the district to support all teachers.

Reflection Questions

1. What effective actions did the director take to address the needs of the DL teachers?

2. Why do you think she selected that specific group of leaders?

3. What could've been the consequences of not addressing the issue?

4. What conditions allowed the team to develop a well-informed DL teacher support plan?

Unpacking the Exemplary Practice Example

Building Leadership Capacity on Multilingual Instructional Practices. As illustrated in the exemplary practice scenario, our field is in urgent need of district and site leaders who will take the courageous and critical steps to ensure that the professional learning needs of DL and biliteracy teachers are given importance equal to the needs of monolingual teachers. There are fundamental differences between monolingual and multilingual instruction that require differentiated professional learning and support. Educators at all levels must come to terms with the fact that instruction in a DL and biliteracy classroom will sound, look, and be structured differently than that of a monolingual classroom and must stop trying to make DL practices fit in a monolingual mold.

For leaders to make informed decisions about the appropriate professional learning that best meets the needs of DL and biliteracy programs, they must be very well versed on the recommendations of research that aligns with

Since the late 1960s and initial federal funding of the Bilingual Education Act, leaders have recognized the importance of professional learning specifically designed for the educators of MLLs. Rubí's thoughtful recommendations are concrete practices that support MLLs, strengthen the DL teacher pipeline, and retain well-trained DL educators and educational leaders.

Lyn

multilingual teaching and learning (Howard et al., 2018). Most DL and biliteracy teachers are well aware of their own professional learning needs; however, they have little to no influence on the type of professional learning their districts provide, and they have to rely on the decisions made by administrators.

Steps must be taken to prepare all educational partners who hold the power over professional learning decisions to understand the research and data on effective multilingual instruction as well as the value of DL and biliteracy teacher voice and choice when they are deciding what professional learning practices and resources to provide. Their educational partners may include district administrators, executive cabinet members, school board members, campus administrators, teacher union leaders, and so on. Leading in DL and biliteracy settings requires that leaders themselves embrace their role as transformative intellectuals and invest in their own development as advocates of effective multilingual instruction.

FIGURE 7.4 **Recommended Professional Learning Practices for Site and District DL Leaders**

1. Provide foundational professional learning sessions offered by organizations with expertise in multilingual instructional practices followed by coaching and consultation to extend learning
2. Organize a book study or article study on topics relevant to multilingual instruction
3. Organize visits to effective DL and biliteracy programs outside the district
4. Organize opportunities to observe effective multilingual instruction within the district
5. Attend conferences that focus on multilingual instruction
6. Join professional networks that focus on topics relevant to multilingual instruction

FIGURE 7.5 **Recommended Professional Learning Topics for All District and Site Leaders**

- History and Foundations of Bilingual Education in the United States
- Federal and State Policies for Multilingual Learner Instruction
- Research on Effectiveness of Multilingual Learner Programs
- Foundations of Effective Instruction for Multilingual Learners
- Foundations of Dual Language and Biliteracy Education
- The Guiding Principles for Dual Language Education
- District-Specific Dual Language Program Model and Instructional Expectations
- Best Instructional Practices in Dual Language Education
- Authentic Methods for Teaching Literacy in the Partner Language
- Translanguaging in Dual Language Classrooms
- Developing and Implementing a District and Site Dual Language Leadership Team
- Best Practices for Dually Identified Multilingual Learners
- Family and Community Outreach Through a Social Justice/Equity Lens

Refinement or Development of Multilingual Professional Learning Systems. By utilizing a multilingual perspective to engage in in-depth reflection of the district's current professional learning initiatives, program leaders will be able to identify the inequitable systems impacting the professional growth of DL and biliteracy educators. This reflection must include the perspectives, experiences, and expertise of key educational partners who can bring positive contributions to the refinement of a more equitable and responsive multilingual professional learning plan.

One recommendation is to establish a multilingual district leadership team made up of key administrators and educators who are well versed on the particular needs of DL and biliteracy programs. This team would engage in a reflection process using resources such as *Guiding Principles for Dual Language Education* (Howard et al., 2018) and *Standards for Professional Learning* (Learning Forward, 2022) to collaboratively create or refine a district's multilingual professional learning plan. A caveat to keep in mind is that this plan would not be secondary to the districtwide general professional learning plan but rather a plan that would include and place equitable priority on the needs of monolingual and multilingual learners (Howard et al., 2018). Figure 7.6 includes sample guiding questions to help lead the reflection process.

FIGURE 7.6 Guiding Questions for Multilingual Professional Learning Planning

1. What do assessment data say about how multilingual learners are performing academically and linguistically in English?

2. What does assessment data say about how multilingual learners in DL and biliteracy programs are performing academically and linguistically in the partner language(s)?

3. Do we have any assessment data on students' sociocultural competence? What does it say?

4. How are we embedding teachers' reflections of their own pedagogical needs in our professional learning plan?

5. How are we embedding students' feedback on classroom instruction in the development of our professional learning priorities?

6. What are the professional learning needs of novice DL and biliteracy teachers?

7. What are the professional learning needs of experienced and expert DL teachers?

8. How can we embed the development of critical consciousness in multilingual professional learning?

9. What are the professional learning needs of educators pursuing a bilingual teacher credential?

10. What are the professional learning needs of teachers returning to teach in DL and biliteracy programs?

11. How are we ensuring that all professional learning programs, sessions, and structures address the needs of all multilingual learners?

12. What are the unique needs of DL and biliteracy instruction that are not being addressed through the professional learning we already provide?

13. How are we addressing the needs of multilingual families through the professional learning programs, sessions, and structures we provide?

(Continued)

(Continued)

14. What opportunities are we providing for teachers of multilingual students to analyze student data and plan for effective instruction?

15. How can we align the professional learning provided to DL and biliteracy teachers with the three pillars of the program?

16. Is the professional learning we provide for DL and biliteracy teachers aligned with the language allocation plan of the program? What training or support must be provided in the partner language?

17. How can we provide comprehensive and sustained high-quality professional learning support to all teachers of multilingual students?

18. How can we ensure that all of the pedagogical, curriculum, technological, linguistic, and human resources are equitably available to address the unique needs of all multilingual programs?

Effective Professional Learning as a Preventative Measure.

Reflection Questions

1. How important is it to invest in high-quality multilingual educator professional learning?

2. What amount of resources should be spent strengthening the pedagogical capacity of multilingual educators?

3. What should take priority when those who control funding allocate build teacher capacity, or provide remedial supports and programs?

Ensuring multilingual learner success calls for an essential mindset shift about the value and significance of effective educator professional learning. Educators cannot control the external factors that may influence student learning, but, when well prepared, they can create the classroom conditions that could mitigate and even leverage some of those factors. By strengthening their collective capacity to deliver effective first instruction, educators will have the tools to appropriately identify and address the needs of a large majority of students, which will potentially decrease the need for future remediation. Building collective efficacy requires a commitment to prioritize the implementation of a comprehensive and sustained professional learning plan that is fully funded, supported, and protected.

It is recommended that funding and recruitment priorities be developed to procure the resources in figure 7.7.

FIGURE 7.7 Resources Needed for Success

Multilingual Human Resources	Multilingual Professional Learning Resources
• Expert External Multilingual Consultants	• Multilingual Professional Learning Books
• District and Site-based Multilingual Instructional Coaches	• Multilingual Instruction Training for Instructional Coaches

Multilingual Human Resources	Multilingual Professional Learning Resources
• Multilingual Professional Learning Specialists • Multilingual Substitute Pool • Full-time Embedded Professional Learning Multilingual Substitutes • Multilingual Professional Learning Coordinator • Multilingual Curriculum Coordinators for All Subject Areas	• Multilingual Instruction Training for Professional Learning Coordinators and Specialists • Funding for Specialized Multilingual Conferences and Trainings • Multilingual Curriculum Resources • Presentation Technological Programs and Tools • Dedicated Professional Learning and Collaborative Planning Time • Materials and Supplies for Coaching, Planning, and Implementation of Strategies

Growing the Multilingual Instructional Leader Pipeline. Talent alone does not make someone exceptional in practice. Even the most talented athletes rely on a team of experts in their sport to guide them and coach them to improve their skills. When they are not playing, they are training, practicing plays, and analyzing how other athletes approach the game. And even though both coaches and athletes have their own individual responsibilities, it's the result of their collective competencies that ultimately matters the most. This example could be useful to informing the field of education because it highlights how the confluence of expertise and talent is essential to the professional growth of both the practitioner and the coach.

Our schools are filled with talented and passionate professionals who are always willing to go the extra mile to guide their students toward success. However, like practitioners in other fields, they require explicit and continuous support from trainers, coaches, and mentors who possess practical experience and in-depth knowledge of effective teaching and learning practices. In essence, to build collective teacher capacity, we must first identify and prepare the instructional leaders and experts who will be responsible for accomplishing that task. Let's keep in mind that an expert teacher does not automatically turn into an expert instructional coach or professional learning specialist when they take on the role. Experts also require training and coaching because working with adult learners is not synonymous with working with children, and teachers must be given the support to grow into highly effective professional learning providers.

In multilingual settings, however, there are additional factors to consider. A bilingual teacher shortage inevitably translates to a multilingual expert shortage. This issue must be addressed as an equity challenge, as there must be a much more intensive and intentional effort on the part of district leaders to increase the pipeline of multilingual experts, coaches, trainers, and instructional teacher leaders who will be needed to support novice and experienced multilingual educators. Therefore, in addition to subject matter and general pedagogical knowledge, specialized professional learning that addresses the unique features of DL instruction and professional learning structures must be a top priority. We must also invest in future leaders who will sustain the success of DL and biliteracy instructional programs.

Figure 7.8 includes a list of the most essential pedagogical and capacity-building skills bilingual coaches and instructional leaders must possess to effectively plan and deliver professional learning in DL and biliteracy programs.

FIGURE 7.8 Essential Pedagogical and Coaching Knowledge for DL and Biliteracy Coaches and Instructional Leaders

- Foundations of Adult Learning Theory
- The Guiding Principles for Dual Language Education
- Developing Critical Consciousness
- Addressing the Sociocultural and Socio-emotional Needs of Educators
- Growth Mindset Theory
- Planning and Delivering Effective Multilingual Professional Learning
- Differentiating Professional Learning Through a Multilingual Lens
- Instructional Coaching Frameworks
- Analyzing Multilingual Learner Data
- Effective Instructional Frameworks for Dual Language and Biliteracy Instruction
- Research on Effective Literacy Instruction in the Partner Language
- State Standards and Instructional Frameworks
- History and Foundations of Bilingual Education in the United States
- Federal and State Policies for Multilingual Learner Instruction
- Ongoing Academic Language Development in Partner Language
- Supporting Dually Identified Multilingual Learners
- Embracing and Building on Indigenous Languages

Recommendations for Effective DL and Biliteracy Educator Professional Learning

With the expansion of DL and biliteracy programs, our district leaders can no longer afford to let the still underlying false narrative that "good teaching is good teaching" preserve the inequitable teaching and learning systems that are failing to meet the needs of multilingual learners. By the same token, we face urgency when it comes to the way leaders approach the professional learning needs of DL and multilingual educators, as what's good professional learning for most is not necessarily good professional learning for all.

Exemplary Practice Example

Mrs. Delgado has been a DL teacher for over 8 years at one of the area's most successful districts. It's a district known for its high teacher retention rate and its culture of continuous learning. Each of the district's twenty-four campuses has at least one site-based instructional coach and an additional DL coach at each DL campus. The district has six district-based instructional coaches, two of them bilingual, who lead the implementation of the district's multilingual professional learning plan. Every spring, Mrs. Delgado completes a districtwide survey designed to gather data on teachers' professional learning interests and needs. The survey is differentiated to address the specific needs of the various instructional programs offered. In addition to the survey, Mrs. Delgado participates in a schoolwide needs assessment facilitated by the instructional coaches to assess the overall professional learning needs of each grade-level team. She also participates in a DL-specific needs assessment session facilitated by the DL coaches. Every year, she has her students complete a survey to provide feedback on their learning experience, a survey is also provided for parents and guardians.

These data, along with disaggregated student academic achievement data, are analyzed to identify district teaching and learning priorities. These priorities will inform the professional learning goals and activities of the following year. Each year, Mrs. Delgado looks forward to attending the yearly summer professional learning summit that offers differentiated pathways of professional learning. In the past, she has participated as an attendee and has even been invited to co-present with one of the DL coaches. However, this year, she was invited to lead one of the foundational sessions offered to novice teachers on inquiry models for science instruction. She will present her session in Spanish since that's the language of instruction for that subject; however, she will make sure to include strategies for bridging across languages because the development of academic English vocabulary was identified as a district priority.

During the school year, Mrs. Delgado is provided with one grade-level backwards planning day each trimester and an additional day to plan with her DL partner. This year, her DL coach is a former colleague who was recently promoted after 10 successful years as a DL teacher. She also attends the planning sessions and is joined by one of the district's DL coaches who will be her mentor through her transition. In addition to the planning days, Mrs. Delgado participates in a coaching cycle facilitated by the site-based instructional coach to address a topic of interest and need in her classroom. Together, they review classroom data to identify a teaching and learning priority and spend 3–5 weeks planning, implementing, reflecting, and refining a high-leverage classroom strategy that will address the priorities they identified. This year, she will also get to shadow her coach because she is interested in pursuing a coaching position in the near future. Mrs. Delgado also participates in a monthly after-school inquiry cycle with all the DL teachers to address the main teaching and learning district priority that derived from the spring data reflection cycle. During these sessions, the DL instructional coaches lead teachers through a cycle of collective inquiry by posing an open-ended question

(Continued)

(Continued)

related to the district's teaching and learning priority. This year, the team will address the following question: "How can we leverage multilingual students' biliteracy skills to build their linguistic capacity to become critical contributors of information?" The team selected *The Translanguaging Classroom: Leveraging Student Bilingualism for Learning* by Kate Seltzer, Ofelia Garcia, and Susana Ibarra Johnson to engage in a book study on the topic. Each month they discuss one translanguaging and one multilingual identity-building strategy, and then they spend the rest of the month trying out the strategy and return to the following session with student work samples and videos of their lessons. The team analyzes the student work and lesson videos. They discuss the challenges they faced and provide each other with feedback. At the end of the cycle, the team presents its findings to the rest of the staff. This year, Mrs. Delgado also had the opportunity to co-lead some of the inquiry cycle sessions because she is working toward building her instructional leadership capacity.

At the beginning of the year, Mrs. Delgado was accepted into a DL instructional leadership cohort designed to build an internal pipeline of DL experts. This cohort is made up of teachers who have at least 6 years of DL experience and aspire to become district DL coaches or campus or district administrators. This team meets once a month to receive targeted professional learning on coaching practices, mentoring strategies, and professional learning expectations in DL programs. The team is also required to participate in at least three instructional leadership capacity-building activities. Thanks to the extensive professional learning opportunities she has been provided, Mrs. Delgado has become one of the most highly regarded DL teachers at the district and has the capacity, confidence, and commitment to share her expertise with her colleagues.

Reflection Questions

1. In what ways do the practices presented lead teachers to become transformative intellectuals?

2. How was teacher agency cultivated through the district's actions?

3. How was professional learning differentiated in this example?

4. What district systems must be in place to support the implementation of a comprehensive professional learning plan?

Unpacking the Exemplary Practice Example

Teachers as Transformative Intellectuals. Language is political. Evidence of this fact has been documented throughout U.S. history. A person's beliefs, ideologies, and cultural identity are all transmitted through language. This turns language into a tool for advocacy and agency, and when one language outnumbers the other languages in a community, it turns into collective power for the members of that language group. That's how English-only based policies and practices help perpetuate the inequitable access to opportunities and resources for speakers of other languages.

Consequently, there is little professional learning available for DL and biliteracy teachers that prepares them to address these sociopolitical factors in their classrooms. As a result, they tend to focus mostly on addressing the first two pillars of the program (bilingualism and biliteracy and high academic achievement), because they often feel unprepared to address the sociocultural competence pillar of the program. For this reason, professional learning designed to develop educator critical consciousness is essential to the success of DL and biliteracy programs (Palmer et al., 2019). Teachers must be provided with the tools to address the power dynamics of language in their classrooms and prepare students to confront the sociopolitical aspects of their multilingual identities as they encounter them in the real world. Professional learning for multilingual educators must aim to develop transformative intellectuals who will build instructional experiences and classroom structures that will lead students to realize and leverage the power of their voice and their biliteracy to create an equitable and democratic world.

Figure 7.9 presents some recommended professional learning topics for developing educator and student critical consciousness.

FIGURE 7.9 Recommended Professional Learning Topics

Level of Support	Developing Critical Consciousness	Affirming Multilingual Identities	Building Sociocultural Competence
Foundational Knowledge	Provide training for all new DL teachers on the history of bilingual education with a focus on the impact on the learning outcomes of multilingual learners.	Provide a session on creating a classroom multilingual ecology to promote multilingual and multicultural identities with a focus on developing educators' critical consciousness through reflection on their own language experiences.	Provide a session to build background on effective strategies for promoting sociocultural competence.
Sustained Implementation	Establish a rotating advocacy committee to provide quarterly updates at PLCs or during team meetings on important legislation, initiatives, and changes to federal and state policies that impact multilingual learner instruction.	Embed an identity development activity in all professional learning provided and ask teachers to bring examples of student work to share at consecutive sessions.	Support teachers who include sociocultural learning objectives in their biliteracy units that align with the academic content and connect to the needs of the community using the social justice standards document found at the Learning for Justice (2022) website. Standards can be retrieved from this link: bit.ly/3NiKajx

Professional Learning Practices That Sustain Transformative Pedagogies

Looking back at my own professional learning journey, I realize that the most impactful professional learning I've experienced involved a lot of wondering, discussing, and reflecting. That is why we must keep in mind that it is through sharing and challenging ideas through reflective discourse that new learning emerges, and as a consequence, learning will lead to a transformation of thought and practice. As illustrated through the exemplary practice example, effective professional learning embeds a coordinated set of learning experiences that facilitate the exchange of ideas, the application of critical reflection, and professional competency and leadership skills.

Figure 7.10 presents some of the professional learning practices that are conducive to building critical consciousness through inquiry, dialogue, reflection, and action.

FIGURE 7.10 Recommended Inquiry-driven Professional Learning Practices

- Professional Learning Communities
- Reflective Co-teaching
- Individual and Small-Group Coaching Cycles
- Book Studies
- Instructional Rounds
- Collaborative Inquiry Cycles
- Cohort-based Professional Learning

Putting All the Pieces Together

Figure 7.11 is a sample differentiated professional learning plan for DL and biliteracy educators. You will notice that the first 3 years focus on building foundational pedagogical knowledge so there will be more time spent covering the essential topics for DL and biliteracy instruction. Don't be alarmed by the large number of topics to cover; keep in mind that some of those topics can be combined and presented in a single professional learning session. For example, one full-day session could cover four topics: an overview of the history of bilingual education, current federal and state policies for multilingual instruction, research on effectiveness of multilingual learning programs, and an introduction to *Guiding Principles for DL Education* (Howard et al., 2018). These topics are meant to be foundational for the first 3 years, but more in-depth study can take place in later years.

You will also notice that as the level of teaching experience increases, the amount of time spent building foundational knowledge on pedagogical practices decreases, but the amount of time spent digging deeper into these topics and building leadership capacity increases.

FIGURE 7.11 Sample Differentiated Professional Learning Plan for DL and Biliteracy Educators

Level of Teacher Experience (Rodriguez & McKay, 2010)	Novice Teachers (0–3 years of DL experience)	Experienced Teachers (4–5 years of DL experience and have a positive impact on student achievement)	Expert Teachers (6+ years of DL experience and have a significant impact on student achievement)
DL and Biliteracy Foundational Knowledge Topics	• Creating a Multilingual Classroom Ecology and Developing Critical Consciousness • History of Bilingual Education at the Federal and State Levels • Federal and State Policies for Multilingual Learner Instruction • Research on Effectiveness of Multilingual Learner Programs • Foundations of Effective Instruction for Multilingual Learners • Foundations of DL and Biliteracy Education • District-specific DL Program Model and Instructional Expectations • Collaborative Learning Structures in DL Education • Authentic Methods for Teaching Reading and Writing in the Partner Language • Translanguaging and Cross-linguistic Transfer in DL Classrooms • Teaching Grammatical Structures of Partner Language • Culturally and Linguistically Sustaining Practices • Designated ELD in DL Classrooms • Integrated ELD and SLD in DL Classrooms • Becoming a Reflective DL Teacher	• Mentoring DL Novice Teachers • Embedding Home Language Varieties in the Classroom • Planning for Designated ELD in DL Classrooms • Creating and Analyzing Multilingual Formative Assessments • Including Families' Funds of Knowledge in the Learning Process • Teacher Selected Topics Based on Self-reflection and Classroom Data • Analyzing Student Writing Through a Biliteracy Lens • Strategies to Address the Socioemotional Needs of Multilingual Learners	• Essentials of Instructional Coaching in DL Classrooms • Teacher Selected Topics based on Self-reflection and Classroom Data • Engaging in Biliteracy Curriculum Planning • Adult Learning Theory • Research Foundations of Effective Multilingual Instructional Frameworks • Leading Inquiry Cycles • Strategies for Planning and Delivering Effective Presentations

(Continued)

(Continued)

Level of Teacher Experience (Rodriguez & McKay, 2010)	Novice Teachers (0–3 years of DL experience)	Experienced Teachers (4–5 years of DL experience and have a positive impact on student achievement)	Expert Teachers (6+ years of DL experience and have a significant impact on student achievement)
Sustained Opportunities for Building Collective Teacher Efficacy	• Participate in student data-reflection cycles in a DL teacher PLC with support. • Based on student data, engage in a collaborative inquiry cycle with other DL teachers to address one common area of need.	• Participate in and co-facilitate student data reflection cycles in a DL teacher PLC with support. • Based on student data, engage in and co-lead a collaborative inquiry cycle with other DL teachers to address one common area of need.	• Participate in and lead student data reflection cycles in a DL teacher PLC with support. • Based on student data, engage in and lead a collaborative inquiry cycle with other DL teachers to address one common area of need.
Individualized Supports	• Participate in coaching opportunities for standards-based backwards planning of biliteracy units. • Participate in coaching cycles to implement teacher-selected foundational strategies.	• Participate in coaching opportunities to refine biliteracy planning. • Participate in coaching cycles to refine a foundational strategy or implement new strategies.	• Participate in coaching opportunities to refine biliteracy planning. • Participate in coaching cycles to refine a foundational strategy or implement a new strategy. • Co-mentor a novice or experienced teacher on biliteracy planning.
Instructional Leadership Development	• Visit other programs or observe experienced or expert teachers. • Practice self-reflection with support.	• Mentor novice DL teachers with instructional coach support. • Co-plan and present professional learning with an instructional coach or experienced teacher.	• Shadow a coaching cycle. • Lead a coaching cycle of a novice or experienced teacher with coaching support. • Lead the planning and delivery of professional learning locally and at state and national conferences.

Conclusion: Key Take-Aways

There is no quick fix that solves the DL and biliteracy teacher shortage issue. This is a critical problem that we can't afford to ignore because it endangers access to equitable instruction for potentially millions of MLLs of diverse linguistic backgrounds. District leaders must transform their professional learning systems through a multilingual lens if they wish to strengthen the pedagogical capacity of new and experienced DL and biliteracy educators. This requires an essential mindset shift because leaders must trust that by building the instructional capacity of multilingual educators, they are also investing in the success of multilingual student populations. We must stop addressing multilingualism as a problem and start treating it as it should be, an asset worthy of investment.

District leaders can help solve these issues if they take the courageous steps to

- accept that pedagogical knowledge and practice are necessary but not sufficient for teaching effectively in a DL program;

- engage key district leaders in critical reflection of their current professional learning systems to address the barriers that prevent DL and biliteracy teachers from receiving the essential professional learning support they need;

- design self-sustaining professional learning systems that will build a pipeline of DL and biliteracy experts and leaders and ensure that equitable professional learning practices continue to extend through the educational system;

- create differentiated professional learning plans that account for the pedagogical, linguistic, sociocultural, and critical consciousness needs of DL and biliteracy educators; and

- become the transformative intellectuals who will serve as critical designers of equitable and just educational structures in DL and biliteracy programs.

> The alignment of investment has to be reflected in the state-, district-, and school-level budgets as well as in how time is spent. State, district, and school leaders need to intentionally demand professional service providers and vendors who have shared beliefs about an asset-based approach to multilingualism. Leveraging federal funds also requires a concerted effort to make sure we can address professional development in intentional ways.
>
> **David**

Reflection Questions

1. How is the bilingual teacher shortage addressed in your district? What strategies are implemented for the recruitment and retention of effective DL and biliteracy teachers?

2. How are the professional learning needs of DL teachers identified and addressed in your district?

(Continued)

(Continued)

> 3. What systems are in place to build capacity among district leaders on DL and biliteracy instructional and professional learning needs?
>
> 4. How are DL teacher voice and choice included in the planning of professional learning in your district?
>
> 5. How is the collective efficacy of DL and biliteracy teachers nurtured in your DL program?
>
> 6. Why must DL teachers be properly trained to address the essential components of DL instruction?
>
> 7. Why is it important that professional learning be provided in the partner language of the program, is of high quality, and expands the educator's bilingual repertoire?
>
> 8. How is the development of critical consciousness addressed through professional learning?
>
> 9. In which ways could you be an advocate for more just and equitable DL professional learning at your district or site?

References

Alfaro, C., & Hernandez, A. M. (2016, March). Ideology, pedagogy, access and equity (IPAE): A critical examination for dual language educators. The *Multilingual Educator*, 8–11.

Bandura, A. (1993). Perceived self-efficacy in cognitive development and functioning. *Educational psychologist, 28*(2), 117–148.

Bartolomé, L. I. (2000). Democratizing bilingualism: The role of critical teacher education. In Z. F. Beykont (Ed.), *Lifting every voice: Pedagogy and politics of bilingualism* (pp. 167–186). Harvard Educational Publishing Group.

Cloud, N., Genesee, F., & Hamayan, E. (2000). *Dual language instruction: A handbook for enriched education*. Heinle & Heinle.

Darling-Hammond, L., Hyler, M. E., & Gardner, M. (2017). *Effective teacher professional development*. Learning Policy Institute. https://doi.org/10.54300/122.311

Escamilla, K., Olsen, L., & Slavick, J. (2022). *Toward comprehensive effective literacy policy and instruction for English learner/emergent bilingual students*. National Committee for Effective Literacy for Emergent Bilingual students.

Every Student Succeeds Act. Pub. L. No. 114-95, 114 Stat. 1177. (2015). https://www.congress.gov/114/statute/STATUTE-129/STATUTE-129-Pg1802.pdf

Garcia, A. (2020). *Grow your own teachers: A 50-state scan of policies and programs*. New America. https://d1y8sb8igg2f8e.cloudfront.net/documents/Grow_Your_Own_Teachers_.pdf

Gibney, D., Kelly, H., Rutherford-Quach, S., Ballen Riccards, J., & Parker, C. (2021). *Addressing the bilingual teacher shortage*. CCNetwork. https://www.compcenternetwork.org/sites/default/files/2.%20Addressing%20the%20bilingual%20teacher%20shortage_Acc.pdf

Giroux, H. (2002). Teachers as transformatory intellectuals. *EDucate, 1*(2), 46–49.

Giroux, H. A. (1988). *Teachers as intellectuals: Toward a critical pedagogy of learning*. Greenwood Publishing Group.

Hattie, J. (2019). *Visible learning for teachers*. Routledge. https://doi.org/10.4324/9781003024477

Horn, C., Burnett, C., Lowery, S., & White, C. (2021). *Texas teacher workforce report*. University of Houston. https://www.raiseyourhandtexas.org/wp-content/uploads/2020/11/Texas-Teacher-Workforce-Report.pdf

Howard, E. R., Lindholm-Leary, K. J., Rogers, D., Olague, N., Medina, J., Kennedy, B., Sugarman, J., & Christian, D. (2018). *Guiding principles for dual language education* (3rd ed.). Center for Applied Linguistics.

Johnson, S. I. (2021). Cultivating pedagogical clarity: Dual-language bilingual education teachers' changing views of literacy practices as influenced by critical dialogue. In S. I. Johnson (Ed.), *Handbook of Latinos and education* (pp. 365–382). Routledge.

Learning for Justice. (2022). *Social justice standards: The learning for justice anti-bias framework*. https://www.learningforjustice.org/sites/default/files/2022-09/LFJ-Social-Justice-Standards-September-2022-09292022.pdf

Learning Forward. (2015, December 10). *ESSA includes improved definition of professional development*. Texas. https://learningforward.org/2015/12/10/essa-includes-improved-definition-professional-development/

Learning Forward. (2022). *Standards for professional learning*. Ohio. https://standards.learningforward.org/

León, J. (2017). *THREAD – An approach for recruitment & retention of bilingual professionals in education*. New Jersey Department of Education. https://www.nj.gov/education/title3/doc/THREAD.pdf

Mitchell, C. (2020, February 07). The invisible burden some bilingual teachers face. *Education Week*. https://www.edweek.org/teaching-learning/the-invisible-burden-some-bilingual-teachers-face/2020/02

National Council of Teachers of English. (2019, July 30). *Shifting from professional development to professional learning: Centering teacher empowerment*. https://ncte.org/statement/proflearning/

Palmer, D. (2018). *Teacher leadership for social change in bilingual and bicultural education*. Multilingual Matters. https://doi.org/10.21832/PALMER1435

Palmer, D., Cervantes-Soon, C., & Dornier-Heiman, D. (2019). *Bilingualism, biliteracy, biculturalism, and critical consciousness for all: Proposing a fourth fundamental goal for two-way dual language education*. https://doi.org/10.1080/00405841.2019.1569376

Piñón, L. (2022). *Texas must build a strong bilingual teacher workforce*. IDRA. https://www.idra.org/wp-content/uploads/2022/09/09.20.22-IDRA-Testimony-on-Texas-Bilingual-Teacher-Shortage.pdf

Rodas, S. (2022, January 30). *To fill shortage, N.J. school district will sponsor teachers from other countries*. NJ.com. https://www.nj.com/education/2022/01/to-fill-shortage-nj-school-district-to-sponsor-teachers-from-other-countries.html

Rodríguez, A. G., & McKay, S. (2010). *Professional development for experienced teachers working with adult English language learners*. Center for Applied Linguistics.

Rutherford-Quach, S., Gibney, D., Kelly, H., Ballen Riccards, J., Garcia, E., Hsiao, M., Pellerin, E., & Parker, C. (2021). *Bilingual education across the United States*. CCNetwork. https://compcenternetwork.org/sites/default/files/Bilingual%20education%20across%20the%20United%20States.pdf

Smylie, S. (2022, March 7). *Illinois hopes a $4 million grant will strengthen the bilingual teacher pipeline*. Chalkbeat Chicago. https://chicago.chalkbeat.org/2022/3/7/22966061/illinois-bilingual-education-teacher-shortage-english-learners

Stavely, Z., & Rosales, M. B. (2021, June 16). *Why training California bilingual teachers just got harder*. Edsource. https://edsource.org/2021/why-training-california-bilingual-teachers-just-got-harder/656558

Thomas, W. P., & Collier, V. P. (2012). *Dual language education for a transformed world*. Dual Language Education of New Mexico – Fuente Press.

Villegas, L., & Garcia, A. (2022, April 7). *Educating English learners during the pandemic*. New America. https://www.newamerica.org/education-policy/reports/educating-english-learners-during-the-pandemic/

Walker, T. (2022, February). *Survey: Alarming number of educators may soon leave the profession*. National Education Association. https://www.nea.org/advocating-for-change/new-from-nea/survey-alarming-number-educators-may-soon-leave-profession

chapter eight

From Monolingual Policies to Dual Language Policies

LYN SCOTT

PREMISE

Educational language policies[1] supporting equity and educational opportunity for multilingual learners (MLLs) are steadily aligning with evidence-based research validating dual language (DL) instruction. In state after state, monolingual (English-only), deficit-based policies have been supplanted by those that support use of multiple languages for teaching and learning. Teachers are the critical change agents who navigate the top-down policies and bottom-up teaching practices to the benefit of MLLs' academic success and multicultural competence.

State-level policies implemented since 2017 such as Massachusetts' Language Opportunity for Our Kids (LOOK) Act and California's Education for a Global Economy (CA Ed.G.E.) Initiative as seen in figure 8.1 emphasize DL programs and policies designed to promote biliteracy and multiculturalism, multicultural competency, and high levels of academic achievement for MLLs. Policies supporting additive teaching practices as discussed in chapter 1

---

[1] The use of the word *policy* (or *policies*) in this chapter refers to Educational Language Policies.

have enabled educators and families in these states and in other communities across the United States to increase the DL educational opportunities for their preschool through high school students. In some communities, existing elementary DL programs are being extended to middle or high school, and in others, new DL programs are being designed as two-way immersion developmental DL, or immersion in a language other than English to support the educational success of MLLs (Gándara & Escamilla, 2017). Such policies effectively reverse two decades of monolingual restrictions that were barriers to equity for multilingual learners.

DL policies validate all students' home language and enable them to use their full linguistic repertoire as they learn and develop multilingually. In the late 1990s, restrictive monolingual policies were implemented at federal, state, and district levels, diminishing or eliminating language-minoritized students' use of their home language. Voter-approved laws in California in 1998, Arizona in 2000, and Massachusetts in 2002 restricted MLLs to an English-only remedial education such as structured English immersion programs. Despite claims to the backers of such policies, such subtractive approaches are unsupported by evidence-based research. At the federal level, monolingual policies such as the English-only testing requirements in the No Child Left Behind Act (2002) undermined multilingual assessments as its consequence, and this continues to persist in many areas under its reauthorization, the Every Student Succeeds Act (2015). In response to these monolingual policies, many schools curtailed or eliminated bilingual education. Figure 8.1 represents recent shifts (or lack thereof) from monolingual policies to DL policies.

FIGURE 8.1 **Examples of Change in Educational Language Policies at the State and Federal Levels**

	From Monolingual Policies	To Dual Language Policies
Massachusetts	**2002 Question 2** **English Language Education in Public Schools Initiative** Ballot language: "all public school children must be taught English by being taught all subjects in English and being placed in English language classrooms." **Modified by the 2017 LOOK Act with dual language policy provisions.**	**2017 LOOK Act** **Language Opportunity for Our Kids Act** Legislation provides schools with flexibility to choose DL programs designed to promote biliteracy and multiculturalism, multicultural competency, and high levels of academic achievement for MLLs; other research-based additive DL programs where all students develop and maintain their home language while adding a second language to their repertoire; and a Seal of Biliteracy for high school graduates. **Implemented in 2018.**

	From Monolingual Policies	To Dual Language Policies
U.S. Federal	**2001 No Child Left Behind Act** Legislation renamed the Bilingual Education Act (BEA) the English Language Acquisition, Language Enhancement, and Academic Achievement Act and removed emphasis on maintaining an MLL's culture and home language by instead emphasizing English-only instruction and quick mainstreaming into general education classrooms. **Replaced by the 2015 Every Student Succeeds Act; however, included no changes to the monolingual policy provisions.**	No recent shift to DL policies at the federal level.
Arizona	**2000 Proposition 203** **English Language Education for Children in Public Schools Initiative** Ballot language: "All children in Arizona public schools shall be taught English by being taught in English and all children shall be placed in English language classrooms." "Foreign language classes for children who already know English shall be completely unaffected." **Implemented in 2001; repeal efforts have failed to date.**	No recent shift to DL policies at the state level in Arizona, which requires voter referendum to reverse Prop 203.
California	**1998 Proposition 227** **English Language in Public Schools Initiative** Ballot language: "Requires all public school instruction be conducted in English." "Provides initial short-term placement, not normally exceeding one year, in intensive sheltered English immersion programs for children not fluent in English." **Repealed by 2016 Prop. 58 California Ed.G.E. Initiative with dual language policy provisions.**	**2016 Proposition 58** **California Education for a Global Economy (CA Ed.G.E.) Initiative** Ballot language: "Authorizes school districts to establish dual-language immersion programs for both native and non–native English speakers." **Implemented in 2017.**

Sources: Information compiled from Arizona (2000), California (1998, 2016), Massachusetts (2002, 2017), No Child Left Behind Act (2002), and Every Student Succeeds Act (2015).

Teachers are at the nexus of practice and policy assuring that MLLs utilize their full repertoire of linguistic resources in their learning. For example, by restructuring English as a second language to embrace inclusive practices such as translanguaging[2] (Kleyn & García, 2019), teachers enact DL policies and

---

[2]See chapters 3, 4, and 7 for further discussion of translanguaging.

validate MLLs' use of their languages in their learning. Teachers, whether monolingual or multilingual themselves, assure that MLLs have equitable learning opportunities by preparing lessons in which their students access and develop both their home language and English or another language. Challenging student teachers to acknowledge and resist deficit perspectives when teaching MLLs may include calling out deficit language and examining the funds of knowledge that MLLs bring from their homes (Ennser-Kananen & Leider, 2018). While DL policies may come from local, state, and national policymakers, teachers, through their practices, are de facto dual language policy implementers who must also be "critical consumers (and eventual producers) of educative materials, curricula, and 'best practices' for MLLs" (Hernández et al., 2022, p. 395).

VIGNETTE

Across the State University campus the linguistic diversity is apparent because students can be heard talking in Spanish, Arabic, Mandarin, Vietnamese, and a mix of English and other languages, while other students can be seen signing American Sign Language. Most of the students are graduates of local high schools and plan to establish careers in the area. Many are from the first generation in their families to attend college. However, only a small percentage of the multilingual student body developed strong biliteracy skills during their elementary and secondary school years because state and federal monolingual policies at the time restricted MLLs' literacy development to English-only.

With recent changes in state law embracing DL policies and establishing a Seal of Biliteracy on the high school diplomas of future graduates who qualify, demand for DL programs in local schools has grown while a shortage of qualified teachers with specialized biliteracy skills has developed. School administrators repeatedly and urgently contact the university's education faculty and dean seeking qualified teachers who are biliterate and hold teaching credentials with bilingual authorization.

The state legislature is debating a JumpStart bill providing funds for universities to hire additional multilingual faculty who can train the needed DL teachers. The dean knows that recruiting and preparing credentialed teachers is not enough, but that the teacher preparation program needs to prepare multilingual teachers with strong biliteracy skills and critical consciousness of the historical and sociopolitical context of schooling. A small team of faculty has been awarded a federal grant to train mentor teachers and student teachers in asset-based approaches such as translanguaging practices to support MLLs' development of biliteracy and multilingualism. They can also offer scholarships to university students to develop the biliteracy skills that they will need to teach effectively in DL programs. With the existing federal grant and the potential state JumpStart funding in mind, the dean approached the provost and faculty with a proposal to transform the teacher education program by recruiting teaching faculty and university students who are multilingual and who will challenge monolingual and deficit-based practices to expand effective DL programs in local schools serving MLLs.

THE URGENCY

One in five public school students is an MLL, yet very few learn in DL programs that develop their biliteracy and multicultural competency. The U.S. Department of Education (2019) considers that there are about 10 million MLLs in public schools speaking over 400 home languages such as Spanish (75%), Arabic (2%), Chinese (2%), Vietnamese (1.5%), and other languages as seen in figure 8.2. Breaking down the monolingual wall is critical to substantially expanding access to DL programs for MLLs and their classmates who attend one of nearly 100,000 U.S. public elementary or secondary schools (Goldenberg & Wagner, 2015).

FIGURE 8.2 Languages Spoken by Most MLLs

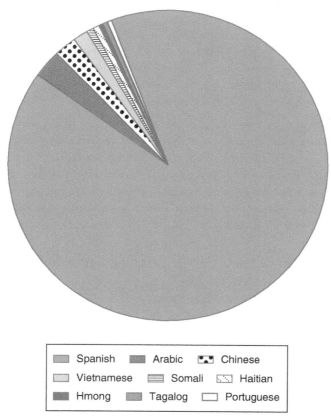

Spanish   Arabic   Chinese
Vietnamese   Somali   Haitian
Hmong   Tagalog   Portuguese

Source: Information compiled from the U.S. Department of Education (2019).

Transforming schools into welcoming spaces of effective multilingual learning does not happen overnight. Educators and policymakers must work in collaboration to realize the promise of multilingual policies. For example, the Common Core State Standards were a time-consuming, monolingual policy effort in math and English language arts that Massachusetts, California, Florida, Texas, New York, Colorado, and other states adopted in 2010. Two years later California adopted Common Core in *Español*, which was developed by the San Diego County Office of Education to provide guidance in Spanish to DL programs. In the decade since, a widely recognized DL policy acknowledging MLLs' biliteracy achievements in two or more languages is the Seal of Biliteracy (SoBL) as discussed in chapters 5 and 6. MLLs are awarded this distinction with a SoBL on their high school diploma. The SoBL was the result of state-level legislation that began with one state in 2012 and grew to forty-nine states and the District of Columbia in 2022.

The changing profile of MLLs in schools in recent years also means adding new linguistic resources to DL programs and updating instructional practices to provide equity and educational opportunity to not only increase MLLs "social and psychological well-being, but . . . also strengthen both their own labor market prospects and the economy of the nation" (Gándara & Escamilla, 2017, p. 11). In response, new policies permitted schools and districts to expand the languages of DL programs. The American Councils Research Center (2021) documented over 3,600 DL programs at the beginning of the 2021–2022 school year. Over 80 percent of the programs partnered Spanish (2,936) with English and over 10 percent East Asian languages such as Chinese (312), Korean (23), Hmong (7), and Vietnamese (6) with English. DL programs included Hawaiian (27), Portuguese (27), and Arabic (5) additionally.

Most important, however, high-quality DL programs require well-trained DL teachers who are currently in short supply as discussed in chapters 1, 6, and 7. In over half the states there is a DL teacher shortage, and this is most severe in the states with the greatest number of MLLs. According to researchers at the Comprehensive Center Network, the teacher pipeline, pay, and working conditions are the main drivers of the shortages as well as the potential policy solutions (Gibney et al., 2021) as seen in figure 8.3.

FIGURE 8.3   **Dual Language Teacher Shortages: Drivers and Policy Solutions**

Drivers of the Shortage	Policy Solutions
Obstacles to recruiting, training, certifying, and retaining teachers	Strengthening the teacher pipeline
Inadequate compensation, lack of incentives	Providing additional financial incentives to teachers working in shortage areas
Poor working conditions	Improving the working conditions of current teachers

Source: Information compiled from Gibney et al. (2021)

As the faculty and dean at the State University in this chapter's vignette take steps to fix a leaky DL teacher pipeline by strengthening and expanding DL teacher training programs that model asset-based practices and pedagogies, policymakers at the district, state, and federal levels urgently need to consider enhanced financial incentives and improved working conditions to attract and retain qualified teachers in DL programs.

Without sustained attention to the DL teacher shortage, poorly trained teachers lacking credentials or working on temporary emergency permits could undermine successful DL programs serving MLLs. The stakes are high: Poorly implemented DL policies could embolden advocates of monolingualism to return to the subtractive policies that have dominated U.S. schools throughout our history.

If we want to retain highly qualified teachers, districts and administrators should try to make bilingual teachers' work environments healthier by adding stipends and providing the support needed. Funding for research-based DL professional development, sending teachers to conferences, and giving them time for collaboration should be included in all School Plans and Local Control and Accountability Plan (LCAP) goals to improve working conditions and retain bilingual-qualified teachers.

Marga

RESEARCH BASE

Prior chapters have underscored the cultural advantages of biliteracy (Goldenberg & Wagner, 2015), social importance (Zentella, 2005), and cognitive benefits of multilingualism (Bialystok, 2001, 2009; Collier & Thomas, 2017); however, linguistic diversity—whether sanctioned by education policymakers or not—has always been a fact of life in North America. The rich linguistic diversity found in communities and schools across the United States reflects a long history of the languages of Native Americans as discussed in chapter 5 as well as those of immigrants from all parts of the world who came after them. For example, speakers of Yup'ik, Lakȟóta, Lushootseed, Makah, Diné, Cherokee, and Hawaiian languages educated their children in their communities before being joined by English-, Italian-, German-, Polish-, French-, Spanish-, Chinese-, and Japanese-speaking communities, to name a few (Nieto, 2009). Today, DL programs in each of these languages and more continue the diversity of languages spoken in communities across the country and used by MLLs in their schools (American Councils Research Center, 2021).

Dual Language Education and the Rise of Monolingual Policies in U.S. History

By the 1800s many states had DL schools in practice (*de facto*) irrespective of formal laws (*de jure*). Over the next two centuries the United States would experience shifts between monolingual and DL policies at the local, state, and federal levels, as seen in figure 8.4. The laissez-faire attitudes toward MLLs at the time allowed communities and schools to set their own course without high-level government interference.

A de facto DL policy characterized many of the practices in European immigrant communities in the Midwest where teachers instructed MLLs in Czech, Dutch, German, Italian, Norwegian, Polish, or Swedish as well as English in their schools. DL instruction in French was common in the Northeast and

Louisiana, and Spanish in the Southwest. Ohio was the first state to have an official de jure DL policy when it enacted a law permitting parents to request DL instruction in German and English in 1839. By the end of the 1890s, more than ten states and territories had enacted official DL policies, including French-English in Louisiana in 1847 and Spanish-English in New Mexico in 1850. Estimates are that DL teachers had instructed one million of the nation's 16 million students in English and another language by 1900 (Kloss, 1998).

FIGURE 8.4 **Change in Educational Language Policies at the State and Federal Levels**

Year	From Monolingual Policies	To Dual Language Policies
Until the late 1800s		Laissez-faire approach, with states and communities having de facto DL policies permitting MLLs to learn in DL schools
1839		Parents could request DL instruction in German and English under Ohio law.
1847		French-English schools permitted under Louisiana law.
1850		Spanish-English schools under New Mexico law.
1868		Fourteenth Amendment's Equal Protection clause protects MLLs' educational rights.
Late 1800s	Bureau of Indian Affairs forces Native American children to attend boarding schools that eradicated Indigenous languages; English language imposed in Southwest	
1906	Nationality Act requires English for naturalization, connecting English and national identity as federal policy	
1914–1918	WWI; German-English bilingual schools close	
By 1923	Thirty-four states require English-only instruction in all elementary schools	
1954		*Brown v. Board of Education* rules "separate but equal" education unconstitutional, guaranteeing MLLs equal educational opportunities under law.
1964		Civil Rights Act prohibits discrimination in federally funded programs and assures MLLs the right to a meaningful education with effective teaching.

Year	From Monolingual Policies	To Dual Language Policies
1968		Bilingual Education Act (BEA) recognizes MLLs' need for specialized instruction and multicultural awareness to receive equal educational opportunities.
1974		Equal Educational Opportunity Act requires that schools take action to remove language barriers so MLLs can equally participate in their instructional program.
1974		*Lau v. Nichols* rules identical educational programs for English- and non-English–speaking students do not provide equal educational opportunity; the school district must take affirmative steps to provide MLLs access to the same curriculum as English-speaking students.
1975–1980s		*Lau Remedies* requires schools to identify MLLs, assess their language abilities, analyze their achievement data, and have a program with realistic time-outcome expectations. Civil rights regulations require that DL instruction be given by qualified teachers.
1976		*Aspira of New York v. Board of Education* Consent Decree provides MLLs in New York City access to transitional bilingual education and English as a second language instruction.
1981		*Castañeda v. Pickard* rules schools act so MLLs overcome language barriers in programs that are pedagogically sound, that are implemented by qualified educators, and that have a system of evaluation.
1984–1994	BEA revisions give English-only programs successively greater portion of federal funding; language-minoritized students in Transitional Bilingual Education are deprioritized	MLLs in two-way immersion prioritized in federal funding of DL programs.
1998–2002	English-only laws in California (227), Arizona (203), and Massachusetts (2) restrict DL education for MLLs	
2002	English Language Acquisition, Language Enhancement, and Academic Achievement Act replaces the Bilingual Education Act in No Child Left Behind legislation	
2012		Seal of Biliteracy law first passed (CA).
2017–present		English-only laws repealed (MA & CA). Seal of Biliteracy laws in DC & forty-nine states.

Sources: Information compiled from Gándara and Escamilla (2017), Kloss (1998), and Nieto (2009).

Native American communities suffered restrictive monolingual policies that only increased through the 1800s as the federal government imposed the English language on Native Americans across the country. By the 1880s the federal Bureau of Indian Affairs forced Native American children to attend boarding schools where assimilation and Native American language eradication was pervasive. While language loss was not entirely complete, monolingual policies succeeded in marginalizing Native American languages and instilling a sense of shame on their speakers and their descendants who used them (Nieto, 2009).

The federal government also imposed English on residents of the Southwest who spoke Spanish by actively working to dilute their political power. The government strategically split Spanish-speaking communities by establishing state borders where a majority of English speakers would dominate the newly admitted state (e.g., California, 1850; Nevada, 1864; Colorado, 1876, and Utah, 1896). Statehood was delayed for other territories without a majority of English speakers until English-speaking settlers populated the state in sufficient numbers to dominate the newly admitted state (e.g., Oklahoma, 1907; New Mexico, 1912; and Arizona, 1912) (Nieto, 2009).

By the early 1900s, the federal government's de facto language policy had become overtly restrictive, favoring English-only communities. With the passage of the Nationality Act of 1906 the federal government's official language policy required, for the first time and with limited physical exceptions, "[t]hat no alien shall hereafter be naturalized or admitted as a citizen of the United States who cannot speak the English language" (p. 599). The connection between English and national identity was thus official law.

With the outbreak of World War I and rising anti-German sentiment during the following decade, German-English bilingual schools were shut down across the country (Gándara & Escamilla, 2017). Soon after the end of the war thirty-four of the nation's forty-eight state legislatures had officially passed laws requiring that all elementary schools, whether public or private, must provide English-only instruction (Kloss, 1998). For the next four and a half decades no significant changes in the federal government's monolingual policies toward education occurred. Intergenerational language-loss increased in homes where languages other than English had been spoken, with many grandchildren unable to speak the languages of their grandparents and many of their multilingual parents having limited biliteracy skills.

While monolingual policies prevailed during this time, a countercurrent took the form of equal protection measures. In 1868 the Fourteenth Amendment to the U.S. Constitution was ratified, guaranteeing that states must give equal protection to each person and never deny anyone privileges granted to others. That protected the educational rights of MLLs in the U.S. Constitution. In 1954 the U.S. Supreme Court ruled in *Brown v. Board of Education* that separate but equal education was unconstitutional. It provided the basis for equal educational opportunities for MLLs and other students. In 1964 the Civil Rights Act became federal law, prohibiting discrimination in any program that is federally funded. Under Title VI of the law, MLLs and other students are assured a right to a meaningful education with effective teaching.

The Bilingual Education Act (BEA) and Equal Educational Opportunities for MLLs

The civil rights movement of the 1960s marked a shift from restrictive English-only, monolingual federal policies toward additive language policies. In 1968 Congress passed the BEA, also known as Title VII of the Elementary and Secondary Education Act. For the first time, federal policy recognized the need to provide equal educational opportunities for language-minoritized students through specialized instruction in languages other than English. The BEA also promoted the inclusion of multicultural awareness in school curricula (Gándara & Escamilla, 2017). While the BEA did not explicitly state that DL instruction should occur, the right of MLLs to be educated in their home language was now in the national discussion (Flores & García, 2017).

The year after the enactment of the BEA, Congress appropriated funds for schools to meet the needs of 27,000 low-income MLLs in four key areas: educational programs, teacher professional development, instructional materials development, and parental involvement projects (Gándara & Escamilla, 2017). No funding was provided for middle- or upper-income MLLs, which cast the BEA as support only for MLLs of low socioeconomic status (SES).

In 1974 three significant events impacting MLLs marked a continued federal policy shift toward DL:

1. Enactment of The Equal Education Opportunities Act (1974). Not only did this landmark legislation prevent states from denying equal educational opportunities to individuals based on race, color, sex, or national origin, but it also required educational agencies to take appropriate action to assist MLLs in overcoming language barriers that impede their equal participation in instructional programs.

2. The Bilingual Education Act was amended to require states and schools serving MLLs to be held accountable for setting goals and measuring their success. It also provided funding to schools serving these students (Gándara & Escamilla, 2017).

3. The U.S. Supreme Court decision in *Lau v. Nichols,* discussed in the following section.

U.S. Court Decisions Impacting Dual Language Policies

The U.S. Supreme Court provided momentum toward DL policies with its landmark decision in *Lau v. Nichols.* The justices ruled that simply providing identical educational programs for English- and non-English-speaking students was not equal educational opportunity (1974). As in the BEA, real access to academic content required specialized language instruction for MLLs (Flores & García, 2017). *Lau* focused on the nearly 2,000 MLLs who spoke Chinese in San Francisco, California, public schools. The court determined that because the students could not understand the monolingual instruction in English, the school district would have to take affirmative steps to provide MLLs access to the same curriculum that English-speaking students received (Gándara & Escamilla, 2017).

The court did not strictly mandate DL education as a result of the *Lau* decision; however, it was one of the possible remedies. Supporting MLLs in gaining proficiency in English was a possible remedy, as was teaching the curriculum in Chinese. The Board of Education was simply ordered to "apply its expertise to the problem and rectify the situation" (*Lau v. Nichols*, 1974, p. 563).

The court built on a constitutional amendment, prior judicial decisions, and interpretation of existing federal legislation in making its ruling. The equal protection clause of the Fourteenth Amendment from the middle of the nineteenth century had established the educational rights of MLLs. Schools could not deprive students of an education or equal protection under the law. And the courts' ruling from the middle of the twentieth century had established equal educational opportunities for MLLs in *Brown v. Board of Education*. Schools could not be "separate but equal" under law. Now, civil rights legislation enacted in the prior decade assured language-minoritized children the right to a meaningful education with effective instruction.

Schools were later guided by the federal Office of Civil Rights (OCR) in inplementing what came to be known as the *Lau Remedies* by developing a compliance plan that identifies language-minority students, assesses their language abilities, analyzes their achievement data, and creates a program with realistic time-outcome expectations. In all cases the *Lau Remedies* were to be seen as a set of minimal expectations that schools were encouraged to exceed based on their local circumstances. Over time additional guidance was added to the *Lau Remedies,* including requirements to hire qualified personnel with appropriate language skills, prohibition of isolating MLLs based on their race or ethnicity, parental notification to families who speak languages other than English, and ongoing program evaluation (Task-Force Findings Specifying Remedies Available for Eliminating Past Educational Practices Ruled Unlawful under *Lau v. Nichols*, 1983).

As a result of the case, language-minoritized students became a protected subgroup entitled to a specialized instructional program and services to receive the educational opportunities that other students receive. Both the OCR and further court rulings have seen DL education as an important means of providing the accommodations MLLs require (Flores & García, 2017), and that most school boards of education have agreed to (Gándara & Escamilla, 2017).

What many consider to be the most important judicial decision for language-minoritized children since *Lau* is the appellate court ruling in

Castañeda v. Pickard (1981). While *Lau* did not provide criteria for determining the effectiveness of a school's approach, Mr. Castañeda, the father of two Spanish-speaking students, sued their school district for segregating students by ethnicity, which was discriminatory, and for not establishing enough DL programs that could benefit his children in receiving an equal education. The father also argued that the school district had no way of knowing if its program actually helped MLLs overcome the school's English-only barriers.

In the ruling favorable to the students, the court established a three-pronged test. First, any program serving MLLs must have a research-based educational theory or an experimental strategy deemed sound by educational experts. Second, the program and instruction must have sufficient resources such as materials, classrooms, and educational staff who can effectively implement the program. And third, the school district must have a system for evaluating the program's success and then implement any necessary changes to make sure the program is helping MLLs overcome English-only barriers.

Court opinions, along with consent decrees in several states and school districts, put added weight on the scale for DL policies benefiting MLLs and less weight for monolingual policies. But, once again, such gains were counterbalanced by a predominant deficit-based perspective on MLLs that played out in the court of public opinion.

Deficit Views of Multilingualism and the Impact of Public Opinion on Dual Language Policies

Since the 1960s when the Bilingual Education Act became law, DL programs for MLLs and court decisions largely held a deficit view of MLLs. English proficiency was widely held as an end-goal, and language-minoritized students were considered as lacking and in need of remediation. The BEA became law as a compensatory program for language-minoritized children from low-SES families, providing funding for what they lacked—English proficiency. In legislative debate there was a tension between the BEA's DL policy, intended to foster a multilingual pluralism recognizing the linguistic assets of MLLs, or a monolingual policy promoting assimilation and viewing MLLs as deficient and lacking English. The final legislation was a compromise that did not provide clarity to policymakers, practitioners, or the public and masked fundamental differences with its vague statement of purpose. What remained was a stigma associating MLLs with poverty and a remedial program for MLLs who have not learned English (Gándara, 2018). Policymakers envisioned the goals, educators implemented the instructional practices, and the public observed the outcome of monolingual development in English.

Rather than being acknowledged for the linguistic assets and cultural wealth that MLLs bring to their learning, they were the recipients of a host of deficit-based labels describing their needs. Limited English Proficient (LEP), Non-English Proficient (NEP), non-English speaker, English Language

Learner (ELL), English Learner (EL), Long-term English Learner (LTEL), and Students with Limited or Interrupted Formal Education (SLIFE) are common descriptors in documents of legislation, court decisions, policy statements, assessment tools, and curricula. Terms describing the multilingual abilities and assets that students bring to their learning were rarely used.

Additionally, students' linguistic resources, often Spanish, were viewed as a problem rather than an asset. For example, the funds of knowledge that Spanish-speaking children from Mexican and Central American immigrant families bring from their homes was not yet recognized (González et al., 2005). Policymakers used examples of vocabulary in their documents—barriers, obstacles, deficiencies, limited, transitional, lacking, needs, and handicaps. Language as a problem rather than an asset dominated policy discussions at all levels, painting a picture of an MLL as a deficient learner (Ruiz, 1984).

Any linguistic assets that MLLs possessed were to be used to speed their transition to English-only classrooms with literacy development only in English as the outcome. Teachers used the MLL's home language, usually Spanish, in instruction until the student acquired sufficient English to be transitioned to an English classroom. After the transition, no attempt to further develop or sustain the MLL's home language and biliteracy occurred.

Thus, from the implementation of the BEA, Transitional Bilingual Education (TBE) was designed as a remedial program that used the home language only until it could be abandoned in favor of English-only instruction. In TBE a language-minoritized student's home language was used only as a bridge to an eventual monolingual education in English—a bridge that could be effectively burned once sufficient English was acquired, causing significant home language loss. Lawmakers proposed policies with a monolingual outcome in each reauthorization of the BEA, rarely including biliteracy and multiculturalism as policy goals, with only transitional approaches adopted at best. Only in the 1994 reauthorization of the BEA was a DL policy inserted into the law by giving funding preference to DL programs where MLLs develop biliteracy in the home language and English (Gándara, 2018; Improving America's School Act of 1994).

While developmental DL programs, including two-way immersion programs having as their goal that MLLs develop biliteracy and multilingual proficiency, became more common in various communities across the country (Nieto, 2009), the remedial and deficit-based notions of TBE instruction remained in mindsets and policy. By the 2000s the movement away from DL policies at the federal level was in full swing with the focus on, and funding of, English taking prominence in legislation, thus strengthening monolingual policies (García & Sung, 2018).

For example, terminology became monolingual and focused on English acquisition. The BEA in Title VII of the Elementary and Secondary Education Act was renamed the English Language Acquisition, Language Enhancement, and Academic Achievement Act. And the Office of Bilingual Education in the Department of Education was renamed the Office of English Language Acquisition (OELA) (Flores & García, 2017; Goldenberg & Wagner, 2015). Also, high-stakes testing in English became law with the passage of the No Child Left Behind Act of 2001. The accountability measures that called on MLLs not yet proficient in English to take these tests in English, with limited exceptions, served as a de facto monolingual policy (Menken, 2006).

Voters in key states approved referendums requiring English-only instruction in public schools with few exceptions. For example, voter guides and titles of the referendum reflected monolingualism, such as *English Language in Public Schools Initiative* in California (1998), *English Language Education for Children in Public Schools Initiative* in Arizona (2000), and *English Language Education in Public Schools Initiative* in Massachusetts (2002). Referendums with similarly chosen titles and monolingual intents nearly passed in Colorado in 2002 and Oregon in 2008 (García & Sung, 2018). The combined efforts had an overwhelming impact in halting the momentum toward DL policies in districts and states across the country and especially in reverting to monolingual policies at the federal level.

Public opinion fueled by sources of information other than evidence-based research was prominent in findings by researchers Lewis and Davies (2018). They found that while 95 percent of evidence-based research articles favored a DL education for MLLs over a monolingual education, only 45 percent of mass media articles were similarly favorable. Also, few media articles available to the public cited evidence-based research and instead relied on anecdotes with increasing frequency. From 2006 to 2016 evidence-based research articles finding that DL education benefits MLLs increased annually; yet reports about legislation impacting policy reflected biases toward the ethnicity of MLLs or immigrant groups rather than scientific findings (Lewis & Davies).

In summary, assuring that a DL policy promotes biliteracy and multiculturalism as educational outcomes necessitates an asset-based foundation, policymakers' advocacy of evidence-based research, and educators' understanding of how the components of DL policy connect to people in the school, home, and community.

Dual Language Policy and Its Components

The underpinnings of DL policy include decades of theoretical work in Educational Language Policy, Educational Linguistics, Language Policy (LP), and Family Language Policy (FLP). The policies described previously in this chapter show how MLLs, schools, and communities have been impacted throughout U.S. history by policies that determined which languages students should use in schools, the languages they should be taught, and what the language or languages of instruction should be. The field of educational linguistics emerged where trained researchers studied language in education by focusing on teaching and learning and the complexity of language used in instruction, the language practices of both teachers and students, biliteracy policies in schools, language and culture, language curriculum, linguistic diversity in schools, equity for language-minoritized students, and educational language policies, to name a few. The evidence-based research that these experts conduct guides policymakers and educators in establishing policies for their programs and schools.

In designing effective DL programs, educators and policymakers consider the everyday DL practices of the school community, their beliefs about language and language acquisition, and plan for how language is used by both students and educators (Spolsky, 2004).

Language Policy Components

1. Language Practices
2. Language Beliefs or Ideology
3. Language Planning or Management

Source: Spolsky (2004)

For example, if MLLs speak different language varieties of Spanish reflecting their families' community of origin, educators examine their beliefs about valuing all varieties. Planning or managing biliteracy practices may involve considering the role of simplified and traditional Chinese characters. Language practices within the family and parents' beliefs about language, known as *Family Language Policies*, impact the entire school community. For example, FLPs consider the language or languages that parents speak with their children or that the children speak with their siblings or grandparents. It also considers home literacy practices, reading habits, and parents' beliefs about their children's language development and biliteracy. Parental control over language mixing or languages permitted to be spoken in the home or at what time also shapes practices that children bring into their schooling.

FLPs also include the aspirations that English-speaking parents have for their monolingual children to become multilingual by joining a DL program. Growth in DL programs in recent years often relies on combining language-minoritized students' needs with those of their monolingual, English-dominant classmates. This requires that school community members design an effective DL program that balances what researchers have identified as global human capital (GHC) and equity/heritage (EH) discourses (Valdez et al., 2016). These discourses, discussed in the following section, are examples of language ideologies or beliefs influencing DL policies.

Global Human Capital and Equity/ Heritage Discourses in DL Policy

GHC discourses focus on the economic benefits of being biliterate. They also highlight how being multilingual improves job marketability and how multilingualism and biliteracy are basic skills in the twenty-first century global community. Such benefits enhance both the individual and the nation. The nation's competitiveness increases by having multilingual citizens who can trade, negotiate, and manage a global workforce. Even the nation's security is strengthened in diplomacy, intelligence gathering, and defense by those who have proficiency in multiple languages (Valdez et al., 2016).

Thus, MLLs' economic outcomes in the global economy are tied to their educational outcome and multilingual proficiency. In fact, recent research shows that MLLs who are in late-exit DL programs are more likely to be promoted at work to higher-level positions and receive significantly higher pay than their peers who lose their home language and speak English only as adults (Gándara & Escamilla, 2017).

MLLs' Likely Economic Outcomes

- Attend late-exit DL programs
  - Promoted to higher levels at work
  - Receive significantly higher pay
- Attend English-only programs and speak English only as adults
  - Fewer promotions at work
  - Receive significantly lower pay

Source: Gándara and Escamilla (2017)

Prior research found insignificant economic benefit among multilinguals in general when compared to all workers; however, a deeper analysis of those findings showed that low-SES and historical disadvantages in the U.S. labor market were the likely cause. Comparisons of classmates from linguistically and culturally diverse communities who become biliterate with those who lose their home language show that there are significant economic benefits for those who gain full literacy in two or more languages (Gándara, 2018).

EH (equity/heritage) discourses explicitly acknowledge that language-minoritized students learn best when the focus is on their heritage. They also emphasize the inequalities in society that MLLs face and that have historically marginalized their home language and culture. Thus, a DL policy must systemically address issues of race, language, and social status in any DL program to provide equity and equal educational opportunity to MLLs (Valdez et al., 2016). This includes continuing to create classrooms that validate MLLs' languages and instill pride in their home cultures while at the same time promoting social justice to remove the institutional barriers and illuminate raciolinguistic ideologies (Flores & García, 2017). We must recognize that all members of society must be advocates for the linguistic human rights of students to an education in their home language as a fundamental right (Skutnabb-Kangas et al., 1994).

Research conducted to understand the social benefits MLLs gain by being multilingual and biliterate shows that the social benefits include having stronger relationships with their family members and within their communities (Gándara & Escamilla, 2017). When multilinguals gain access to these social networks, they can receive help in finding work, and their labor market outcomes increase (Gándara, 2018; Rumbaut, 2014). Additional benefits include gaining a better sense of self and reduced behavior problems in school (Darling-Hammond et al., 2018; Gándara, 2018).

Validating Academic Achievement in DL Policy

Successful educational outcomes for MLLs are fundamental in equitable DL policies. Research on child (Cummins, 2001) and brain development substantiates the benefits of giving MLLs the opportunity to learn in their home language. Cognitive advantages that MLLs develop relative to their monolingual peers include metalinguistic awareness, increased working memory, better abilities solving spatial problems, greater cognitive flexibility, enhanced focus, and problem-solving skills (Darling-Hammond et al., 2018; Gándara & Escamilla, 2017). Evidence-based research also found that effective DL programs promote multilingualism and biliteracy without sacrificing proficiency in English (Goldenberg & Wagner, 2015).

MLLs in well-designed DL programs often achieve above grade level and have higher academic achievement than MLLs in English-only programs. This is true in every secondary subject (Darling-Hammond et al., 2018). MLLs who are in late-exit DL programs are more likely to graduate from high school and more likely to go to college, and those who are Latinx are more likely to go to 4-year colleges (Gándara & Escamilla, 2017).

In the last decade school districts across the country have begun awarding biliterate MLLs the SoBL on their high school diploma as discussed in chapters 5 and 6. The potential exists for MLLs to earn the SoBL by successfully completing their DL program, world language course credit, or demonstrating their home or heritage language proficiency, as well as English (Subtirelu et al., 2019). The SoBL exemplifies the twenty-first century skill of communication, important for graduates in the increasingly interconnected world, and provides a reward that colleges and employers recognize. It also creates excitement for multilingualism among students, educators, families, and the community.

The SoBL is one example of a DL policy vision that guides and validates the importance of linguistic and multicultural competence for MLLs.

IMPLICATIONS FOR PRACTICE AND IMPLEMENTATION

A dual language policy for MLLs' successful educational outcomes is a federal-, state-, and district-level commitment to MLLs' academic achievement, biliteracy, and multicultural competence. It guides the implementation and adequate funding of well-designed DL programs in alignment with evidence-based research and fully staffed with qualified DL teachers. It supports MLLs in developing and utilizing their full repertoire of linguistic and cultural assets in their education, homes, communities, and future careers. Teachers with critical consciousness are the change agents whose instruction and advocacy implement DL policies and effective teaching practices to integrate biliteracy development with content learning for their MLL students' academic success and multicultural competence.

State-level commitments to DL policies such as the SoBL and legislation supporting DL education are furthered by policymakers who provide adequate funding and accountability measures for school districts. District-level commitments include implementing family engagement strategies, providing educators with professional learning opportunities, and aligning biliteracy pathways with evidence-based DL programs from early childhood through high school graduation (Olsen & Aguila, 2019). Federal-level commitments include the return to the original aims of multilingual education, prioritizing the lives and realities of students from linguistically and culturally diverse communities, as expressed in the civil rights movement.

Aligning Dual Language Policies With Evidence-based Research and Best Practices

Evidence-based research is the systematic and transparent use of objective information such as student performance data, school metrics, DL program evaluation data, or teacher details that build on prior peer-reviewed research to answer educational questions with validity. Evidence-based research questions that guide DL policies can be about any concept or strategy, such as teaching practice, multicultural competence, preventing home language loss, eliminating deficit terminologies and viewpoints, or how to support MLLs' utilization of their full repertoire of linguistic and multicultural assets in school, to name a very few topics. Successful DL policies aligned with evidence-based research focus on and support MLLs' academic success and multicultural competence.

The Massachusetts LOOK Act (2017) and its implementation is a DL policy aligned with evidence-based research. The act calls for DL programs to be research based and designed as additive multilingual programs that promote high levels of academic achievement for both English speakers and language-minority students. All students are to develop both their home (or partner) language and English while receiving the state's core curriculum for all students.

> Alternative instructional programs shall include, but shall not be limited to transitional bilingual education and dual language education. Programs shall be research-based and include subject matter content and an English language acquisition component. Programs shall be based on best practices in the field and the linguistic and educational

needs and the demographic characteristics of English learners in the school district. (Section 52, p. 9)

Evidence-based research informs best practices for teaching MLLs. Best practices are asset based and include embracing translanguaging, promoting multicultural competence, utilizing the full repertoire of students' cultural and linguistic resources, supporting identity development, and developing multicultural appreciation, to name a few (Howard et al., 2018). In their evidence-based research, Sánchez et al. (2018) found that translanguaging affordances and a language allocation policy that validates, rather than marginalizes, the home language empowers MLLs. Teachers use best practices to assure that all students meaningfully participate in classroom learning regardless of their language or learning abilities.

Fully Staffed and Expanded Quality Dual Language Education Programs

Well-designed DL programs that support MLLs' academic success, biliteracy, and multicultural competence require DL teachers with subject matter competency and language pedagogy skills. Implementing DL policy means that districts must fully staff DL programs. Districts learned from prior experiences that DL teacher shortages undermine the effectiveness of DL programs. For example, California currently lacks sufficient qualified DL teachers to meet the growing demand in DL programs as discussed in chapters 1, 6, and 7. From 229 schools in the state with DL programs in 2011, to 407 in 2017, and 747 or more by 2019, school districts scrambled to hire qualified DL teachers (Hernández et al., 2022). In 150 out of 200 districts surveyed at the start of the 2016–2017 school year, districts reported a shortage of qualified teachers and the fact that the shortages were increasing annually. This caused districts to rely on teachers who were not fully credentialed or had not completed teacher training programs demonstrating subject-matter competency (Darling-Hammond et al., 2018).

While severe shortages of DL teachers exist nationwide in urban and rural schools and those schools with high percentages of low-SES, low-achieving, or minority students (Aragon, 2018), California experienced a 50 percent drop in credentialing new DL teachers between its peak in the 1990s and the 2010s. In the year when voters passed California's Proposition 58 (2016), allowing districts to more easily expand DL programs, only 700 new DL teachers received credentials statewide. Returning the DL teacher pipeline to its peak in the mid-1990s, of 1,800 newly credentialed DL teachers annually (Darling-Hammond et al., 2018), requires concerted efforts by policymakers at all levels.

For example, a fully implemented DL policy requires investment in the DL teacher pipeline and higher education. When voters passed California's Proposition 227 (1998), teacher education programs across the state eliminated or reduced their DL teacher preparation programs. By the mid-2010s only half of the states' eighty teacher education programs offered bilingual authorizations to teachers, even though new standards for preparing DL teachers occurred in 2009 and again in 2021 (California Commission on Teacher Credentialing, 2021). The current DL teacher preparation requirements include examination and coursework options or a mix of the two. Fieldwork integrated with the coursework option provides teachers an understanding of language-minoritized students' schools and pedagogies for their biliterate development. Also, in 2017 the state's budget provided funding to recruit teacher assistants, many of whom are multilingual, to become fully credentialed teachers through the Classified School Employee Teacher Credentialing Program (Carver-Thomas & Darling-Hammond, 2017).

Teachers as Change Agents Who Have Critical Consciousness

Throughout U.S. history, teachers have been front-line advocates for their MLLs' educational outcomes. Teachers with critical consciousness (Broughton, 2019; Broughton et al., 2020; Heiman & Yanes, 2018; Palmer et al., 2019) create cracks in the monolingual wall, opening windows of educational opportunity for their students from linguistically and culturally diverse communities. In their daily instruction, teachers choose effective DL teaching practices and reflect on the optimal management or planning of language in the classroom. They interpret and implement top-down policies—or delay implementation—by advocating changes that their students need based on their cultural and linguistic assets (Hernández et al., 2022).

Recently, critical consciousness has become part of teacher professional learning initiatives building on the history of teachers' advocacy roles in calling out and acting to support increased equity and social justice in DL education.

Critical consciousness involves critical listening, integrating power, historical understanding of marginalized groups, and embracing discomfort in this process (Palmer et al., 2019).

> Both monolingual and multilingual educators have preconceived ideologies toward multilingual education based on their own experiences with language or language learners. In DL programs, a division of the two groups can develop when these ideologies conflict with each other. By providing professional learning that focuses on building critical consciousness and defines language as a resource and a right for all educational partners, we can foster true collegiality and partnership among DL and non-DL educators.
>
> **Rubí**

Critical Consciousness

1. Critical listening
2. Integrating power
3. Historical understanding of marginalized groups
4. Embracing discomfort in this process

Source: Palmer et al. (2019)

Fostering the critical consciousness of parents and students in addition to that of teachers adds a fourth pillar to DL education (Heiman & Yanes, 2018; Palmer et al., 2019), joining the original three goals of academic rigor, biliteracy and multiculturalism, and multicultural competence (Howard et al., 2018).

Teachers' beliefs about DL education and multilingual development are crucial in their decision making. Ruiz (1984) outlines three prominent orientations toward the DL education of MLLs.

Orientations Toward Language

1. Language-as-a-problem
2. Language-as-a-resource
3. Language-as-a-right

The first orientation views language-as-a-problem and is prominent in deficit views of restrictive monolingual English-only instruction. This orientation does not support DL policies and views language-minoritized children as deficient. Teachers with critical consciousness compare the evidence-based research that exposes the outcomes from this orientation, such as home language loss, with the other two orientations, which are more asset-oriented.

The belief that language is a right (Coady et al., 2022) reflects the EH discourse previously discussed in this chapter. The civil rights movement and the enactment of the BEA drew heavily from this orientation. Both language-as-a-right and language-as-a-resource discourses have the potential to guide DL policy toward asset-based practices that support MLLs' maintenance and development of their biliteracy and multilingualism throughout their PK–12 schooling.

The global human capital discourse presented earlier in this chapter is an example of a language-as-resource orientation. When teachers implement DL policies, they must also critically examine the limitations of this discourse, for example, whether it ignores or dismisses the social and historical context of their community in favor of privileging biliteracy as an economic asset to English-dominant families (Flores & García, 2017). If teachers do not address the inequities and social class conditions of their MLLs then multilingualism becomes only a commodity, and language-minoritized children's linguistic resources become commodified for English-dominant children's benefit (García & Sung, 2018). Recent evidence-based research provides numerous examples of prioritization of the needs of English-dominant children learning Spanish over the needs of language-minoritized Spanish-speakers (Flores & García, 2017).

Professional learning communities (PLCs) also provide an excellent forum for discussing DL policy implementation and building teachers' critical consciousness. For example, in a PLC discussion, teachers could compare the school district's requirements for awarding MLLs the SoBL for world language proficiency with the requirements for home language proficiency. The PLC could examine evidence-based research finding that schools with students from low-SES families or a high percentage of language-minoritized students have low numbers of graduates who earn the SoBL (Subtirelu et al., 2019). They could also consider whether their district's SoBL requirements recognize the linguistic repertoires of language-minoritized students or whether requirements advantage the biliteracy of English-speaking students enrolled in world language courses.

The Call for Action

DL policy breaks down the monolingual wall when elected officials, judges, voters, educators, parents, advocacy organizations, government employees, and other policymakers work in concert to further additive policies that nurture and develop MLLs' academic success, biliteracy and multiculturalism, and multicultural competence. Efforts in five states exemplify the work of individuals and groups across the country heeding a call for action by creating and implementing DL policies in support of MLL students.

Massachusetts: Voters' English-Only Initiative Reversed by DL Policy in the LOOK Act

When Massachusetts voters approved Question 2 in 2002, a ballot measure in support of a monolingual policy, they reversed the Commonwealth's 1971 DL education law, which had been the first state-level DL policy of its kind following federal legislation from the 1960s civil rights movement (Gándara & Escamilla, 2017). The passage of Question 2 immediately prohibited home language instruction by credentialed DL teachers with authorization to teach in languages reflecting the language diversity in the state's public schools, such as Arabic, Armenian, Cape Verdean, Chinese, Haitian-Creole, French, German, Greek, Hebrew, Hmong,

Massachusetts LOOK Act

Hungarian, Italian, Japanese, Khmer, Korean, Polish, Portuguese, Russian, Spanish, Ukrainian, and Vietnamese. The new English-only policy did not require teachers to have special training or preparation to teach students who did not speak English and required only that teachers be fluent in English. Districts such as Boston Public Schools immediately moved to implement the monolingual policy that would hold sway for the next fifteen years.

In 2017 bipartisan support for a DL policy shift broke down the monolingual wall and once again restored DL education in the state's public schools. Most important, passage of the LOOK act provided guidance for the Department of Elementary and Secondary Education (DESE) to establish a comprehensive DL policy. First, school districts have flexibility in designing programs to best meet the needs of their MLLs. This means DL programs can fully implement the pillars of DL education established in *Guiding Principles for Dual Language Education* (Howard et al., 2018). Second, the DESE gains oversight of all new programs with the mandate to conduct comprehensive reviews. For example, this provides the mechanism for developing a state-level DL policy identifying evidence-based research and best practices for program accountability to MLLs. Third, DL policy requires teacher credentialing for all programs serving MLLs. Fourth, districts with significant numbers of MLLs must establish parent advisory councils. And fifth, the law establishes a SoBL award for graduating high school seniors who meet specific biliteracy criteria.

California: From English-Only to DL
Call to Action in CA Global 2030 Initiative

Global California 2030 Initiative

When nearly 10 million Californians voted for the CA Ed.G.E. Initiative known as Prop 58 (2016), they joined educators, parents, advocacy organizations, community and business leaders, and elected officials who were incrementally developing and implementing DL policy initiatives such as the EL Roadmap and the State Seal of Biliteracy throughout the 2010s (Olsen & Aguila, 2019). Prop 58 passed with more than 73 percent of the vote, demonstrating the widespread public support for a multilingual California and rejecting the monolingual mandates in Prop 227 (1998), which had required English-only instruction for the vast majority of MLLs in the state.

In 2018 the State Superintendent of Public Instruction validated the ongoing DL policy implementation from his platform as the state's highest elected education official with the Global CA 2030 Initiative and a call to action.

We are inviting educators, parents, legislators, and community and business leaders to join us on the road to a multilingual California. We need support from everyone as our K–12 education system expands access to world language classes, programs, and experiences; trains more bilingual teachers; and improves the quality and availability of advanced language classes. By 2030, we want half of all K–12 students to participate in programs leading to proficiency in two or more languages, whether through a class, a program, or an experience. By 2040, we want three out of four students to be proficient in two or more languages, earning them a State Seal of Biliteracy." (California Department of Education, 2018, p. 4)

The initiative furthered both DL policy and respect for the diverse languages, cultures, and heritages in the state. Its goals included aligning instruction and assessment for MLLs' academic success and providing equitable funding to meet MLLs' needs. It also set a target for half of high school graduates to receive the SoBL in 2030 and 75 percent by 2040. A fully implemented DL policy can meet this goal since over 40 percent of K–12 students already spoke a home language other than English at the time of the report, and 60 percent of even younger children were growing up with a home language other than English. The call to action, then, was a call to maintain and develop every child's home language and stem the language loss that California's children experienced in recent decades.

Florida: Community Activism for DL Policy

After fleeing the Cuban Revolution in the late 1950s, leaders in Florida's Cuban community embraced DL education as they actively sought success in English for their children while also assuring that they would maintain their culture and Spanish language. The DL programs that educators developed are considered among the most successful in the United States (Goldenberg & Wagner, 2015). While district-level DL policies reflected the local business and community leaders' advocacy, DL policies at the state level were not fully implemented.

In the 1980s the League of United Latin American Citizens (LULAC) and other civil rights organizations sued the Florida State Board of Education to implement policies supporting MLLs. Before going to trial the state and the parties negotiated a settlement entering a consent decree (*League of United Latin American Citizens et al. v. Board of Education*, 1990) into the court record. This consent decree continues to guide the state's compliance with federal laws and court orders regarding the education of MLLs. For example, it provides for DL education in English and the home language of the MLL. Qualified teachers with appropriate materials must teach the home language, and the state must develop or identify appropriate standards for evaluating DL instruction.

Florida Consent Decree

Texas: Parent Advocacy and Court Action Advance DL Policy

From 1918 until 1973, Texas law forbade teachers from using any language other than English in schools or textbooks except in high school world language classes. The teachers who violated the law risked a misdemeanor

Parent Advocacy in Texas

fine for speaking or teaching in their MLL students' home languages. Legislative debate at the time of enactment connected English with U.S. identity and bilingualism with inferior intelligence (Nieto, 2009).

In the nearly five decades since repeal, DL policy implementation has advanced through statewide mandates to districts and parents taking legal action against districts on behalf of their children. For example, state policy mandates a DL education when twenty or more students at any grade level in a district have the same home language and are developing English proficiency. Additive, late-exit DL programs are among the possible program options for districts (U.S. Department of Education, 2015).

The persistence of Mr. Castañeda on his daughters' behalf exemplifies parents' struggles to force districts to effectively implement a DL policy. Fifteen years of advocacy in a small town in Texas became a significant court decision impacting MLLs, as discussed earlier in the *Castañeda v. Pickard* decision. Texas Rural Aid and the *Castañeda* parents spent thousands of hours resisting the district's lack of implementation of policies and procedures for an appropriate DL program for language-minoritized students in their community. While the parents' efforts originally focused on the Mexican American community, the court decision had national ramifications for all language and cultural groups, notably in the Denver Public Schools in 1983 and with the Office of Civil Rights issuing the *Castañeda* Test in 1991 (Meehan, 2013).

Colorado: A Shift to Asset-Based Terminology Furthers DL Policy

Official State Guidance in Colorado

Over 100,000 students speaking more than 280 languages attend Colorado public schools. The Colorado Department of Education (CDE) had used deficit terms to refer to students in this group. However, at the start of the 2022–2023 school year, the CDE announced a shift to asset-based terminology to reflect its belief system. A memorandum in the form of a Dear Colleague letter (Colorado Department of Education, 2022) informed districts that the CDE's approach would no longer label students in terms of the language they had not yet learned but instead would use the term MLL to acknowledge the MLLs' language and culture as strengths while validating biliteracy.

The CDE guidance acknowledged that districts and schools make their own decisions about whether to adopt the new terminology; however, the memo was clear that the CDE would be using the language and hoped districts and schools across the state would join them in this asset-based belief system reflective of the diversity in the state's classrooms and communities.

Conclusion: Key Take-Aways

Educational language policies can be monolingual or DL. We must implement policies aligned with evidence-based research that are beneficial for all students but are *essential* for MLLs. Monolingual policies do not benefit all students and do not promote biliteracy and multicultural competency. DL policies are evidence-based and promote biliteracy and multiculturalism, multicultural competence, and high levels of academic achievement for MLLs.

Educational language policies can be de facto, meaning in practice without being formally codified, or de jure, meaning in formal law such as federal and state legislation, court actions, negotiated consent decrees, executive orders, voter referendums, district mandates and implementation, and community decisions, to name a few. In the absence of formal measures, established practices serve as policy. Both de facto and de jure policies ultimately rely on teachers to interpret and implement the policies and best practices that will support their multilingual students' development.

Federal law has never mandated DL education; however, at times federal policy has promoted evidence-based research finding strong academic outcomes for MLLs in DL programs. In recent decades federal monolingual policies have focused on English-acquisition and student assessment in English-only without validating biliteracy or the home language development of language-minoritized students. Changes in federal policies could eliminate deficit-based mindsets, promote the asset-based strengths of MLLs, and provide support and validation that DL education is beneficial for all students and optimal for MLLs.

DL policies must keep in mind the needs of language-minoritized children. It is a civil rights issue as well as a human rights issue. MLLs learn best when their home language is developed, validated, and viewed as an asset for biliteracy and multilingual competency. Ensuring equity and educational opportunity for MLLs not only increases their academic, social, and psychological well-being but also strengthens their career prospects and the nation's economy as a whole.

State-level policies impact the implementation of DL programs. Recent legislation in Massachusetts and California, current articulation of policy in Colorado, and ongoing judicial action in Florida and Texas provide guidance in those states and concrete examples of DL policies for other states as well as the federal government. Reversing monolingual policies in states such as Arizona requires ongoing advocacy efforts involving educators and parents such as the Castañeda family in Texas.

A teacher shortage exists in key areas including well-trained and credentialed DL teachers. The DL teacher pipeline, financial incentives, and improved working conditions are important to training and retaining qualified DL teachers. Without enough qualified DL teachers to staff DL programs, those advocating English-only policies could force schools to return to subtractive, monolingual policies, which were common in schools throughout U.S. history. Well-designed DL programs rely on qualified DL teachers.

The economic benefits of multilingualism are important to all students, and the demands for DL programs by families who speak English currently outpace the supply. Each DL program needs to be addressed within the school, as well as at the district level so that language-minority students are not denied a place in DL programs. The Bilingual Education Act, which came out of the 1960s civil rights movement, focused the need for language-minority students to have access to DL education as an equity issue.

The Seal of Biliteracy has strong support across the country. It needs teacher support for full implementation of its potential at every grade level and in every subject area. The District of Columbia and forty-nine states have legislation implementing it.

The teacher is at the nexus of instructional practice and implementation of educational language policies. All teachers, including monolingual and multilingual teachers, need critical consciousness to understand and challenge monolingual views. Evidence-based research finds that critical consciousness involves critical listening, integrating power, historical understanding of marginalized groups, and embracing discomfort in this process. Teachers, students, and families create cracks in the monolingual wall, opening windows where DL policies can provide educational opportunities for students from linguistically and culturally diverse communities.

Reflection Questions

1. How is your state moving from monolingual policies to DL policies?

2. How can you engage your school community in discussing evidence-based research aligned with an additive approach toward your students' multilingual development and avoid language myths, deficit terminologies, and remedial views of MLLs' academic success?

3. What language policies can your school community consider to welcome and involve the families of your MLLs?

4. How has your school district determined the requirements for MLLs to earn the Seal of Biliteracy on their high school diploma?

5. What can you do at your grade level or subject area to support your MLLs' biliterate development so that they will earn the Seal of Biliteracy when they graduate from high school?

6. How can your school and community reverse the DL teacher shortage with improved working conditions, financial incentives, and professional opportunities?

7. What instructional practices might you include to implement a DL policy in your classroom to support your students' multilingual development, whether you are monolingual or multilingual yourself?

References

American Councils Research Center. (2021). National Canvass of Dual Language Immersion Programs in U.S. Public Schools. https://www.americancouncils .org/sites/default/files/documents/pages/2021-10/Canvass%20DLI%20-%20 October%202021-2_ac.pdf

Aragon, S. (2018). Targeted teacher recruitment: What is the issue and why does it matter? Policy snapshot. *Education Commission of the States.* https://www.ecs.org/ wp-content/uploads/Targeted_Teacher_Recruitment.pdf

Arizona. (2000). Proposition 203: English Language Education for Children in Public Schools Initiative. https://www.azed.gov/sites/default/files/2017/03/ PROPOSITION203.pdf?id=58d003651130c012d8e906e5

Bialystok, E. (2001). *Bilingualism in development: Language, literacy, and cognition.* Cambridge University Press.

Bialystok, E. (2009). Bilingualism: The good, the bad, and the indifferent. *Bilingualism: Language and Cognition, 12*(1), 3–11. https://doi.org/10.1017/ S1366728908003477

Broughton, A. J. (2019). *Cultivating educators' critical consciousness of learning and language needs in emergent bilinguals* [Doctoral dissertation]. University of South Florida. https://digitalcommons.usf.edu/etd/8340

Broughton, A. J., Scott, L., & Barreto, J. (2020, February 25–28). *"You helped me crack open the window!" Pairing Evidence-based Language Practices with Cultural Competence* [Conference session]. National Association for Bilingual Education Annual Conference, Las Vegas, NV, United States.

Brown v. Board of Education, 347 U.S. 483. (1954). https://www.oyez.org/ cases/1940-1955/347us483

California. Proposition 227: English Language in Public Schools Initiative. (1998). https://vigarchive.sos.ca.gov/1998/primary/propositions/227.htm

California. Proposition 58: California Education for a Global Economy (CA Ed.G.E.) Initiative. (2016). https://vigarchive.sos.ca.gov/2016/general/en/ propositions/58/

California Commission on Teacher Credentialing. (2021). *Bilingual authorization educator preparation preconditions, program standards, and bilingual teaching performance expectations.* https://www.ctc.ca.gov/docs/default-source/educator-prep/ standards/bilingual_authorization_program_standards_btpes.pdf

California Department of Education. (2018). *Global California 2030.* https://www .cde.ca.gov/eo/in/documents/globalca2030report.Pdf

Carver-Thomas, D., & Darling-Hammond, L. (2017). *Addressing California's growing teacher shortage: 2017 update.* Learning Policy Institute.

Castañeda v. Pickard, 648 F.2d 989. (5th Cir. 1981). https://openjurist.org/648/ f2d/989

Civil Rights Act of 1964, Pub. L. No. 88-352, 78 Stat. 241. (1964). https://www .govinfo.gov/content/pkg/STATUTE-78/pdf/STATUTE-78-Pg241.pdf

Coady, M. R., Ankeny, B., & Ankeny, R. (2022). Is language a 'right' in US education?: Unpacking *Castañeda's* reach across federal, state, and district lines. *Language Policy, 21,* 305–329. https://www.doi.org/10.1007/s10993-021-09604-1

Collier, V. P., & Thomas, W. P. (2017). Validating the power of bilingual schooling: Thirty-two years of large-scale, longitudinal research. *Annual Review of Applied Linguistics, 37,* 1–15.

Colorado Department of Education. (2022). Multilingual Learner (MLL) Dear Colleague Letter. https://www.cde.state.co.us/cde_english/new-ml-letter-clde-announcement

Consent Decree, League of United Latin American Citizens (LULAC) et al. v. Board of Education (No. 90-1913, S.D. Florida, August 14, 1990). https://www.fldoe.org/core/fileparse.php/7582/urlt/Consent-Decree.pdf

Cummins, J. (2001). Bilingual children's mother tongue: Why is it important for education? *Sprogforum, 7*(19), 15–20.

Darling-Hammond, L., Sutcher, L., & Carver-Thomas, D. (2018). *Teacher shortages in California: Status, sources, and potential solutions.* Learning Policy Institute. https://learningpolicyinstitute.org/product/teacher-shortages-ca-solutions-brief

Ennser-Kananen, J., & Leider, C. M. (2018). Stop the deficit: Preparing preservice teachers to work with bilingual students in the United States. In P. Romanowski & M. Jedynak (Eds.), *Current research in bilingualism and bilingual education* (pp. 173–189). Springer. Multilingual Education, 26. https://doi.org/10.1007/978-3-319-92396-3_10

Equal Education Opportunities Act of 1974. Pub. L. No. 93-380, 88 Stat. 514. (1974). https://www.law.cornell.edu/uscode/text/20/1701

Every Student Succeeds Act. Pub. L. No. 114-95, 114 Stat. 1177. (2015). https://www.congress.gov/114/statute/STATUTE-129/STATUTE-129-Pg1802.pdf

Flores, N., & García, O. (2017). A critical review of bilingual education in the United States: From basements and pride to boutiques and profit. *Annual Review of Applied Linguistics, 37*, 14–29. https://doi.org/10.1017/S0267190517000162

Gándara, P. (2018). The economic value of bilingualism in the United States. *Bilingual Research Journal, 41*(4), 334–343. https://doi.org/10.1080/15235882.2018.1532469

Gándara, P., & Escamilla, K. (2017). Bilingual education in the United States. In O. García, A. Lin, & S. May (Eds.), *Bilingual and multilingual education. Encyclopedia of language and education* (pp. 439–452). Springer. https://doi.org/10.1007/978-3-319-02324-3_33-2

García, O., & Sung, K. K. (2018). Critically assessing the 1968 Bilingual Education Act at 50 years: Taming tongues and Latinx communities. *Bilingual Research Journal, 41*(4), 318–333. https://doi.org/10.1080/15235882.2018.1529642

Gibney, T. D., Kelly, H., Rutherford-Quach, S., Riccards, J. B., & Parker, C. (2021). *Addressing the bilingual teacher shortage.* Comprehensive Center Network. https://www.compcenternetwork.org/resources/resource/6898/addressing-bilingual-teacher-shortage

Goldenberg, C., & Wagner, K. (2015). Bilingual education: Reviving an American tradition. *American Educator, 39*(3), 28.

González, N., Moll, L., & Amanti, C. (2005). *Funds of knowledge: Theorizing practices in households, communities and classrooms.* Lawrence Erlbaum Associates. https://doi.org/10.4324/9781410613462

Heiman, D., & Yanes, M. (2018). Centering the fourth pillar in times of TWBE gentrification: "Spanish, love, content, not in that order." *International Multilingual Research Journal, 12*(3), 173–187. https://doi.org/10.1080/19313152.2018.1474064

Hernández, S. J., Alfaro, C., & Martell, M. A. N. (2022). Bilingual teacher educators as language policy agents: A critical language policy perspective of the *Castañeda v. Pickard* case and the bilingual teacher shortage. *Language Policy, 21*, 381–403. https://doi.org/10.1007/s10993-021-09607-y

Howard, E. R., Lindholm-Leary, K. J., Rogers, D., Olague, N., Medina, J., Kennedy, B., Sugarman, J., & Christian, D. (2018). *Guiding principles for dual language education* (3rd ed.). Center for Applied Linguistics.

Improving America's Schools Act of 1994, Pub. L. No. 103-382, 108 STAT. 3518. (1994). https://www.congress.gov/103/statute/STATUTE-108/STATUTE-108-Pg3518.pdf

Kleyn, T., & García, O. (2019). Translanguaging as an act of transformation: Restructuring teaching and learning for emergent bilingual students. In L. C. de Oliveira (Ed.), *The handbook of TESOL in K–12* (pp. 69–82). John Wiley & Sons. https://doi.org/10.1002/9781119421702.ch6

Kloss, H. (1998). *The American bilingual tradition* (Reprint ed.). Center for Applied Linguistics and Delta Systems.

Lewis, K., & Davies, I. (2018). Understanding media opinion on bilingual education in the United States. *Journal of Social Science Education, 17*(4), 40–67. https://doi.org/10.4119/jsse-1096

Massachusetts. An Act Relative to Language Opportunity for Our Kids, Ma. General Laws § 138. (2017). https://malegislature.gov/Laws/SessionLaws/Acts/2017/Chapter138

Massachusetts. Question 2: English Language Education in Public Schools Initiative. (2002). *Official information for voters.* https://archives.lib.state.ma.us/bitstream/handle/2452/114615/ocm18711581-2002.pdf?sequence=1&isAllowed=y

Meehan, J. P. (2013). *Castañeda v. Pickard: The struggle for an equitable education— One family's experience with resistance* [Doctoral dissertation]. Baylor University. https://baylor-ir.tdl.org/handle/2104/8844

Menken, K. (2006). Teaching to the test: How No Child Left Behind impacts language policy, curriculum, and instruction for English language learners. *Bilingual Research Journal, 30*(2), 521–546. https://doi.org/10.1080/15235882.2006.10162888

Nationality Act of 1906. Pub. L. No. 59-338, 34 Stat. 596. (1906). https://scholarscollaborative.org/PuertoRico/items/show/79

Lau v. Nichols, 414 U.S. 563. (1974). https://www.oyez.org/cases/1973/72-6520

Nieto, D. (2009). A brief history of bilingual education in the United States. *Perspectives on Urban Education, 6,* 61–72.

No Child Left Behind Act of 2001. Pub. L. No. 107-110, 115 Stat. 1425-2094. (2002). https://www.congress.gov/107/plaws/publ110/PLAW-107publ110.pdf

Olsen, L., & Aguila, V. (2019). *Towards a multilingual California: Recommendations from the Dual Language Instruction Transition Team.* California Department of Education English Learner Support Division.

Palmer, D. K., Cervantes-Soon, C., Dorner, L., & Heiman, D. (2019). Bilingualism, biliteracy, biculturalism, and critical consciousness for all: Proposing a fourth fundamental goal for two-way dual language education. *Theory Into Practice, 58*(2), 121–133. https://doi 10.1080/00405841.2019.1569376

Ruiz, R. (1984). Orientations in language planning. *NABE Journal, 8*(2), 15–34. https://doi.org/10.1080/08855072.1984.10668464

Rumbaut, R. G. (2014). English plus: Exploring the socio-economic benefits of bilingualism in Southern California. In R. M. Callahan & P. C. Gándara (Eds.), *The bilingual advantage: Language, literacy, and the US labor market* (pp. 182–205). Multilingual Matters.

Sánchez, M. T., García, O., & Solorza, C. (2018). Reframing language allocation policy in dual language bilingual education. *Bilingual Research Journal, 41*(1), 37–51. https://doi.org/10.1080/15235882.2017.1405098

Skutnabb-Kangas, T., Phillipson, R., & Rannut, M. (1994). *Linguistic human rights.* De Gruyter Mouton.

Spolsky, B. D. (2004). *Language policy.* Cambridge University Press. https://doi .org/10.1017/CBO9780511615245

Subtirelu, N. C., Borowczyk, M., Thorson Hernández, R., & Venezia, F. (2019). Recognizing *whose* bilingualism? A critical policy analysis of the Seal of Biliteracy. *Modern Language Journal, 103*(2), 371–390. https://doi.org/10.1111/ modl.12556

Task-Force Findings Specifying Remedies Available for Eliminating Past Educational Practices Ruled Unlawful under *Lau v. Nichols.* (1983). https://web.stanford .edu/~hakuta/www/LAU/IAPolicy/IA3ExecLauRemedies.htm

U.S. Department of Education, Office of English Language Acquisition (OELA). (2015). *Dual language education programs: Current state policies and practices.* https://www.air.org/sites/default/files/downloads/report/Dual-Language-Education-Programs-Current-State-Policies-Feb-2017-rev.pdf

U.S. Department of Education, Office of English Language Acquisition (OELA). (2019). *The top languages spoken by English learners (ELs) in the United States.* https:// ncela.ed.gov/files/fast_facts/olea-top-languages-fact-sheet-20191021-508.pdf

Valdez, V. E., Freire, J. A., & Delavan, M. (2016). The gentrification of dual language education. *Urban Rev, 48,* 601–627. https://doi.org/10.1007/s11256-016-0370-0

Zentella, A. C. (Ed.). (2005). *Building on strength: Language and literacy in Latino families and communities.* Teachers College Press. https://doi.org/10.1080/ 19313150709336867

GLOSSARY OF TERMS

Assessment *as, for,* and *of* **Learning:** These three approaches represent a model that centers multilingual learners and their relationships with others as it is operationalized across education sectors (Gottlieb, 2016, 2021, 2022a). Together these approaches offer a comprehensive balanced system that humanizes assessment and exemplifies assessment equity.

Assessment: This multiphase process consists of planning, gathering, analyzing, interpreting, reporting, and using data from a variety of sources to make educational decisions. Assessment occurs in multiple contexts, from state to classroom levels, with multiple purposes, from documenting accountability to informing teaching and learning.

Bilingual Paraprofessionals: May serve as translators, both for individual ELs immersed in English classes and for events such as individualized education plan or parent meetings, as required by federal law. May provide small-group or individual instruction to ELs under teacher supervision. May perform noninstructional duties (e.g., supervising recess, lunch, and school transitions or interacting with parents).

Bilingualism: Bilingual refers to a person who can speak two languages fluently. Although some ELL students may not yet be fully bilingual, the goal for these students is to attain strong communication skills in English and in their first language.

> **Additive bilingualism:** Additive bilingualism refers to when a student's first language continues to be developed while he or she is learning a second language. Such students often have opportunities to use both languages inside and outside of school, and they have a desire to maintain both. Additionally, if a child is from another culture, his or her first culture is also valued and respected in the classroom.

> **Subtractive bilingualism:** Subtractive bilingualism refers to when students learn a second language at the expense of their first language. In this case, the child will usually lose the ability to speak the first language over time. Children who develop subtractive bilingualism may not have opportunities to practice their first language and may even feel that their first language or culture is unwelcome in class.

Biliteracy: Biliteracy is the ability to effectively communicate or understand written thoughts and ideas through the grammatical systems, vocabularies, and written symbols of two different languages.

Black Lives Matter: Although the Black Lives Matter movement officially started in 2013, and the culturally responsive research base emerged in 1995, the era of advancing biculturalism and biliteracy officially took hold during the pandemic. The movement returned to national headlines during the global George Floyd protest in 2020, following his murder by Minneapolis police officer Derek Chauvin. An estimated 15 million to 26 million people participated in the 2020 Black Lives Matter protests in the United States. As such, a 2020 Pew Research Center poll found that 67% of adult Americans expressed some support for the Black Lives Matter movement.

California Bilingual-Bicultural Act: With this act, bilingual education became a right for ELs. The California Bilingual and Bicultural Act was also referred to as the Chacon-Moscone Bilingual-Bicultural Education Act of 1976. The purpose of the act was to require California school districts to offer bilingual learning opportunities to each pupil of limited English proficiency (LEP) enrolled in public schools and to provide adequate supplemental financial support to achieve such purpose.

Castañeda v. Pickard: The case of *Castañeda v. Pickard* was tried in the United States District Court for the Southern District of Texas in 1978. This case was filed against the Raymondville Independent School District (RISD) in Texas by Roy Castañeda, the father of two Mexican-American children. Castañeda claimed the RISD failed to establish sufficient bilingual education programs, which would have aided his children in overcoming the language barriers that prevented them from participating equally in the classroom.

Certified Bilingual Teachers: Provide instruction in primary language and/ or English to ELs. They have both a base credential and an additional endorsement (also called a certification, authorization, credential, or extension).

Consent Decree: A legal decree that a judge makes with the consent of all parties involved in a lawsuit.

Critical Consciousness: The ability to analyze and identify inequity in social systems and to commit to take action against these inequities (Freire, 1970).

Cultural Wealth: Skills, knowledge, experiences, and assets shared by members of marginalized groups and people of color.

Culturally Sustaining Pedagogies: Culturally Sustaining Pedagogy builds on decades of asset-based pedagogical research, including Culturally Relevant Pedagogy (Ladson-Billings) and Culturally Responsive (Gay & Hammond) and Linguistic (Hollie) Pedagogy. Culturally Sustaining Pedagogy affirms and respects the key components of the Asset-Based Pedagogies that preceded it, but also takes them to the next level. Instead of just accepting or affirming the backgrounds of students of color as seen in Culturally Relevant Pedagogy or connecting to students' cultural knowledge, prior experiences, and frames of reference as we see in Culturally Responsive Pedagogy, Culturally Sustaining Pedagogy views schools as places where the cultural ways of being in communities of color are sustained rather than eradicated.

De Facto: Policies that exist in practice but that are not legally codified.

De Jure: Policies that stem from formal laws.

Deficit Views of Multilingualism: The belief that monolingualism and monolingual approaches improve student learning; the use of deficit-oriented terminology in describing language learning and learners; and assumptions that multilingualism confuses learners.

Dual language education (DLE): Dual language as a form of bilingual education in which students are taught literacy and content in two languages. The goals of DLE are **bilingualism** and **biliteracy**. Thus there should also be sustained instruction in the partner language for at least 6 years (Grades K–5). Additionally, at least 50% of instruction during the day should be in the partner language throughout the program. Last, language arts and literacy instruction should occur in both program languages (CAL Dual Language Program Dictionary, 2004).

Dual Language Learners and Multilingual Learners: Chapter 5 refers to the students enrolled in dual language programs as dual language learners and multilingual learners. Some students may be those who were referred to the program as English learners. Other students may be those named as English speakers. In chapter 5 we emphasize the need to leverage all students' cultural and linguistic richness. Dual language programs may include learners who are becoming bilingual, those who are becoming multilingual, and those with multiple home languages, both named and unnamed.

Dual Language Teacher Pipeline: Financial, academic, advising, recruitment, and retention supports for individuals to earn their teaching certification and be hired as teachers. These supports are at each level of the individual's progress to becoming a teacher.

Educational Language Policies: Official policies through legislation or court decisions or informal practices that determine how language is used in schools or educational settings.

English Learner (EL) or English Language Learner (ELL): The federal statutory classification for the subset of multilingual learners who have been identified as eligible for English language support, which public, state, and local education agencies are required to provide.

Equity/Heritage Discourse: Explicitly acknowledges that language-minoritized students learn best when the focus is on their heritage; emphasizes the inequalities in society that MLLs face that have historically marginalized their home language and culture.

ESL (or ELD) Teachers in Bilingual Placements: Provide instruction in English or, in some cases, in the ELs' primary language. They nearly always have both a base teaching credential and an additional ESL certification. Typically, they have to demonstrate additional competencies and/or complete coursework or professional development related to teaching ESL.

Every Student Succeeds Act: Every Student Succeeds Act (ESSA) is the 2015 reauthorization of the 1965 Elementary and Secondary Education Act. ESSA includes a number of new requirements for the education of English Learners (ELs), including standardized criteria for identifying EL students and inclusion of English proficiency as a measurement of school quality. Unlike its predecessor, the No Child Left Behind Act, ESSA pushes back on the states' critical decisions such as how quickly schools must improve and how states can intervene with struggling districts. It shifted such decision making to state governments—along with provisions within ESSA requiring stakeholder engagement.

Evidence-Based Research: Systematic and transparent use of objective information such as student performance data, school metrics, DL program evaluation data, or teacher details that builds on prior peer-reviewed research to answer educational questions with validity.

Funds of Identity: Coined by Esteban-Guitart and Moll (2014) as an extension of "funds of knowledge," this set of resources helps shape people's self-definition, self-expression, and self-understanding.

Funds of Knowledge: Stemming from the research of González et al. (2005), the findings reveal rich expertise that has been developed in multilingual multicultural home and community spaces for schools to tap as grounding for curriculum, instruction, and assessment. Investigation into this knowledge base uncovers a shining light and promise for the education of multilingual learners.

Global 2030: Written by then California State Superintendent of Education, Tom Torlakson, and continued by Tony Thurmond, current California State Superintendent of Education, a document whose purpose was to undo 20 years of subtractive policies that extinguished language and multilingual identities in PK–16 and put into place specific additive policies that now promote bilingualism systematically across the state.

Global Human Capital Discourse: Focuses on the economic benefits of being biliterate, job marketability, basic skills in the twenty-first century global community for trade, negotiation, and management.

Home Language: In chapter 5 this term to refers to the students' languages that are used and practiced in homes and communities outside of the traditional school setting. We recognize that some of these languages are named while others are not. In conjunction with the focus on collaboration we also honor the richness and multidimensional aspects of all the home languages within dual language programs. Lachance and Honigsfeld (2023) remind us to advocate the recognition of home languages as a critical part of multilingual engagement. In this way, multilingual learners are afforded equitable opportunities to use their funds of knowledge from their home and community lives. Ultimately, honoring home languages helps position MLLs to embrace and build upon their linguistic identities.

Improving America's School Act (IASA): Also known as the 1994 reauthorization of the Elementary and Secondary School Act, this federal law first required state academic content standards to be aligned with annual state assessments in reading/language arts and mathematics for students in grades 3–12 as part of state systems. It had no specific provisions for assessment for multilingual learners, which at the time, were named "Limited English Proficient" students.

Language Loss: When children cannot speak their home language (i.e., intergenerational language loss).

Late Exit or Developmental bilingual education: This model encourages bilingual and biliteracy development of multilingual learners as programmatic goals where use of multiple languages is not diminished.

Lau v. Nichols: This was a violation for not providing ELs language support. Specifically, a lawsuit was filed by Chinese parents in San Francisco in 1974, which led to a landmark Supreme Court ruling that identical education does not constitute equal education under the Civil Rights Act. Instead, school districts must take "affirmative steps" to overcome educational barriers faced by non-English speakers (Lyons, 1995).

Linguistic Assets: Multiple strengths that students possess, including language and communication skills in one or more languages, understanding of vocabulary and grammar, abilities to work within different language registers and communication styles, and utilization of appropriate social skills within diverse contexts.

Local Educational Agencies (LEAs): These districts, townships, or counties are legally constituted within a state; they have administrative control over schools through a board of education.

LOOK Act (Massachusetts, 2017): Legislation providing schools with flexibility to choose DL programs designed to promote biliteracy and multiculturalism, multicultural competency, and high levels of academic achievement for MLLs.

Multicultural Competency: The ability to understand and accomplish cross-cultural communication, appreciate and interact with people from diverse cultures and belief systems.

Multilingual Language Learner: In this book, we are specifically focused on those students who come from homes where a language other than or in addition to English is spoken in the home and students who come from cultures outside the dominant culture. Multilingual learners is *not* simply an assets-based replacement label for English learners. It refers to a broad group that includes those receiving services (English learners); those who have exited out; "never English learners" who come from linguistically and culturally diverse backgrounds; and Heritage language learners.

No Child Left Behind: The No Child Left Behind Act (NCLB) passed Congress with overwhelming bipartisan support in 2001 and was signed into law by President George W. Bush on Jan. 8, 2002. The NCLB law—which grew out of concern that the American education system was no longer internationally competitive—significantly increased the federal role in holding schools responsible for the academic progress of all students. The best thing that NCLB did for ELs was to make sure that they, and other subgroups—such as students with special needs—were also making strides in achievement. States that did not comply risked losing federal Title I money.

Professional Learning Communities (PLC): A team of educators who meet and work together in building common ideas for improving their teaching practice to create learning environments that support students' success.

Program Languages and Partner Languages: The diversity in dual language programs shaped the mention of the two languages in dual language programs as either program languages or partner languages in chapter 5. In the United States English is most often one of the two program languages, partnered with a language other than English. We honor that in some cases the two program languages do not include English. For example, Spanish may be partnered with an Indigenous language. With this in mind, the dual language program languages must partner together.

Promoting the Educational Success of Children and Youth Learning English Promising Futures: This 2017 report the National Academies of Sciences, Engineering, and Medicine points to the multidimensional patterns of under-representation and over-representation of multilingual learners at the national, state, and district levels in PK–12 for all disability categories. Furthermore, it states that those who become proficient in both a home or primary language and English are likely to reap benefits in cognitive, social, and emotional development. Most important, the cultures, languages, and experiences of multilingual learners constitute assets for their personal development as well as the nation.

Proposition 203 (Arizona, 2000): English Language Education for Children in Public Schools Initiative requiring that "all children in Arizona public schools shall be taught English by being taught in English and all children shall be placed in English language classrooms."

Proposition 227 (California, 1998): English Language in Public Schools Initiative requiring that "all public school instruction be conducted in English." Repealed by Proposition 58 (CA Ed.G.E.) in 2016.

Proposition 58: The California Education for a Global Economy Initiative, which unanimously passed in 2016, undoing the restrictive English only Proposition 227 from 1998, where instruction had to be taught overwhelmingly in English.

Question 2 (Massachusetts, 2002): English Language Education in Public Schools Initiative requiring that "all public school children must be taught English by being taught all subjects in English and being placed in English language classrooms."

Seal of Biliteracy: Graduating high school students receive the Seal of Biliteracy on their diploma for demonstrating proficiency in two or more languages. States, districts, and/or schools award the SoBL to recognize and encourage students to pursue biliteracy and multilingualism. First adopted in 2011 by the California legislature, the State Seal of Biliteracy is now approved in 49 states and the District of Columbia.

Sheltered Content Instruction: Generally designed for middle and high school multilingual learners, this methodology makes grade-level content area instruction in English comprehensible to the learners. In essence, sheltered instruction facilitates multilingual learners' academic progress while they simultaneously develop English.

Sociocultural Consciousness: The awareness that your worldview is not universal and the belief that your worldview is not superior to the worldviews of others.

Socioculturalism (Socio-cognitivism): This theory of language affirms learning as a social activity that accepts multiple modes and languages in contact or translanguaging as a valid communication mode. It reflects and values effectiveness of communication where meaning is negotiated among individuals in social and cultural contexts.

State Educational Agencies (SEAs): These governmental entities set rules, regulations, and policies for districts and schools based on federal and state legislation. SEAs are also responsible for establishing funding formulas and monitoring their distribution. Most SEAs issue annual report cards on student assessment results.

Structuralism (Cognitivism): This theory of language assumes a hierarchical ordering of the components of language (from sounds to words to sentences to discourse). It is generally rule-bound with proper use of language in oral and written expression as the standard, with reliance on error correction and accuracy of communication.

Structured English Immersion or English Language Development: A program designed to eventually impart English language skills necessary to succeed in an English-only classroom.

Subtractive Schooling: An institutionalized process in which students who are outside the dominant culture have their linguistic, cultural, and historical identities stripped away by schools' curriculum and policies (Valenzuela, 1999).

The National Literacy Panel on Language Minority Children and Youth: In the mid-2000s, the Stanford Research Institute International and the Center for Applied Linguistics were awarded a contract from the Institute of Education Sciences to convene a National Literacy Panel composed of expert researchers from the fields of reading, language, bilingualism, research methods, and education. The charge to the panel was to conduct a comprehensive, evidence-based review of the research literature on the development of literacy among language minority children and youth.

Transitional Bilingual Education (TBE), or early exit bilingual education: Two-way or dual language programs are programs where the goal is for students to develop language proficiency in two languages by receiving instruction in English and another language. Similarly, according to the Center for Applied Linguistics (CAL), "[m]any people use the term *dual language* to refer to programs that have a balance of native English speakers and native speakers of the partner language. This model is also called *two-way immersion* or *two-way bilingual immersion*" (CAL Dual Language Program Dictionary, 2004).

Transitional bilingual education or English as a Second Language: A program for English language learners in which the goal is proficiency in oral and written English. The students' native language is used for instruction for a number of years (1–3 is typical) and is gradually phased out in favor of all-English instruction.

Translanguaging: Described as the natural and fluid interweaving of languages among bilingual and multilingual learners, this practice has been widely applied to language education as multiple language use has gained acceptance as part of schooling (García & Wei, 2013). As language policy and practice, translanguaging can be interwoven into all classrooms with multilingual learners and bilingual and multilingual program models.

NAME INDEX

SUBJECT INDEX

Solutions
YOU WANT

Experts
YOU TRUST

Results
YOU NEED

INSTITUTES

Corwin Institutes provide regional and virtual events where educators collaborate with peers and learn from industry experts. Prepare to be recharged and motivated!

corwin.com/institutes

ON-SITE PROFESSIONAL LEARNING

Corwin on-site PD is delivered through high-energy keynotes, practical workshops, and custom coaching services designed to support knowledge development and implementation.

www.corwin.com/pd

VIRTUAL PROFESSIONAL LEARNING

Our virtual PD combines live expert facilitation with the flexibility of anytime, anywhere professional learning. See the power of intentionally designed virtual PD.

www.corwin.com/virtualworkshops

CORWIN ONLINE

Online learning designed to engage, inform, challenge, and inspire. Our courses offer practical, classroom-focused instruction that will meet your continuing education needs and enhance your practice.

www.corwinonline.com

PLSN209A8

Visit www.corwin.com

CORWIN

A Sage Company

CORWIN HAS ONE MISSION: to enhance education through intentional professional learning.

We build long-term relationships with our authors, educators, clients, and associations who partner with us to develop and continuously improve the best evidence-based practices that establish and support lifelong learning.